Historical Vocal Pedagogy Classics

Berton Coffin

The Scarecrow Press, Inc.
Lanham, Maryland, and London

SCARECROW PRESS, INC.

Published in the United States of America
by Scarecrow Press, Inc.
4720 Boston Way, Lanham, Maryland 20706
www.scarecrowpress.com

4 Pleydell Gardens, Folkestone
Kent CT20 2DN, England

British Library Cataloguing in Publication Information Available

The hardback edition of this book was previously cataloged by the Library of
Congress as follows:

Coffin, Berton.
    Historical vocal pedagogy classics

        Bibliography: p.
        1.   Singing—Instruction and study—Book reviews. I. Title.

MT820.C69   1989   783'.007 89-6258
ISBN 978-0-8108-4412-4

ISBN: 0-8108-4412-5   (paper)

Manufactured in the United States of America.

♾™ The paper used in this publication meets the minimum requirements of
American National Standard for Information Sciences—Permanence of
Paper for Printed Library Materials, ANSI/NISO Z39.48-1992.

To my wife,
MILDRED COFFIN,
who has been my right arm,
editor, typist, and the main source of
encouragement in all my writings concerning
vocal repertoire and the pedagogy of the singing voice.

Contents

v

Berton Coffin, 1910–1987

Dr. Berton Coffin, internationally known vocal pedagogue, Professor Emeritus, and former Chairman, Division of Voice, College of Music, was a member of the faculty from 1946 until mid-1977. He was selected by the Faculty of the College of Music in 1987 for the first "Distinguished Faculty" award.

Dr. Coffin's contributions to the College of Music and the University of Colorado at Boulder included his long teaching career, with his love of teaching and personal interest in his students; establishing and implementing the Doctor of Musical Arts degree in vocal performance and pedagogy; the building and recruitment of an excellent vocal program and faculty; the creation of the Festival Chorus which blended "town and gown"; and his recognition as one of the leading authorities in voice and pedagogy due to his inquisitive mind and practical research with outstanding acousticians in Europe and the United States.

His numerous volumes, of which two will be published posthumously, and professional writings dealing with vocal techniques, phonetics, translations, and repertoire had basic underlying principles of the acoustics of the voice and the pitch of vowels. Professor Coffin's major concern was always for vocal improvement in his students, and his investigations of techniques were to enable him to delve into the "why" of the singing voice (from his own singing experience and a teacher's viewpoint); and the relationship to languages, with optimum resonance a primary goal. He credited the talented ears of his singer-concert-manager-

This Citation is located in the Music Library of the University of Colorado, Boulder, in recognition of the outstanding service to the College of Music by Berton Coffin, and was prepared by Mildred W. Coffin and Dr. Robert R. Fink, Dean, College of Music.

wife, Mildred, and her editorial assistance, as being a significant influence in formalizing his observations of a lengthy pilgrimage in the *Sounds of Singing*, and other volumes.

The dedication and generosity in imparting vocal knowledge and encouragement to Berton Coffin's singers went beyond these statements since he wanted them to learn vocal independence, be they University students or professional singers in 21 European opera houses in five countries, and in the United States at the Metropolitan, San Francisco, and Houston Opera companies.

A Citation of Recognition presented to Dr. Coffin in September of 1985 by the College of Music stated that his early Quaker training and background helped to mold and instill a love and passion for producing something peaceful and beautiful in his students and colleagues. This further reflects his keen sense of integrity and dedication which emanated from him to his loyal students. Many of these students and singing teachers have written that his books have been and will continue to be a mainstay in their vocal lives. Professor Coffin's unique sense of humor, his healthy, deep sounding laughter, and his warmth of personality endeared him to students, colleagues, and other teachers of singing. These memories will linger together with his written legacy of vocal teaching principles.

Preface

I have done a considerable amount of research in areas related to the art of singing and have reviewed and interpreted eighteen books that are vocal pedagogy classics in the light of contemporary observations and findings.

Extensive fragmentary research has been done in various laboratories of the world, but many teachers have debated as to how those efforts could be related to the art of singing. Many of the researchers are not singers nor are they hearing many live performances of high-quality singing because of lack of interest, travel distance, the pressure of time, expense, etc.

The pertinent question is: How can a teacher teach high-quality live vocal performance if he has not heard it? How can a chef teach cooking without a taste for good foods? This implies that all teachers of singing should hear as much good-quality live performance as possible. With "live" (not dubbed) television performances, teachers and singers can see and hear how the world's best artists are singing. This relates to posture and mouth openings for the various pitch levels, dynamics, and languages. Recordings are not to be trusted implicitly because many of the audible sounds of poor singing can be filtered out. A sound engineer's responsibility is to sell records, not to "tell it as it is." He is in the cosmetic business!

There are many types of oblivion. The great teachers of the past are no longer known when the careers of their singers come to an end, unless they taught teachers of singing or had assistant teachers. Many of the famous and effective teachers did not write their thoughts, preferring to keep their procedures secret. How can singing best be taught? By both sound and sight! A picture (live or synchronous as in television) is worth a thousand words,

ix

although much of what occurs is invisible inside the throat and body of the performer.

I have reviewed what teachers of the past have had to say about their art.[1] I will compare what they said about the state of singing at that time with present-day singing. The printed page is not necessarily correct; many written statements are partial truths. We need to know when something is true and when it is not. Most of the books reviewed are out of print, and part of my exciting quest has been to locate them in this country and in Europe.

Recent books are specialized—some on the breath, some on the muscles and cartilages, some on sounds, etc. All facets are involved with the singer's art, but not consciously. The study of nature (science) is cold and calculating, but can be a partial basis for technique. The singing art is inspirational and intuitive, but its very foundation is vocal technique which enables the spark of emotional expressiveness to flourish in song.

The teaching of singing has frequently been involved with fads. On the occasion of Garcia's 100th birthday, in 1905, it was stated that "Musical and medical science are in the present day brought very much together, so that it is often difficult to guess whether some learned expatiator on the last method of producing the voice is a singer who dabbles in surgery or a surgeon who has a taste for singing." Since that time, we have had Symposiums on the Care of the Professional Voice, usually looking at the vocal cords as the total source of singing. Naturally the vocal cords are essential but are not the entire story. There has also been the fad of speech therapy which is certainly related to the teaching of singing, but unrelated to the projection of tone in large opera houses and/or concert halls. Now the fad is the Alexander Method, which has a relationship to posture and coordina-

---

1. These reviews first appeared in the *NATS Bulletin* [now *Journal*], the official publication of the National Association of Teachers of Singing, Inc., between 1981 and 1984. Further comments have been added.

tion based on the experiences of an actor from the spoken stage around 1903. The postures of speech and of singing are different because of pitch height. I consider Alexander's writing primary to those individualized approaches based on his method. People interested in the Alexander Method should go back to his original statements. In other words, read the "Bible" and not what is said about it. The teachings of Garcia, Marchesi, Stockhausen, and Lamperti have been diluted in three generations until they are practically nonexistent.

It is the purpose of this book to bring those truths to the attention of teachers who are learning the art of singing from the "neophyte," from those who have had long careers and usually teach their own techniques, and are now beginning to teach. Singing has not been at a lower level than it is now. As a case in point, check the Metropolitan Opera Roster of 1926 and 1986. There are exceptions because there always are great singers, but other forms of athletics have increased in quality and quantity. The low-quality versus the lack of high-quality singing is due to the void of knowledge of vocal technique and should encompass a thorough knowledge of the vocal instrument. There are many young singers constantly found through competitions who are potentially great singers if they have an established and dependable technique. However, they are often pushed into large and demanding roles before vocal maturity. Thus they are quickly worn out before they reach their zenith. If something is not done soon, many operas will disappear from the repertoire and the lyric art will fade into oblivion.

The song recital is in a state where only established, outstanding artists can attract a large paying audience. There seems to be no promise of increased activity in this area.

Perhaps we should return to the principles of Maurice Grau, who was Director and General Manager of the Metropolitan Opera and Covent Garden at the same time. He managed a concert bureau from his office and split the profits fifty-fifty with the singers. Grau said that his half was enough to pay Plançon's salary at the "Met." That was in 1903, the time of the Golden

Age of Opera. All the singers of that era knew their technique, but sang so long that few learned the technique of teaching singing. Among those who did were Jean de Reszke and Lilli Lehmann, who are included in this text.

The basic thrust of this text is directed to the reader audience of teachers of singing, performing singers, and vocal pedagogy students. Vocal pedagogy is taught in few schools of music in colleges and universities. One reason is, as a friend of mine said of teachers of singing, "Thou shalt have no other Gods before me." It is hoped that this collection of reviews will assist this reader audience in an understanding of their heritage and give them a perspective on which to base their teaching in their own individual ways. The teaching of an art and a skill must be within that framework. No two teachers are the same, and no two students are the same.

There are many negative factors working against today's singers, as I have discussed in my books. Concert pitch is now higher than 440 in many places and higher than the 421.6 of Mozart's time. Orchestras are louder than ever (decibels are higher) because of the development of instruments. American houses are larger than European opera houses and salons for which classical music was written. There are presently more opera houses giving opera, which dilutes the diminishing number of quality singers available for each performance. Some vocal coaches and conductors have little knowledge of the voice and are demanding pure vowels and consonants of the singers they coach. This is impossible if there is a pitch change in the melodic line. Fortunately, there are those singers with a singing sense who understand this.

Furthermore, the great singers are being worn out by jet travel and shorter periods of rest. With the din of sounds from television and recordings, there is a possibility that our sense of hearing is being dulled.

I hope this condition is cyclical and that there can be a rebound of *bel canto*. In summation, there cannot be an enduring art without an enduring technique. It is to this enduring technique that this opus; *The Sounds of Singing; Overtones of Bel Canto;* and the Chromatic Vowel Chart are dedicated.

Berton Coffin
June 15, 1986

Editorial Note: Since most of these books, as reviewed, are now out of print, Professor Coffin wanted to preserve them for the future of vocal pedagogy classes in colleges, universities, and conservatories; hence the compilation of this volume. (*Mildred W. Coffin*)

Historical Background

The art of opera began in rooms, salons, and small theaters which were the meeting places of society in Italy. At one time there were as many as sixteen "theaters" in Venice. The singers were from orphanages and had been trained for singing opera in small places with light instrumental accompaniment. Italian opera invaded Munich, and its acoustical housing is best observed in the princely, rococo Cueveille Theater which stands next to the State (National) Theater in all its classic splendor. The Cueveille Theater represents the period of the emasculated male voice which retained its soprano range. This fitted in very well with the visual and auditory tastes of the rococo, and is further explained in Appendix A.

The first two books reviewed in this text, Tosi and Mancini, are about the male soprano voice. Later the center of singing shifted to Bologna where the Teatro Communale still stands and is used. The castrati were trained and taught there. The name most closely associated with that type of singing is Farinelli who was taught by Porpora. Thus we see that architecture is related to a style of singing. Later Teatro San Carlo was built in Naples where Garcia I studied and upon which his review is based. By that time theaters were becoming larger, the orchestras less like guitars, and the vocal dynamics were louder than that of the *bel canto* singing that originated in the compositions of Rossini, Bellini, and Donizetti. Also, there had been a law against the brutal preparation for the male soprano voice (castrato), so that the teachers of that time were castrati who passed along the agility and beauty of their art.

The book of Garcia II told of an enormous change in the technique of singing. He described the clear and sombre timbres

xv

used in the differentiation of lyric and dramatic singing. Alfredo Kraus states that the art of singing today was established by Garcia II. This book is very closely related to his teachings and those of his students, Marchesi and Stockhausen. The dramatic singing (sombre timbre) has been more in vogue since that time. Violins have steel strings for higher tunings (the harpist in the Vienna Philharmonic tunes to 447), but the human voice still has human tissue.

A very large percentage of international artists will cancel in Vienna when they encounter difficulties involved with higher pitch. The string players say their instruments sound more brilliant at the higher pitch. They also have a partial control in the selection of the General Music Director. We have international singers but not an established international pitch that is adhered to. I am including a pronouncement on this question by the American Academy of Teachers of Singing on the effect it has on the voice (see Appendix B).

Fewer and fewer international singers are coming out of Italy, and the supply of German singers is not enough so that all the Wagnerian operas can be given at Bayreuth even when calling upon international singers. Singers from all countries will benefit in emulating the *bel canto* style of singing described in this text.

1

Pier Francesco Tosi:
Observations on the Florid Song

INTRODUCTORY NOTE

Since the Papal Declaration by Pope Urban in 1586 that no female voices be used in the sacred services of the church, the use of Spanish falsettists and the castrati voices took their place. Tosi's book is primarily concerned with the castrato voice and has little to do with the training of the male voice. It is the basis of the many techniques of the female voice which became very important in early opera and lighter music. The book was written in England at the time Honeywell Hall was built in Oxford. (It still stands next to Blackwell's Music Company.) This was the first concert hall in Europe. The falsetto-castrato voice was not large and the size of the hall was optimum for the beginning of the recital era.

Castrato voices in choruses could be heard in the cathedrals, however. The castrato was a different species of man with a large chest and the voice of a boy. This enabled him to perform many vocal feats acceptable to operatic and other types of music. This was the basis of the vocal music that was to follow.

This first jewel on the teaching of singing was written in 1723 by the male soprano Pier Francesco Tosi (b. Bologna 1647, d. Faenza 1732), who was trained in Bologna by his father, sang in.

Reprinted from the *NATS Bulletin* [now *Journal*], January-February 1981.

Italian theaters in his native country, England, and Germany. He was giving regular concerts in London in 1693, and after losing his voice taught in London and was court composer in Vienna from 1703–1712. The text was written in Bologna in Italian, was translated and annotated by the theater oboist and composer Gaillard, who surely knew Tosi's artistry as a soprano, composer, and teacher of singing. This classic was also translated into German with explanations and additions by Agricola, a student of J.S. Bach.

OBSERVATIONS FOR ONE WHO TEACHES A SOPRANO

In the training of the soprano voice Tosi recommended first the study of solfeggio to unite articulation with the vowel and to establish good intonation. The voice should be trained in Head Voice (*voce di testa*) and Chest Voice (*voce di petto*). The head voice was to be taken softly so that it did not shriek like a trumpet. The roulades and scales (*divisions*) were to be taught on the open vowels without separation of [h] or [g]. Of the five Italian vowels [a,e,i,o,u] Tosi states that fast passages should be taken on the first vowel, never on the third and fifth vowels, and in the best schools the close form of the second and fourth vowels were avoided. "Whoever would be curious to discover the feigned Voice of one who has the Art to disguise it, let him Notice that the Artist sounds the Vowel [i] or [e] with more strength and less Fatigue than the Vowel [a] on the high notes."

Other suggestions were that the teacher should teach all of the intervals and that vocalises proceed from the easy to the difficult. The singer should always stand with a reasonable appearance and with an expression more towards a smile than of too much gravity, avoiding grimaces and tricks of the head.

In the beginning, the singer should hold out the length of the notes without shrillness and trembling. Later the *messa di voce* (swell and diminuendo) could be taught. He believed that teaching should be done on the three open vowels [a], [ɛ], and [ɔ] and not always on [a] so that the singer could more easily come to the words.

To teach the continuity of tone, there was to be a gliding between the tones. A dragging of the voice from high notes to lower notes should be taught, but the drag upwards was considered to be in bad taste. This is a technique which cannot be gained from sol-fa-ing.

The *appoggiatura* is the most important grace and should be taught, but used within the limits of good taste which he defined very carefully. A refined ear was considered the final arbiter of taste.

In the soprano voice (male or female) the trill is a necessity, and the singer's technique is incomplete without it—he had found no rules for teaching it. He gives aesthetic rules for its use. However, after the trill has been taught it is necessary that the singer be able to sing without it; such study can make the voice tremulous.

Tosi points out that there is a tendency for teachers to always keep the voice in motion. There should be an easy velocity, but when taught exclusively the voice can lose in size. If the teacher hastens the tempo in runs, he can quickly free a voice (unbind it) and bring it more "volubility" [my guess is that this is round, full, purer with fewer overtones].

Correct pronunciation should be achieved, with care taken to distinguish between single and double consonants. If words are not understood there is little difference between the voice and the instruments.

The teacher should teach both *forte* and *piano,* but his experience showed that the *piano* was not to be trusted, "and if any one has a Mind to lose his Voice, let him try it." "The Piano of a good singer can be heard because of the profound Silence and Attention of the Audience." [One must keep in mind the size of auditoriums and the loudness of accompanying instruments. At the time of this writing there were no concert halls in Europe—the first one (1748) in Oxford, England, seats about 300 and still stands next to Blackwell's Music Store. The first large opera houses were still to be built. The singer's art was of the court theater.]

Tosi was especially noted for his recitatives, of which he said

there were three styles—of the Church—of the Theater—and of
the Camera (Chamber Music). That of the Church was to be with
sanctity and devotion—of the Theater it was accompanied by
action and should be done in the manner "with which Princes
speak"—of the Chamber Music there should be a skill of the
words, to move "the most violent Passions of the Soul." Tosi
felt that a teacher who disregards *recitative* probably does not
understand the words, with the consequence that he cannot teach
the singer expression in it.

OBSERVATIONS FOR THE STUDENT

• Study with the mind when one cannot with the Voice. Hear
  [and see] the most celebrated singers and instrumentalists.
• Too much practice and beauty of voice are incompatible, but
  art is dependent upon much practice.
• Imitate the *cantabile* of those who are best and the *allegro* of
  those who excel in that skill.
• "The best Singer in the World is still a Learner, and must be
  his own Master."
• ". . . Women, who study, may instruct even Men of some
  Note."
• "Let him [the student] shun low and disreputable company,
  but, above all, such as abandon themselves to scandalous
  Liberties."
• Arrogance is ignorance in masquerade but "amiable Humility,
  the more the Singer has of it, the more it depresses him."
  "Who would sing better than the arrogant if they were not
  ashamed to study?"
• "Interest will persuade you to conform to the Taste of that
  Nation (provided it be not too depraved) which pays you."
• To copy is the part of a student, that of an artist is to invent.

"It may seem to many, that every perfect Singer must also be
a perfect Instructor but it is not so; for his Qualifications (though
ever so great) are insufficient, if he cannot communicate his

Sentiments with Ease, and in a Method adapted to the Ability of the Scholar; . . . and a manner of instructing, which may seem rather an Entertainment than a Lesson, with the happy Talent to show the Ability of the Singer to Advantage, and conceal his Imperfections; which are the principal and most necessary Instructions.''

These are a few of the basic principles which should entice the reader to further valuable investigation of this classic.

REFERENCES

Agricola, J. H. (1757), (1966). *Anleitung zur Singkunst*. H. Moeck Verlag-Celle (includes copy of original Italian of Tosi, original German of Agricola plus Preface and Appendix by Erwin R. Jacobi).

Tosi, Pier Francesco (1743). *Observations on the Florid Song*. Tr. and annotated by Gaillard. J. Wilcox, London. Reprinted 1926 by William Reeves Bookseller Ltd., London.

2

Giambattista Mancini: *Practical Reflections on the Figurative Art of Singing*

INTRODUCTORY NOTE

This is the first book that speaks extensively on the registers of the voice, since it mentions the moral obligations to take into consideration the talent of the child before the preparation to become a singer. Mancini discusses the castrati and also comments on the two registers which he has called "chest" and "head" or "falsetto." Very little is said about the male voice because the castrati were the teachers of the time and those techniques were used in the teaching of all singers.

Today we speak of three or more registers, but the blending of them is fairly well described by Mancini. The ornamentation is that of the castrati—the male voice had not come into its own at the time this book was written. I believe that the three-register approach used by some teachers and singers today is traceable to this document. Later, the extent of the full voice is told by Garcia II and Lilli Lehmann.

Much **of what we know** of singing today has its first statement in the stellar book of the castrato soprano Giambattista Mancini (b. 1714 Ascoli, d. 1800 Vienna), who was a student of Bernacchi, the founder of a school of singing in Bologna after the precepts of his teacher Pistocchi. Bernacchi's most famous students were

Reprinted from the *NATS Bulletin* [now *Journal*], March-April 1981.

Senesino (for whom Handel wrote many operas over a period of ten years in London), Carestini (who sang for Handel for two years), and tenor Anton Raaff (for whom Mozart wrote the title part of *Idomeneo*. Raaff was the teacher of Ludwig Fischer, for whom Mozart wrote the part of Osmin in *Abduction from the Seraglio*). Mancini, as well as being a student of Bernacchi, was also a composition student of Padre Martini, as was Mozart for a short time. Both Martini and Mozart were members of the Accademia Filarmonica of Bologna. His *Practical Reflections on Figured Singing* was written in 1774, fifteen years after he was employed in the court of Maria Theresa of Vienna, to whom the book is dedicated.

The enlarged 1777 edition was translated by Pietro Buzzi in 1912 and dedicated to lyric tenor Alessandro Bonci, who in his acceptance of that honor stated, ''If the modern scientific discoveries would blend themselves with the old Italian Method, using the latter as a foundation, then the Art of Song would again be raised to its former high standard.'' Foreman has translated the 1774 edition and shows the changes in the 1777 edition with added historical information.

Mancini stated that during his time there were ''many presuming to teach the art of singing who in truth never learned the rules.'' It seems the first rule was, that to avoid the unhappiness of failure, certain talents were necessary in a boy or girl before their parents dedicated them to singing in either the theater or the church. Success could come only to those with a good voice backed by natural musical intelligence. Then, there should be an elevated chest, harmonious proportions of the vocal organs, symmetry of the mouth and teeth, and nose neither too short nor too long, because imperfect organs and physical defects are incurable and inevitably result in imperfect singing. Mancini added that a homely, inexpressive face ''will not be tolerated unless the person is unexcelled in the art of singing.''

At that time teachers thought of the voice as having two registers, chest and head (or falsetto). These should be equalized by following ''the natural instinct, but to never force Nature.''

Of interest to present-day teachers and singers is what Mancini has to say concerning the opening of the mouth. "I am of the opinion that to know well how to shape it [the mouth] can reasonably be kept as one of the essentials most important to a singer. Without this knowledge, although he may possess all the other abilities of the profession, he will never be able to please, and will often render himself ridiculous and disgusting." [Have you, when you are pleased by a singer, observed how the mouth was being opened? The positions are those of resonation.] He acknowledged that all faces differ in structure, and some are better proportioned for singing than others; nevertheless certain positions were best for a smooth, pure quality of tone, and certain positions would bring out a suffocated and crude tone (too open) or a nasal tone (too closed). He thought the Italian vowels [a,e,i,o,u] could be sung on each note in the position of a smile with the [o] and [u] being slightly rounded. [We must remember that the upward extension of the soprano voice had not yet been found.] Mancini felt the [i] vowel was difficult and should be sung in the position of a "composed smile."

He felt rules should be brought to life. "The general precepts are usually of little value, just as the practiced applications are good. In giving the precise rules to a student, let the teacher not only tell him and explain to him, but let him illustrate his meaning by making himself an example, by assuming the different positions of the mouth, the wrong as well as the right position, in order that *the student may see and also hear the corresponding tone which comes from each corresponding position.*" [Reviewer's italics. We can all be aware of the relationship of tone and position now as never before with the use of tape recorders, mirrors, television, or video cameras.]

"As for myself I always acted with my pupils like a dancing master. I used to call my pupils one by one in front of me, and . . . placed them in the right position . . . if you lean your head forward on to your chest your side muscles of the neck are tense, and they are also tense if you lean your head back." When the head is erect and natural the vocal organs remain relaxed and flexible.

"The voice cannot come out natural and spontaneous if it finds the throat in a strained position which impedes the natural action. Therefore, the student must take the trouble to accustom his chest to give the voice with naturalness and to use the throat smoothly and easily. If the union of these two parts [the breathing and the pronunciation] reaches the point of perfection, then the voice will be clear and agreeable. But if these organs act discordantly, the voice will be defective and the singing will be spoiled."

Students should be taught according to the nature of their voices. In the case of a raw, robust, harsh, and shrill voice, the teacher should endeavor to purify it and to make it sweet, especially the upper voice, so that it is emitted without shriekiness. Following this the entire range should be equalized. At that time the voice could be expanded slowly in such a way that the roughness and crudity are eliminated.

The weak voice which was limited in range was considered worthless, but the weak voice which had an extended range with good high notes should sing chest notes for a period each day. Mancini suggested the use of even and quiet solfeggi with a round pronunciation to deepen the tone.

But basically there was only one way to place a voice and that was "to exercise it with sustained tones (whole notes) rendered with repose and taken one by one with due graduation." "At the beginning of the tone, the mouth should be but slightly open, thus helping to draw the voice in its sweeter and softer quality. Then gradually reinforce the tone, by opening the mouth as wide as the rules of art prescribe." [He does not mention that in the diminuendo the reverse occurs.] This practice should be undertaken with the greatest care since there was the risk of fatiguing the chest.

Mancini thought that "the graces and beauties that the art of singing use to enrapture the human heart are: Portamento di voce, Appoggiatura, Messa di voce, Trillo and Mordente." The portamento was a part of Italianate singing and unsuited to French. He felt the trill was the most important embellishment and was taught by the old masters in the beginning of study. He observed that "agility cannot be perfect unless it is natural." In that case he felt time would be wasted in trying to acquire it. "A run and all kinds of agility must be supported by a robust chest, assisted by the graduation of breath, and a light 'fauces' [the lower extensions of the soft palate] in order that each note can be distinct, although executed with the greatest velocity.''

He felt it very beneficial for a singer to read portions of poetry aloud daily in a loud voice to form the habit of making all those necessary changes and shades of voice. Besides, one learns to recite well in public—this leads to the technique of recitative, which "will always be languid unless it is supported by convenient action. Movement gives life and strength and value to speech.''

COMMENTARY

Just as our country has had many developments since 1776, so has our singing art. There are many things in our American Constitution that are as valid today as when they were formulated by our forefathers, but there have been several amendments. The same is true of our art. Most of Mancini's principles can be taken as currently being constitutionally valid for the art of singing, but the first amendment, as viewed today, would concern the smiling position in singing. If still valid, it is only partly valid, and in only the very high and light female voice. Mancini's statement referred to the male soprano voice [the "boy's" larynx above a man's enlarged chest—the female voice was referred to as "cantatrice" as late as 1777, according to Duey]. The smiling position with light "fauces" enabled the great agility and vocal displays of the first *bel canto* period. The development of pedagogical viewpoints on various mouth positions will be treated in a future discussion. Meanwhile, the other statements by Mancini, based on tactile sense and the senses of hearing and seeing, may be taken as quite valid, and if applied would enrich the art of singing today.

REFERENCES

Duey, Philip A. (1951). *Bel Canto in Its Golden Age: A Study of Its Teaching Concepts.* King's Crown Press, Columbia University, New York.

Mancini, Giambattista (1777). *Practical Reflections on the Figurative Art of Singing.* Tr. by Pietro Buzzi (1912). Richard G. Badger, The Gorham Press, Boston.

Mancini, Giambattista (1774, 1777). *Practical Reflections on Figured Singing.* Compared, tr. and ed. by Edward Foreman (1967). Pro Musica Press, Champaign, Illinois.

Pleasants, Henry (1966). *The Great Singers: From the Dawn of Opera to Our Own Time.* Simon and Schuster, New York.

3

Manuel Garcia I (Père):
Exercises and Method for Singing

INTRODUCTORY NOTE

With Manuel Garcia (Père) we begin to have a statement on the teaching of the male voice. He had few fundamental statements to make on placing the voice, but had extensive exercises that were later used or adopted by his son, Garcia II, as well as by Marchesi and Stockhausen. These concerned all the styles of singing and were based on the teaching of Ansoni, who had a beautiful tenor voice. The exercises in all these styles should be used by today's singers to maintain their flexibility and youth, coupled with the tuning of vowels and vowel pitch. This is only one relationship of vowel sound to pitch and that was on an Oh on C above middle C. As a teacher, he was a tyrant and made his son sing bass in The Barber of Seville *at twenty years of age. The* Barber of Seville, *which was written for Garcia Père, included in it "Non più mesta," later used in* La Cenerentolla. *This will give some idea of the agility required by the* bel canto *composers Rossini, Bellini, and Donizetti. Much of that agility training and/or exercises have been omitted by today's type of voice building, which contributes much to the decline of today's singing.*
What do Marilyn Horne, Joan Sutherland, Beverly Sills, and

Reprinted from the *NATS Bulletin* [now *Journal*], September-October 1981.

Dietrich Fischer-Dieskau have in common? Much of their art of singing can be traced to Manuel del Popolo Vicente Garcia né Rodriguez (1775–1832), whose principles of singing were the roots of many outstanding teachers of the nineteenth and twentieth centuries. Garcia was an eminent tenor who had a remarkably flexible voice; because of this facility, and because of his inventiveness, he excelled in the lighter, florid music. (From about 1919 onward the name Garcia was spelled without the accent in all publications of the family, no student of the Garcias used it, and Manuel Garcia the son signed the facsimile of his centennial portrait by Sargent without the accent. [Frontispiece— *Garcia the Centenarian*. He should have known by then how the name should appear!] It is of interest to note that the 1980 Grove's Dictionary article on the Garcias uses the accent, although the author of the Grove article uses the name without accent in her 1964 biography of Pauline Viardot Garcia, *The Price of Genius*.)

It would take years of study and travel to trace the musical activities and influence of the Garcia family and their artistic descendants. No more exciting and rewarding investigation for teachers interested in the art of singing and vocal pedagogy can be recommended. Space, time, and purpose of this review do not allow such a discourse, but an introductory bibliography is given for those who would like to begin such a project. Without the Garcias the art of song could not have achieved many of its highest moments.

A shortened version of the Garcia story would begin with an illegitimate six-year-old boy whose mother had just died and who was introduced to the *maestro de capilla* of the Cathedral of Seville by his stepfather, Garcia by name. There he was taught by Antonio Ripa and Juan Almarcha, and by the time he was 17 he had the reputation of being a fine singer, conductor, and composer. His travels led him to Cádiz, Málaga, and Madrid. He left Spain in 1808, never to return; his international career led him to Paris, Turin, Rome, and Naples (1811). There he became a friend of Rossini, who wrote the role of Almaviva in ''The Barber of Seville'' specifically for the tenor from Seville. While in

Naples, Garcia furthered his Italianate singing and style by extensive study with Giovanni Ansoni, described by Burney as having
one of the sweetest and most powerful voices of his generation.
Gervasoni (according to Levien 1932) stated that Ansoni had "a
very rare truth of intonation, great power of expression and the
most perfect method, both of producing the voice and of vocalization." Ansoni's style and technique came from the old
Neapolitan maestro Porpora. It was in Naples, and in the Neapolitan vocal style, that Garcia began his teaching.

In 1816 the Garcia family returned to Paris, where Garcia sang
at the Théâtre Italien and continued his teaching, for which he
achieved great fame. Garcia was described in a London tribute to
his son in 1905 as not being a voice placer (a professor of voice
production or anything of that kind), but as a great singer who
knew how to communicate the secrets of his art to others. He was
the teacher of, among others, Adolphe Nourrit, the famed tenor
of the Paris Opera, and of his own children, Josepha Ruiz-Gar-
cia, daughter by an early marriage, Maria (Malibran), and Manuel Garcia, the famed teacher of singing.

Exercises Pour La Voix

Sometime between 1819 and 1822, Garcia published in Paris
Exercises Pour La Voix with preliminary discourse in Italian and
French and with figured bass accompaniment (UCB). This was
republished in 1824 by Boosey in London with the foreword
translated into English (BML). In 1868 the text was republished
with pianoforte accompaniment (NYPL). Without doubt, this
classic of vocal pedagogy includes the secrets of the old Italian
School divulged to him by Ansoni, and is the basis of the most
rigid and thorough-going method by which he trained his students
in Paris and London between 1816 and 1832.

By the time of the 1824 edition, Manuel Garcia was a member
of the Accademia Filarmonica di Bologna [as were Mozart, Tosi,
and Mancini], Primo Tenore della Reale Cappella Palatina di

S.M. il Re delle due Sicilie, e Primo Tenore della musica par-
ticolare del Re di Francia.

RULES

Garcia I states that the Art of Singing is subject to rules and
principles as are all other arts, so he has written 340 exercises to
remove any obstacle that can be met in the management of the
voice.

The preliminary discourse was only four pages long, since he
did not deem it necessary to explain how each example should be
used, believing that numerous explanations would more likely
confuse than assist the student. He felt the instruction of a Master
would explain any difficulty the singer might meet. However, he
did give several rules for those who did not have a Master.

RULE 1

The exercises throughout were written in Do (C), yet he desired that they be transposed beginning with the lowest tone of
the voice and ascend by semi-tone to the highest tone without
forcing the voice.

RULE 2

All of the exercises were to be sung on the five vowels, beginning with [a], [e], [i], [the other two Italian vowels were [o], and
[u]]. They were to be sung distinctly, not in a staccato manner,
nor with the "unpleasant sounds of /ha/, /he/, /hi/, /ho/, /hu/"
which he said was "a defect but too general."

RULE 3

Garcia I embellished the three cadences in several ways with a
view to opening an extensive range within which a diligent student might employ his imagination to sing with inspiration.

RULE 4

"The position of the Body must be erect, the Shoulders
thrown back, with the arms crossed behind, this will open the
chest and bring out the Voice with ease, clear and strong without
distorting the appearance either in Face or Body." [This should
be read again by many singers, teachers, and coaches I have
known in this country and in Europe.]

RULE 5

He advised, "never to commence singing in a hurry, always to
take breath slowly and without noise, which would otherwise be
unpleasant to those who listen and injurious to the Singer. . . ."

RULE 6

"The Throat, Teeth and Lips, must be sufficiently open so
that the Voice may meet with no impediment since the want of a
strict attention to either of the three is sufficient to destroy the
good quality of the Voice and produce the bad one, of the Throat,
Nose etc., besides, a proper attention to the Mouth will give that
perfect and clear pronunciation indispensable in singing and
which unfortunately few possess." [Voice placement by ear.] He
states that many of his scholars had imagined themselves as having limited voice, or even one of bad quality, who with his aid in
pointing out defects obtained at least a pleasing voice if not a
powerful one.

RULE 7

After taking the breath slowly and noiselessly, ". . . the Tone
must be commenced as piano as possible gradually increasing its
force to the utmost, returning again by the same method to the
extreme piano, without renewing the breath," taking care that the
intonation neither rises nor falls, which is the nature of the voice.

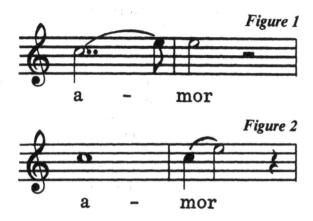

Figure 1

a - mor

Figure 2

a - mor

RULE 8

To sing in the Italian manner, the greatest attention is necessary to the carrying or slurring of the voice. A passage on the word "amor" on two notes a third apart was to be sung as in Figure 1, not as in Figure 2 (see Figures 1 and 2).

EXERCISES

The first exercise involves Rule 7, which concerns the crescendo and diminuendo of the voice, the famous *messa di voce* of the castrati. The second, third and fourth exercises involve the connection of tones with slurs, crescendi, and diminuendi. These are followed by exercises of agility, encompassing the problems of the Rossini-Bellini-Donizetti *bel canto* period of which Garcia was a part [and in which style he himself wrote many operas].

The exercises are progressively difficult in agility and range. Particular care was to be paid to certain intervals; one page involves the [o] vowel [a favorable vowel at that point in the scale and a form of covering] around c^1 and c^2 (C_4 and C_5, U.S.A. Standards Association). One page was devoted to preparation of the trill, and many pages were directed to variations and cadenzas.

Exercises and Method for Singing is the work of the genius founder of the family which according to Chorley (1926) "impressed a permanent trace on the record of the methods of vocal execution and ornament."

These rules and exercises were to be expanded and rearranged by the son of Manuel Garcia, who at 19 years of age had been trained for nine years by his father, and who within the year would travel to America with the first Italian opera company to perform on our shores. This classic of vocal pedagogy, *Exercises and Method for Singing*, led to the methods of Manuel Garcia II (see Vocal Pedagogy Classics, *NATS Bulletin*, May-June 1981), Mathilde Marchesi, and others which will subsequently be reviewed.

REFERENCES

Chorley, Henry F. *Thirty Years' Musical Recollections* (1926). Edited with an Introduction by Ernest Newman. Alfred A. Knopf, New York.

Fitzlyon, April. *The Price of Genius* (1964). [The biography of Pauline Viardot Garcia.] Appleton Century, New York.

Garcia, Manuel, I. *Exercises Pour La Voix* (c. 1820). A. Parite, Paris, [University of Colorado, Boulder.]

Garcia, Manuel, I. *Exercises and Method for Singing* (1824). Boosey, London. [British Museum Library.]

Garcia, Manuel, I. *340 Exercises-Thèmes Variés et Vocalises* (1868). 4th Edition. Heugel, Paris [with piano accompaniment by E. Vauthrot]. [New York Public Library.]

Grove's Dictionary. 1956 and 1980 Editions.

Levien, John Newburn. *The Garcia Family* (1932). Novello, London.

4

Manuel Garcia II (Patricio Rodriguez): *Memoire on the Human Voice*

Singing and the terminology of singing come to us from the techniques and writings of the teachers of the castrati. The clearest line is through Manuel Garcia I (Manuel Popolo Vicente Garcia [Rodriguez], 1775–1832), whose pedagogical principles are found in most of the historical lines of the great teachers of singing. Garcia's book, which contains rules and exercises for training the singing voice, was published in both Paris and London. Garcia's son, Manuel Garcia II (Manuel Patricio Rodriguez Garcia, 1805–1906), based his treatises on singing upon his father's book.

Manuel Garcia II presented a *Mémoire sur la voix humaine* to the French Academy in 1841, which, significantly, was five years after the introduction by Gilbert Duprez of the *do di petto* (chest-voice high C), and two years after the suicide of the elder Garcia's celebrated tenor pupil Adolphe Nourrit, who took his life because he sought the *voix sombre* and had become despondent over its effect on his voice. The *Mémoire* was presented (and accepted by the French Academy) three years after the termination of the career of Nourrit's famous pupil Marie Falcon, whose name still is used to describe a particular type of dramatic soprano voice. I detect these dramatic stories behind the explanation of *clair* (clear) and *sombre* (dark) timbres in relationship to the

Reprinted from the *NATS Bulletin* [now *Journal*], May-June 1981.

structure of the throat and to vocal registers, and in the extent to which they have affected the history of the development of the art of teaching singing.

In the introduction to the *Memoire on the Human Voice,* Garcia points out reciprocal actions among the vibrations of the cords, the breath, and certain parts of the vocal tube through which sound travels; it is by these physical activities that the voice is formed. Garcia's observations took place in Parisian military hospitals, where he studied the physiology of the larynx, and voice production. The *Memoire* (the Paschke translation is here cited) opens with a short description of the vocal apparatus:

> The human voice submits to the influence of age, sex, constitution, and undergoes innumerable modifications . . . there are also an unlimited number of nuances belonging to the organ of a single individual.

The sounds of the cry, the exclamation, the high or low speaking voice, the singing voice throughout its range, and the intensity of sound—all come from a small number of principles. It can be established that the human voice is composed of two registers— *chest* and *falsetto-head* (the lower part designated as *falsetto* or *middle,* the upper as *head*). In addition, there are two timbres, the *clair* and the *sombre;* all sounds of the same register are consequently of the same nature, whatever the modification of timbre or the degree of force used. And in a certain part of the voice, tones can belong to two different registers at the same time. This takes place between the *chest* and the *falsetto,* which coincide for the range from g to d^2. [The Helmholtz system and the more current U.S.A. Standard Association system of pitch designation may be compared on page 43, Music Review Section of *Bulletin.*]

Garcia states that chest register is the basic essential of the female, as well as of the male voice, and that ordinarily the chest voice in women does not exceed g to g^1. In male voices, as a whole, the chest extends from the low C of the serious bass to the c^2 of the tenor. It is the fundamental part of the man's voice. It is loud, round, and clear, and usually comprises a range of two

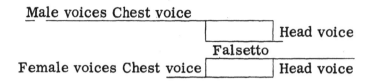

The general scale of the three registers is as follows:

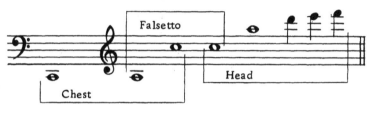

octaves in each voice. Men always speak in this register; women seldom do. In Garcia's terminology, the falsetto register extends from about *a* or b-flat to the c-sharp^2 in both female and male voices. The tones resemble somewhat the low tones of the flute.

The head voice is a distinct and brilliant part of the woman's *falsetto* voice, and it makes its first sound on c-sharp^2 or d^2, and extends to the extreme high. Most men lose the *head* voice as the result of mutation, but occasionally in the high tenor [and countertenor] the *head* voice remains. Garcia points out that the register systems of male and female voices are essentially the same in that the *falsetto* register, in his terms, has the same extension. The difference is that the *chest* voice extends much lower in the male voice, while in the female voice, the *head* voice extends much higher. [This is an observation that has been overlooked by all but the most recent researchers of the singing voice.]

Timbre is the peculiar and infinitely variable character which can occur in each register. When the sound is emitted from the larynx, the pharynx takes possession and modifies it. A *clear* timbre carried to exaggeration makes the voice shrill and produces a yelling quality. *Sombre* timbre gives penetration and roundness to the voice, and enables the singer to give all the volume to the sound. However, if this timbre is carried to excess it muffles the tone. The action of the timbres is less obvious in the low portion of the voice than in the higher register. When the tones between e^1 and b^1 are given *sombre* timbre they acquire dramatic character in both men and women. [Such tones have been called mixed voice. In my tone analysis, I have found that in this area of the voice, the first and second partials are equally reinforced.] The *sombre* timbre in the *head* voice has a remarkable effect of making the tone pure and limpid. [An acoustical analysis of head voice shows that the fundamental is strengthened, that the partials are few, and that the scratchy effect of the 3000 Hz sound is filtered out.]

In *clear* timbre the larynx, serving as the base of the vocal tube, must necessarily rise to shorten the tube of the pharynx, and must lower itself to permit the tube to lengthen. In the process, the pharynx can vary its shape and its diameter. [The associated colors are denied to those who teach that the larynx should always be in the low position. This was probably Nourrit's problem.] Garcia further points out that in the ascending scale in the chest register, the larynx initially lies in a position a little lower than the position of rest. The larynx then follows the voice in its pitch rise, carrying itself slightly forward. When the voice reaches the extreme pitch of which it is capable in that register, the larynx moves against the jaw, and the tone becomes thin and strangled. In higher pitches, the head tips back a little in order to facilitate the elevation of the larynx. The larynx and head movements occur when ascending through *falsetto* (middle) and *head* registers in the *clear* timbre, the larynx taking the lower position at a register change and then ascending by a slight movement, note by note.

Garcia states that in *sombre* timbre the larynx is fixed in the lower position. The lowering becomes especially apparent when the individual exaggerates the timbre and gives the voice all the volume of which it is capable; in this latter situation, the larynx remains immovably fixed in the lowest position for the entire compass of the register. One is obliged to facilitate this position by leaning the head forward a little.

As for the head tones, the larynx almost always produces them while rising rapidly. One could not prevent these movements; trying to do so to swell the voice would be a dangerous and often useless effort.

Garcia notes that when *clear* and *sombre* timbres are alternated, the larynx rises for the *clear,* and lowers for the *sombre.* The movements of the pharynx correspond to the different positions of the larynx. The form of the pharynx is principally controlled by the action of the velum and the tongue: ". . . it is especially to the movement of these two organs that the attention of the singer should be paid." The velum can act to direct two currents of air, one to pass through the nasal passage to take on some nasal resonance, and the other to flow through the mouth. These two currents have different importance according to the angle of palatal inclination. If the palate rises, it blocks the entrance to the nasal passages; then the air column strikes against the palatal arch, which presents itself best at a right angle, and the mouth alone constitutes the echoing tube. If the velum is completely lowered, the column of air immediately behind it rises into the nasal passages, which offer the only escape for the sound. In these movements of the velum, the tongue always follows the action of the larynx, to which it is attached, and moves in an opposite direction to that of the velum. When the velum is bent, the tongue hollows itself deeply along the mid-line from the back, and the passage of the throat presents the shape of an oval. As the velum lowers, the tongue rises and broadens at the base. In such a case, the resultant shape is similar to a crescent.

Vowels can be used to attain these formations for the colors of voice: the open vowels [a], [ɛ], [ɔ], as in Italian, are modifications of the *clear* timbre. The close vowels [e], [o], as in Italian, as well as the vowel [u], are modifications of the *sombre* timbre. Garcia states that the vowel [i], not having any character of its own, can receive the two timbres equally. The exaggeration of volume can take place only in the conditions of *sombre* timbre, and with greater effort. These are the two timbres from which all others are borrowed, whether as variations of vowels or as sounds made under the influence of the emotions.

The capacity of the vocal cords to vibrate, the dimensions of the
larynx, the thorax, the lungs, the pharyngeal, buccal and nasal
cavities, the disposition of these cavities to resonate, constitute
the absolute power of the voice of an individual . . . the singer,
in order to dominate the material difficulties of his art, must have
a thorough knowledge of the mechanism of all these pieces to the
point of isolating or combining their action according to the need.

REFERENCE

Garcia, Manuel, II. *Memoire on the Human Voice,* translated into En-
glish in full, 1970, by D. V. Paschke, 49 pages, from the original
French language part of Garcia's *Schule oder die Kunst des
Gesanges,* B. Schotts Söhnen, Mainz 1841. (This translation avail-
able only from Dr. Donald V. Paschke, 228 Kansas Drive, Portales,
New Mexico 88130.)

5

Garcia (Manuel Garcia II):
New Treatise on the Art of Singing

Manuel Garcia II (1805–1906) was twenty years old when he journeyed with his parents, sister, Maria, and several Italian singers to New York for the first season of Italian opera on the North American Continent. There he made his debut as Figaro in *The Barber of Seville,* with his sister Maria (later to be called Malibran) as Rosina, his father as Almaviva, and his mother as Berta. He had been trained by his father for 10 years, and during the troupe's stay in New York City and Mexico City had occasionally been called upon to substitute for his ailing father in tenor roles. Finding that his voice was deteriorating, the son returned to Paris for further study. This was followed by an unimpressive debut in Naples, whereupon he gave up singing—the only one of the singing Garcias not to follow that career. No doubt this stimulated his desire to know more about the voice, and led to his *Memoires on the Human Voice* (reviewed in this column May-June 1981). In 1840 he published his *Traité complet de l'Art du Chant.*

In Stockholm, about that time, the twenty-year-old Jenny Lind, after several years of a career asked the Italian baritone Bellite where she could learn the Italian style and technique. He answered, "In Paris under Manuel Garcia, the brother of Malibran." When she sang for Garcia, a period of rest was recom-

Reprinted from the *NATS Bulletin* [now *Journal*], November-December 1981.

mended, but by September 1841 Jenny Lind was having two lessons a week, "working again from the beginning, singing scales up and down, slowly and with great care, practicing the shake [trill] and gradually losing her hoarseness." She wrote that her voice was "becoming clear and sonorous and acquiring more firmness and agility." Signor Garcia was of infinite use to her in the management of the breath, the production of the voice, and the blending of the registers. Her voice was restored and her Italianate schooling completed in ten months. In 1847 Manuel Garcia published Part II of the *Traité complet de l'Art du Chant*, which was concerned with the interpretation of song. This was dedicated to the King of Sweden as a tribute to the nationality of Garcia's famous student, Jenny Lind.

What were Garcia's principles of developing the vocal instrument for the music of that period? Part I of an 1870 revision of the *Art of Singing*, which incorporates changes made after his invention of the laryngoscope and subsequent observations of the vocal organ by its use, will be considered here. This is the same document as the poorly-proofed American version which exists without date or publisher.

BREATHING

Garcia used breathing exercises to give power and elasticity to the lungs. From this the voice acquired steadiness, power, and expressiveness. The exercises were to be done with the head erect, "the shoulders thrown back without stiffness and the chest expanded," the diaphragm lowered without any jerk, and "the chest regularly and slowly raised." This was the complete inhalation called *respiro*. He also taught the half-breath termed *mezzo respiro*. In the first two exercises air was to be taken through pursed lips. *First* the student should slowly inhale over a period of several seconds as much air as the chest could contain. *Second*, after the deep breath the air should very slowly be exhaled, and *Third*, after the lungs have been filled, the breath should be held for the longest possible time. A fourth exercise was omitted in *Hints on Singing* (1894). The exercises were admittedly fatiguing and should be done separately and with intervals of rest.

EQUALIZATION OF FEMALE VOICES

In essence Garcia said that female voices should first attempt the chest voice on open vowels between a-flat and c^1, and if well managed the sound would come out pure and ringing. (The Helmholz pitch designations used by Garcia are retained in this discussion.) The pupil may ascend by half tones to f^1, after which she may descend, also by half tones, as low as the voice will permit. "Whether the voice is or is not capable of ascending high in the chest register, experience shows that the pupil should never in studying pass e^1 or f^1." When the pitches between d^1 and a^1 were difficult or feeble, he recommended short attacks on the five Italian vowels. If the quality of the sound was thin and childlike Garcia recommended correcting it by using the close timbre with the vowel [a] or [ɔ]. He suggested that this process sometimes be used at c^2 sharp and d^2 because, if not rounded, those notes form too great a contrast with the first notes e^2 and f^2 of the head, which are round and clear [Round Vowels—the meaning of *Umlaut*]. The most essential feature of the head voice is roundness. High notes were to be gained by rapid passages before being sustained. "Each note conquered should be allowed time to become firm before the next above is attempted."

EQUALIZATION OF MALE VOICES

Garcia describes the open, round, and close vowel relationship for bass and tenor voices. (In the interest of brevity, the one given for tenor voices is here presented.) He described the bass scale a minor third lower [the baritone would be a major or minor second below the tenor, although Garcia did not make a statement concerning that voice].

Tenors should attack their chest voice at d and e [below middle C]. The sounds g—b-flat offer a phenomenon worthy of attention. Unless care be taken, it becomes very difficult to produce them of a clear quality; the larynx always tending to render them sombre, and then they are a source of trouble to the singer. The only way to combat this tendency and give firmness to a voice, is to employ the clear timbre, emitting /A/ and /E/ with more and more openness. Tenors should begin to round gently at b^1 and c^1, for the actual clear quality would be too thin. [This is where his father used Oh in one page of his exercises.] The reader will remark that the word rounding, and not closing, is here used.

Garcia said that between d^1 and f^1

the two qualities agree [open and close]; but that the closed timbre in these sounds should not be practiced till a pupil has mastered the bright timbre. . . . If this caution be neglected there is a risk of the voice being veiled or muffled. The bright timbre alone can make the voice light and penetrating.

He stated that the chest voice existed within the 10th of d to f^1. The tenor should abandon the bright (voice) on f-sharp^1 [Pavarotti says real tenors should cover on fa, f^1]. "The tones g^1 to b^1 should be sung only in the close timbre because the sound in clear timbre would be too shrill [spread] even in a very large room."

Thus in both female and male voices there should be a rounding for the extension of high tones. In *Hints on Singing* (1894), when asked if this method introduced a real inequality in the vowel sound, Garcia answered

It does; and the apparent equality of the notes in the scale will be the result of actual but well-graduated inequality of the vowel sound. Without this manoeuvre, the round vowels which are suitable to the higher notes would extinguish the ringing of the middle and lower notes, and the open vowels which give éclat [ring] to the lower would make the higher notes harsh and shrill.

It is our loss that Garcia did not have access to the International Phonetic Alphabet (IPA) so he could define more accurately how clear and sombre timbres on certain pitches apply to the singing of languages. *In other words, for a vocal line to be equal there must be vowel modification, or inversely, if there is no vowel modification there is not an equalized vocal line.* In this development, Garcia differs from his father, who said that his exercises were to be sung on the five Italian vowels. Perhaps this is one of the reasons the younger Garcia had a short and undistinguished career, and the reason that Malibran was said to have had an uneven voice. Perhaps it is also the reason that the Earl of Mount Edgcumbe referred to the elder Garcia as being a "good musician, but (to my ears at least) a most disagreeable singer." The modifying of vowels where covering or rounding should take place in female and male voices is both a matter of voice placement and a method of preserving vocal health. This principle seems to be unknown or ignored by "one-vowel" teachers. The spread and white tone places excess tension on the cricothyroid muscles in such a manner that the resultant hyperfunction is detrimental to the health, growth, and survival of the voice.

A curious footnote of greatest importance must be related. Garcia states that sometimes when the female voice attempts to sing b^2 and c^3 it unconsciously flips to d^3 and e^3 in a thin but pure voice. He also found this phenomenon to be advantageous in extending the range of male voices, giving clarity and *mezza voce* to the high voice. [This technique has assumed great importance in the singing of today's artists.]

Garcia's techniques of articulation were discussed in *The NATS Bulletin* Feb/March 1976, and are here omitted.

EXERCISES

Manuel Garcia based his *Method* on that of his father but changed the order of the exercises. He states that studies must be made of passing alternately from one register to another on the notes d^1—f^1 in both female and male voices. Consequently, the first three exercises are on this technique, which was followed by many of his father's exercises that connect tones by portamento and agility. My impression is that the exercises of Manuel Garcia

II, as compared to those of his father, are more orderly and complete, but less improvisatory and inspirational. Manuel Garcia II has been criticized by Manén for introducing his father's first exercise of "swelled sounds [messa di voce]" so late in the text—after 167 exercises.

In conclusion, I quote another of Garcia's great singers, Sir Charles Santley.

> . . . he taught singing and not surgery. I was a pupil of his in 1858 and a friend of his while he lived . . . and I never heard him say a word about larynx or pharynx, glottis or any other organ used in the production and the emission of the voice.

Garcia knew the physiological instrument but did not mystify his pupils by its structure since he felt it "could serve no good purpose in acquiring a knowledge of the art of singing."

A comparison of several editions of Part II was published by Paschke in 1975, and a comparison of several editions of Part I is expected momentarily.

REFERENCES

Earl of Mount Edgcumbe (1834). *Musical Reminiscences of London.* John Andrews, London. 1973 Reprinted, Da Capo Press, New York.

Garcia, Manuel (1847, 1872). *A Complete Treatise on the Art of Singing,* Part II, 1975, Da Capo Press, New York. Collated, edited, and translated, Donald V. Paschke.

Garcia, Manuel (c. 1870). *New Treatise on the Art of Singing.* Cramer, London.

Garcia, Manuel (1911). *Hints on Singing.* Includes corrections and footnotes by Hermann Klein, regarding 1894 edition. Ascherberg, Hopwood and Crew, agents. Chappel, London.

Mackinlay, M. Sterling (1908). *Garcia, The Centenarian and His Times.* Appleton, 1976. Reprinted Da Capo Press, New York.

Manén, Lucie. *The Art of Singing* (1974). Faber Music, London.

Maude, Mrs. Raymond (1926). *The Life of Jenny Lind.* Cassell, London. [Mrs. Maude was Jenny Lind's daughter.]

Santley, Charles (1908). *The Art of Singing.* Macmillan, New York.

6

Mathilde Marchesi (1826–1913): *Theoretical and Practical Vocal Method;* and *Ten Singing Lessons*

The story of Nellie Melba is unique in the history of singing. After she had auditioned for Arthur Sullivan in 1886, she was told that if she would study singing for a year he might give her a small part in the "Mikado" (Melba 1925). After an audition with an agent she was given a London recital which Hermann Klein, the critic, described as being "decidedly amateurish and mediocre." During a subsequent audition with Mathilde Marchesi she was asked, "Why do you screech on your high notes—can't you sing them piano?" So she sang the B-flat^{2}natural [Helmholtz] pianissimo, continuing to E-flat^{2}natural. Suddenly, Marchesi left the room to tell her husband, Salvatore, "At last I have found a star." Within a year of instruction Nellie Melba made her debut in the Théâtre de la Monnaie in Brussels as Gilda, to great acclaim, which led to a world career of thirty-nine years. Her studies did not stop with her debut; Melba never lost contact with Marchesi during her teacher's professional life. What was Marchesi's magic with Nellie Melba, Ilma di Murska, Emma Eames, Emma Calvé, and many other singers?

After four years of study with Garcia, Marchesi was thoroughly trained in his techniques. While still his student she taught

Reprinted from the *NATS Bulletin* [now *Journal*], January-February 1982.

for him during a time when he was incapacitated. A superb musician, she, like Garcia II, had an unexceptional voice. Marchesi had a limited but highly artistic career before teaching in Vienna, Cologne, and Paris. She published many books of exercises and had singers auditioning for her from all parts of the singing world. Marchesi knew a natural voice and exceptional talent when she heard it—she developed it according to strict principles to such an extent that she is historically considered unrivaled as a teacher of the female voice. (She taught only female singers.) Her principles are set forth clearly in her *Theoretical and Practical Vocal Method* and *Ten Singing Lessons.* Melba said of Marchesi that she was a great enthusiast and philosopher [one who loves wisdom] of the art of singing. This was shown in her *lengthy* teaching career.

Marchesi's credo was, "In song, the formation of the voice is the first requisite, as it is the foundation of an artist's afterwork and the future of every singer; neglect means loss of all." She felt that what was worth doing was worth doing herself. She had no assistant teachers, but did have a conductor from the Paris opera to coach her opera class, and an outstanding accompanist to coach her concert class. She alone taught the class on voice formation, and only her students knew how to carry on her traditions.

In Melba's case, after a few private lessons, she went into the opera class. Other singers participated in the vocal formation class, in which Marchesi recommended from her thirty-six books of vocalises those which best suited individual voices. She demanded of her students enthusiasm and intelligent energy or she sent them away. Before she would accept a worthy student she had to know the singer would be with her a minimum of two years to complete the student's vocal formation. She found that in her own case, four years of study with Garcia was not too much.

Marchesi said there was only one *right* method of singing— that based on the nature of the voice [W. J. Henderson, in his introduction to Marchesi's method said that such a proper method was equally right for Brahms, Bellini, Gounod, and Wagner].

The teacher of female singers needed to have a comprehension of the different types of voices and of the three registers as bestowed by nature. Marchesi abhorred the bleating sound caused by undue pressure on the larynx. She observed that when one sings the highest notes violently for years, the voice becomes weary and the tones become tremulous and unavailable. [This is one reason young singers should not sing dramatic music.] Marchesi was greatly averse to the nasality of her American female students and felt that it was a retarding factor in their instruction. She thought humming was detrimental to the formation of the singing voice.

She advised against strenuous exercise, singing after meals, exposure to excessive heat or cold, loud speech, and too frequent theater parties. [There are many other things to be avoided today!]

Marchesi had frequent musicales in her home with such composers as Gounod and Massenet as accompanists. Is it a wonder they knew voices and that she knew opera?

MARCHESI'S BASIC PRINCIPLES

1. The attitude of the singer should be natural and as easy as possible with the body held erect. She recommended, as did Garcia I, that her students sing with the arms behind the back (during practice periods).

2. The beauty of a voice may be spoiled by a faulty position of the lips since they are a part of the vocal resonating tube. She was averse to the smiling position on /A/ because it "is absurd, and quite contrary to the laws of acoustics" because it gives the *voix blanche* [white voice]. Her desire was to have the jaw dropped and kept immovable during the entire duration of sound. [Close and repeated observations of television video tapes of singing do not prove this to be true at the present time—although in many cases the movement is very subtle. Perhaps a better statement would be to internalize as much of the mechanics of singing as possible.]

3. Respiration—she believed in normal breathing in which the

lungs are expanded at the base to give the greatest quantity of air—this she called *diaphragmatic* or *abdominal* breathing. She did not believe in corsets which would cause lateral breathing and prevent inflation of the lungs at the base. She advised against

> a crushed posture of the head, which interferes with the free and natural rising and falling action of the larynx. And there are teachers that seek to prevent this motion by pressure of the forefingers. Alas for such ignorance! I have seen its victims suffering from cramps of the larynx and ultimately losing their voices.

4. Attack—she desired to have the spontaneous action which has been developing since the first cry of birth in which the air bursts through the vocal cords at the moment of expiration. This was the *coup de glotte* which she considered to be a natural and normal event.

   Marchesi states that the firmer and more complete the approximation of the lips of the glottis, the less air it will take to set the *vocal cords* vibrating. The sound will, as a consequence, be longer and the vibrations more equal. She felt that staccato was very wearisome and should be practiced sparingly—the attack of each is a small *coup de glotte*.

5. Registers—she considered the treatment of the registers as "the touchstone of all singing methods, old and new." She believed there were three—Chest, Medium, and Head, and that a voice without a chest tone was like a violin without a G string.

> To equalize and blend the Chest and Medium register, the pupil slightly closes [darkens] the last two notes of the former in ascending, and opens [makes clearer] in descending.

The Chest in soprano voices could be taken as high as e^1 or f^1 and for mezzos and contraltos to f^1 or f-sharp^1. The same closing of vowels in ascending and opening of vowels in descending should occur at the juncture of *Medium* and *Head* voice. Marchesi did not agree with Garcia II that there was a register change at c². [In the overtone observations of registers there *is* an harmonic shift at that point.]

Marchesi stressed that f-natural² was the last note of medium voice and that "whoever sings or has sung the high notes in medium tones, is bound ere long to bleat like a goat." She felt that more time was needed for the development of the *head* voice since it is not used in speech. And most of all, she wanted the passage from register to register to be undetected.

6. The method of study was based on the principle that a singer can think of only one thing at a time. So the exercises are progressively more difficult and singing should not tire the voice with too long a period of practice—better five or ten minutes three or four times a day than too long. "A conscientious professor will never allow the lesson to last longer than half an hour." She recommended practice "with the full volume of tone" without forcing or shouting in order to develop the power, extent and equality of the voice.

7. Vocalization should be advanced before vowels were combined with consonants—she preferred the Italian language to German because of the gutteral vowels of German—despite the fact that she was born in Frankfurt. The defect of the French language was the uvular [ɓ].

8. The consonants involving the tongue [l,d,t,s,z,r,n,c,g,k,x] should be practiced until the action of the tongue is independent of the laryngeal actions. This study can be followed with that of the Recitative and Air.

9. Style—her feeling, after having resided in Germany, Italy, and France was that there were only two styles: the *good,* from which the best results are obtained, and the *bad,* from which the reverse is the case.

10. Marchesi believed in class instruction because others could learn from hearing a singer being taught. [Singers were not vocalized together.] The individual singer would stand on a platform and take up to a 15-minute lesson in front of the other students in a small class. The singers sang words only after vocalization was clear—transition was made to songs

and arias by means of her vocalises, which were combined with words. They were selected for the individual needs of the singer. Marchesi was too rigid and exacting a taskmaster to ask her students what they thought—she was indomitable, and her principles were too basic to be changed by the untrained ear or by student tastes.

11. Finally,
   A singer who has learned how to breathe well, and who has equalized the voice, neatly blended the registers and developed the activity of the larynx and the elasticity of the glottis and resonant tube in a rational manner, so that all possible shades of tone, power and expression can be produced by the vocal organs, would most assuredly be able to sing well, and without fatigue and effort the long and declaimed modern phrases.

Times have changed, but not her basic principles of the singing voice. "First technique and afterwards aesthetics."

REFERENCES

Marchesi, Blanche (1923). *Singer's Pilgrimage.* Small, Maynard, Boston.
Marchesi, Mathilde (1898). *Marchesi and Music.* Harper and Brothers, New York.
Marchesi, Mathilde (1901). *Ten Singing Lessons.* Harper and Brothers, New York.
Marchesi, Mathilde (1970). *Theoretical and Practical Vocal Method.* Reprinted with Introduction by Philip Miller, Dover, New York.
Melba, Nellie (1925). *Melodies and Memories.* Thornton Butterworth, London.

7

Julius Stockhausen:
Method of Singing

When Dietrich Fischer-Dieskau was asked the source of his technique and interpretation, he replied that both of his teachers were students of Julius Stockhausen, a student of Manuel Garcia II, and that most of the answers could be found in the writings of Stockhausen and Garcia (Sugg 1973). In contrast to the Garcia family and their singers, who were basically involved with opera, Stockhausen was most closely identified with the Lied. In fact, his biography by his daughter was entitled, *Julius Stockhausen: Der Sänger des Deutschen Liedes.* Between 1848 and 1868 his activities extended to most of the musical centers of Europe. He gave the first public performance of *Die Schöne Müllerin;* his first public performance of *Dichterliebe* was with Brahms at the piano; and Brahms wrote the *Magelone Lieder* for him. The trio of Stockhausen, Joachim, and Brahms concertized extensively during this period. He was at the Opera Comique in Paris from 1856 to 1859, but his main vocal activity was in recital and oratorio. He sang in the first performance of the *German Requiem* by Brahms. As with Mathilde Marchesi, his extension of the Garcia technique is highly significant.

Sir George Grove (1965) in speaking of Stockhausen stated, "The rich beauty of the voice, the nobility of the style, the perfect phrasing, the intimate sympathy and, not least, the intelligible way in which the words were given—in itself one of his

Reprinted from the *NATS Bulletin* [now *Journal*], March-April 1982.

greatest claims to distinction—all combined to make his singing a wonderful event.'' All of these points are touched upon in Stockhausen's *Method of Singing* (1884). He taught many famous singers in Frankfurt am Main, including Hermine Spies, Anton van Rooy, and Karl Scheidemantel, all of whom were excellent *Lieder* singers; the last two were opera luminaries of the first magnitude. Max Friedländer, the noted editor of *Lieder*, was a pupil of both Garcia II and Stockhausen.

Stockhausen stated there are three elements of singing:

1. Pitch—which must be true, and is from the larynx, directed by the ear;
2. Power—which may be loud or soft, and is caused by the lungs giving more or less amplitude of vibration; and
3. Quality—which is determined by the method of its production in the cavity of articulation [the vocal tract] and which changes forms in the larynx by means of the lips, tongue, soft palate, and epiglottis through the formation of vowels.

He hoped that his work would show how these three elements work together in the six types of vocalization which form the whole of the technique of the art of singing.

The tone *must* be pure (in tune) ''. . . purity of tone [he does not say purity of vowel] may be described as *absolute*, a necessity. Power of the voice is *relative* and the *quality* is inherent.''

Julius Stockhausen noted that quality is partly due to the types of vibration from the larynx, known as registers. The sound [pa] assists in the emission of the chest register, the sound [ba] in the emission of the middle register.

The purity of tone is involved with sustaining the voice, carrying and uniting tones, execution of ornaments, and exercises. The power and quality of the voice are involved with expression when they are in harmony with inward emotions. Stockhausen agreed with E. Seiler that a beautiful tone is the first and most important basis of the art of singing, and that it alone in its highest perfection can serve as interpreter of the varied feelings which find their expression in song. He professed his allegiance to the school which makes formation of tone precede technique, and which never sacrifices beauty to mere execution.

This artist-teacher goes further than Garcia in the study of articulation and the effect upon the vocal cords and expression. [I have transcribed his observations of vowels and consonants to current IPA symbols, which I believe will do a great deal to facilitate the combination of word and music in song.] He said that vowel and consonant are as inseparable in singing as in speech. "The emission of consonants acts on the vocal cords almost like blinking does on the eye."

He believed that all sounds in the singer's alphabet should be studied, and that the study of all vowel forms was indispensable to the beauty of tone. He observed that the open vowels [a, a, ɛ, U, ɔ, Y, ɪ] can strengthen a weak voice, and that the close vowels [e,ø,o,u,y, and i] can give mellowness and roundness to hard voices.

Stockhausen pointed out that the vowel attacks should be as varied as the attacks on [pa], [ba], and [ma], and that by watching the lips in these sounds the singer could form a concept of the occurrence in the larynx. This quantifies Garcia's shock of the glottis, which he states should be accomplished by a lowering of the larynx. Otherwise, the notes will be poor and thin.

Stockhausen believed the smile of the old Italians was a thing of the past, and that [o,u,ø, and y] could be sung with the lips drawn back and [i] and [a] with the lips pushed forward. Otherwise, it would be impossible to produce vowels distinctly with different expressions of the face.

He believed that *mezza voce* solfaing was the best way of acquiring unimpeded tone and suggested that at first the consonants [d,r,m,f,s,l] be articulated *senza voce*—whispered. Later, voice and consonants could be used together. In fact he stated, "One should sol-fa first and only vocalize when the emission of the voice has become quite unimpeded by the use of syllables. The vowel attacks will after a while have neither throaty nor nasal quality." [May I state that the [r] should be flipped and [l] should be bright, neither of which is an American sound.] Stockhausen preferred to begin the study of singing with the limited range of a hexachord. In solfaing the larynx was to be lower than in speech. He later stated that songs with difficult words should at first be sol-faed.

Little is said of breathing, except that diaphragmatic breathing is sufficient for the half breath [*mezzo respiro*] and that for the full breath [*respiro pieno*], the extension of the ribs was indispensable.

He pointed out that the notes from d^1 to f-sharp^1 were common to all voices and that near this area lay the problem of the *passaggio,* or the changing and blending of registers. This could be accomplished by close vowels in ascending, and by open vowels in descending. The progression of the vowels [u,I,*a*,I,u] on the same note would facilitate the *messa di voce.* As a rule Stockhausen stated that the *messa di voce* could only be executed with the help of two registers, with the exception that above f^2 the head register suffices for high soprani; below b for bass voices, the chest suffices. His nomenclature for registers was similar to that of Garcia.

Of the six styles of singing, *tenuta di voce,* in which notes are sustained with "equal and medium power," is the chief manner by which musical phrases are executed. It is by contrast with this technique that the other dynamic and artistic techniques are effective.

The second type of vocalization is *portamento.* By it "the singer gets his breathing and vocal apparatus under full control." This could best be acquired by the help of the *messa di voce,* since the *portamento* can be executed either with equal power, *crescendo* or *diminuendo.* [And as Tosi said, "Those who want to perfect themselves in this must listen more to the dictates of the heart than to the laws of art."] The *portamento* itself essentially tends to blend the registers.

The *legato* runs should be performed on single vowels only, without aspiration. The [h] was to be used only to clarify the repetition of a note. *Decrescendo* in ascending passages and *crescendo* in descending passages will assist in equalizing the voice.

The *staccato,* or pointed vocalization, is a technique in which the notes are attacked by a slight shock of the glottis and immediately quitted—thus the value of each note is slightly shortened. "In this style of vocalization the student should concentrate his attention chiefly on the closing muscles [of the larynx]." ". . . the quick inspirations required for staccato we practice from earliest childhood in laughing and sobbing." The *staccato* should be accomplished with a soft vowel attack.

The *martellato* is related to the *legato* in that there is a continual breath flow, the exception being that in the *martellato* the muscles of the diaphragm give a fresh impulse for each note. "The contact of the vocal cords is never interrupted and they never cease to vibrate." He found the *martellato* most favorable for the male chest register and the female falsetto [medium] register, and that it gave great energetic expression. He felt the *staccato*, being lighter and brighter, was more easily executed by sopranos than by other voices. When both styles are practiced he recommended executing the *staccato* very slowly and the *marcato* with a faster tempo. His *martellato* exercises for the female voice extend to a^2 and for the male voice to e^1. He stated that it is advantageous to practice the high notes *martellato* with the result being more fullness and greater flexibility.

His examples and exercises of the six types of vocalization are extensive. In conclusion, Stockhausen stated that a good voice and a lively imagination are not enough for becoming a good singer; they are the preliminary conditions of artistic singing, which can only be attained by unremitting and careful study. "What will always distinguish him from the untaught singer, who is lacking in control over his breath, or in flexibility, or in distinctness of pronunciation, is that he perceives at once the meaning of the artistic task before him, and enters into it with full command of the means necessary for its interpretation." And for our composer friends, I must add this final quote: "Music has always found its chief resource in song, and this is what has preserved instrumental music from degenerating into empty jingle and meaningless noise." Oh yes, he was conductor of the Hamburg *Philharmonische Konzertgesellschaft,* 1863–1867.

REFERENCES

Grove's Dictionary (1965). *Die Musik in Geschichte und Gegenwart.*
Bärenreiter, Basel.
Stockhausen, Julius (1884). *Method of Singing.* Translated into English
by Sophie Löwe. Novello, London.
Sugg, James Ferrell (1973). *Comparisons in Historical and Contemporary Viewpoints Concerning Vocal Techniques.* M.M. Thesis, Baylor University, Waco, Texas.
Wirth, Julia (1927). *Julius Stockhausen: Der Sänger des Deutschen Liedes.* Verlag Englert und Schlosser, Frankfurt am Main.

8

Enrico Delle Sedie: *Esthetics of the Art of Singing and of the Melodrama* (1885)

Gerhard Hüsch, after his first recital in Berlin in 1932, was considered one of the greatest *Lieder* singers of his time. During his career he sang in the major opera houses of Europe. His teacher was Hans Emge, a student of Enrico Delle Sedie, who formed one of the most remarkable of the vocal pedagogy classics. Delle Sedie (1822–1907) was one of the early Verdi baritones who sang in the principal theaters of Italy, in Paris at the Théâtre-Italien, and in London, where he sang Renato in the first performance of *Ballo in Maschera* at the Lyceum in 1860. Although his voice was small, his musicianship and style were outstanding. He concluded his career as a teacher of singing in Paris. His *L'estetica del canto e dell'arte melodrammatica* was published in Livorno, Italy in 1885, in Italian, French, and English, in four books: I, Solfeggio; II, Formation of the Voice; III, Exercises of Vocal Flexibility, Use of Words; and IV, Concepts of Acting.

The unique thing is that an Italian artist authored the first text to take into account the resonance of vowels found in Helmholtz' *On the Sensations of Tone* (1877) and in the research of early investigators. Furthermore, Delle Sedie included a "Vowel Chart" which he must have devised in response to sensations noted in his operatic and teaching career. The Chart (Figure 1)

Reprinted from the *NATS Bulletin* [now *Journal*], May-June 1982.

43

TAVOLA COMPARATIVA DELLE GRADAZIONI FONICHE INE. RENTI ALLA SCALA VOCALE	TABLE COMPARATIVE DES NUANCES PHONIQUES INHE. RENTES A LA GAMME VOCALE	COMPARATIVE TABLE OF THE PHONICAL SHADES IN. HERENT TO THE VOCAL SCALE
La parola posta contro la nota musicale serve per indicare l'accen. tofonico della vocale corrispondente al suono di quella nota. Questa vo. cale è messa in evidenza per mezzo di segni speciali apposti alla voca. le citata.	Les mots mis en regard des notes servent à indiquer l'accent phoni- que de la voyelle correspondant au son vocal et celle-ci est signalée par des lignes speciales posées auprès de la voyelle même	The words placed at the sides of the notes serve to show us that the phonic accent of the vowel corre. sponding to the vocal sound, is marked by special lines and plac- ed after the same vowel.
a aperta come nel la parola Bando	a ouvert comme dans l'a de Climat	ā open as in the word .. Bär
a semioscura come nella parola Baulta	a un peu sombre com- me dans l'a de Courage	a a little closed as in the word. : Father
ā oscura come nel la parola Parmaco	a sombre comme dans l'ā de Caprice	ā closed as in the word.....Cāto
â grave come nel la parola Gâudio	â grave comme dans l'â de Grâce	â grave as in the word .... Wâs
a aperta come nel la parola Bando	a ouvert comme dans l'a de Climat	a open as in the word..... Bär·
â grave come nel. la parola Gâudio	â grave comme dans l'â de Grâce	â grave as in the word ..... Wâs
ò chiusa come nel. la parola Dolce	ò fermé comme dans l'ò de Idôle	ò closed as in the word...... Or
ô grave come nel. la parola Dôlo	ô grave comme dans l'ô de Pôle	ô grave as in the word ..... Pôle
eu chiuso come nel. la parola francese Jeune	eu fermé comme l'eu dans Jeune	eu closed as in the french word .. Jeune
eu grave come nel. la parola francese Feu	eu grave comme l'eu dans Feu	eu grave as in the french word . Feu
ē muta come nella parola francese Nature	ē muet comme l'ē dans Nature	ē mute as in the word.... Nature
e muta oscura co. me nella par. fr. Refrain	e muet couvert com. me dans l'e de Refrain	e mute covered as in the word. Her

Figure 1: Delle Sedie's modifications of the French A in the Modulated Voice o Singing (Articulated Voice is used in speech). For a larger version of this chart see Appendix K, pages 300–301.

which came into my hands indirectly from Gerhard Hüsch some years ago, led me to a copy of this book in the British Museum Library, the second part of which I here review.

Delle Sedie observes that the human voice is divided into two categories: the *articulated voice,* and the *modulated voice* which constitutes singing, but articulation is not indispensable to it. This is the difference between speech and singing, a fact unknown to this day to many people including singers, singing teachers, coaches, and conductors.

He stated the pharynx and the oral cavities must be considered as the mobile resounding body of the vocal organ, the different motions of which determine in great part the timbre of the voice. He was also aware that some observers had called the cavity of the larynx a resonator [now believed to be the source of the "singer's formant"].

Delle Sedie observed as did Stockhausen that the intensity of the voice depends on the vigor with which the vocal cords put sound into vibration—similar to the act of the [m], [b], [p], action of the lips [the concept possibly came from Fournié]. He desired to teach the attack in a "way to vibrate the vocal sound without incurring the defect of a weak emission called *humming."* He had exercises utilizing [me], [be], and [pe], varying the attacks.

He believed that the breath should be *sustained* [he did not like the word *support*] in such a way that there would be "time for the vibrations to complete themselves in the resounding body so that the intensity of the voice could be transmitted far." In that way "the mouth then acts as a speaking trumpet." He stated that a forced pressure "gives to the respiratory apparatus a useless fatigue and will greatly destroy the sonority, flexibility and mellowness of the voice," and that the listener will hear "the noise of the reed [vocal folds] instead." The forced and compressed *support* "in time may engender a disease in the larynx and trachea." He suggests obtaining the *sustained* breath by counting in a low voice from 1,2,3 to as high a number as a person can easily attain without tension and complete exhaustion of the breath—this to be done without escape of air between the syllables. This exercise should not exceed the limits of the middle of the voice.

THE DELLE SEDIE PHONIC ORDER

In Delle Sedie's opinion, when the voice is exercised by the aid of natural conditions and without being strained, it becomes stronger without interruption up to an advanced age. The natural conditions of the voice of which he speaks involve sympathetic resonation which is the basis of *modulated voice*. He cites Koenig's investigations (1870) of vowels with organ pipe diapasons in which the mouth could be brought into certain forms to "vibrate in unison with the exterior motor." He concludes ". . . the modifications brought to the oral cavity by the motion of constriction given to the lips, must exercise an appreciable influence on the tone of the voice . . ." [Whereas Koenig's "exterior motor" was a diapason pipe, today we can use the Echophone with amplifier and a Casio VL-Tone to resonate the vowels not only in unison but at harmonic distances from the unison found in the Chromatic Vowel Chart—(Coffin 1974, 1977, 1980)]. Although the vowel values on which Delle Sedie based his phonic order are not in accord with Helmholtz' vowel values and overtone relationships of vowels, his deductions are in the right direction and usable. His notation is quite involved, as will be any work of this kind notating the slight modifications of any vowel in an ascending scale. "The slight modifications brought to the initial vowel by the different sounds of the scale are so minute that the ear could hardly perceive them if not aided by precise appreciation and demonstration" [or by an Echo phone]. He was persuaded "that these changes [of vowel quality] are imposed by the *musical tone*."

He was also convinced that when the whole vocal tract was brought into vibration one "finds a kind of repercussion in the upper part of the thorax, hence the term chest voice applied to the low notes" [below e^1 or "the break"], and that the study "of going from one register to another consists simply in the gradation of vocal sound obtained by displacing the harmonics."

It is evident in this work that the movements of the tongue indicated for the formation of the vowels must be effected in general with its back part, for those which exact the action of the front part are used especially for the articulation of the consonants.

Delle Sedie states, "The vowels corresponding to the conditions of height of the vocal sound [as shown on his vowel chart], will be identically the same for all voices, excepting a few modifications subject to the character of each voice." [It has been found that vowels of the female voice are 10 to 15% higher than those of comparable classifications of male voices.] His chart is concerned with the French /A/ vowel but he states similar changes occur in other vowels. His observations concern the front, umlaut, and back series of vowels. An interesting statement on *messa di voce* is that the vowel is enlarged for *crescendo* and diminished in size for the *diminuendo*.

Regarding the various timbres of the singing voice, he spoke of the *closed timbre, somber voice,* and *open timbre, clear voice;* of the particular timbre of an individual's voice; of the timbres constituted by degrees of height of voice [related to phonic order shown on his chart]; of the intermediate timbres or vowels between the ten which he used; and of the sentiment used to express the emotions of the soul. He felt he was not forming a new school of singing but reestablishing the old school of singing by "the practical application of vowels corresponding to the sounds of the vocal scale." His vowel scale was divided into four parts, C-A, A-C, C-E, and E-G. The exercises using these vowels were noted in different clefs, indicating that the "phonic order" was to be used by all voices, male and female. The pupil was to use his memory and his ear as guides for the appreciation of the phonic intervals in the vocalises and in songs.

The limitations of his chart are due to the crude means of observations at that time. It lacks the harmonic definition of vowels and vowel colors in the highest and lowest extensions of the voice. Nevertheless the text is filled with astute observations on the use of vowel resonance before the term "formant" had been coined by Hermann in 1890.

It is Delle Sedie's belief that "The esthetic study made, proves that art and science aiding intuition, may obtain a strong development of the vocal organs, from which singing, declamation and the correct dramatic expression may draw the greatest advantage." This is a statement from a baritone who made his debut within twenty years of the beginning of the Italian baritone voice classification. His was a great career in the extended range and color of the Italian *bel canto*. And his influence exists to this day in *Lieder* and operatic singing.

REFERENCES

Coffin, Berton (1980). *Overtones of Bel Canto*. The Scarecrow Press. Metuchen, New Jersey.
Coffin, Berton (1977). *The Sounds of Singing: Vocal Techniques with Vowel-Pitch Charts*. The Scarecrow Press. Metuchen, New Jersey.
Coffin, Berton (1974). "The Instrumental Resonance of the Singing Voice." *The NATS Bulletin*, 31,2.
Delle Sedie, Enrico (1885). *L'estetica del Canto e dell'arte Melodrammatica*. Leghorn, the author.
Grove's Dictionary. 1980 Edition.
Helmholtz, Hermann L. F. (1877). *On the Sensations of Tone*. Translated by Alexander Ellis, 1885. Reprint. Dover Publications, New York.

9

Emma Seiler:
The Voice in Singing

INTRODUCTORY NOTE

Linking paragraphs between Marchesi, Stockhausen, and Delle Sedie are not described in this text, but Emma Seiler needs clarification. She was a student of Helmholz, a Professor of Physiology, who wrote in the Translator's Preface to her book Voice in Singing *(1866) that she had rare scientific attainments and should be recognized in this country where she had recently taken up abode in Philadelphia. He published testimonials of her position in her own country (Germany).*

She taught singing in Heidelberg for a number of years and had the reputation of being a very careful, skilled, and learned teacher of singing, with a delicate musical ear and cultivated taste.

Emma Seiler was interested in the formation of vowel tones and registers of the female voice. This coupled with a scientific culture of music was a rare combination, as was her interest in the anatomical study of the vocal organs. Establishment of the conditions of the formation of the voice (the larynx) and its production was important to her. She finalized a formation of "fistel tones" (head tones).

That this much practical research, including investigations

Reprinted from the *NATS Bulletin* [now *Journal*], September-October 1982.

*with Helmholtz, was done in the mid to late 1800s by this in-
quisitive woman is unique. Her writings provided approbation of
both the physiologist and the singing master. Even today, men
seem to be more in the limelight, but whoever is doing the research, let us hope it will be practical and meaningful. The
writers of the books reviewed after Seiler follow some of the more
well known principles of singing and need less explanation.*

One of the most curious occurrences in the history of vocal
pedagogy is one which did not happen. Manuel Garcia, although
he spoke of vowel colors and forms in the singing of the scale of
male singers, ignored *On the Quality of Vowels,* which Helmholtz published in 1859, and the four revisions of *On the Sensations of Tone,* all of which were published before Garcia's *Hints
on Singing,* 1894. However, he did mention Helmholtz's definition of frequencies the ear could perceive. It took an unsuccessful
singer, Emma Seiler, to further Garcia's visual and aural observations and to assimilate them with Helmholtz's discoveries into
the teaching of singing.

Emma Seiler's case was one of vocal misfortune. She was
trained in the art of singing in the best of both the "German and
Italian tuition," and often sang in concerts with favor. In order to
become a good teacher she studied with the best teachers, each of
whom had his own rules but no reason for them. Under one of
them she completely lost her voice. After this she studied with
Frederick Wieck, father of Clara Schumann, in order to become a
teacher of piano. While living in Dresden she took the opportunity of hearing Jenny Lind whenever possible. [How strange
that she did not go to Garcia for study!] She studied singing in
Italy, where she gathered "no sure and radical knowledge" and
found that the historical cultivation of the singing voice was nonexistent. This was due to the fact that there were no longer the
castrati who could pass along their art of vocal formation and
expression.

When convinced that the only sure way was scientific investigation, she sought the counsel of Hermann Helmholtz, who in the
introduction to her book wrote that he was assisted by Emma
Seiler in his essay upon the formation of the vowel tones and the
registers of the female voice. E. du Bois-Raymond stated that she

stood by the side of the celebrated physiologist Helmholtz while
he was engaged in his physiologico-acoustic work upon the generation of the vowels and the nature of harmony (1866).

Emma Seiler felt that the human voice was the most natural of
all instruments and the the cultivation of beautiful tone of voice
should be the foundation and first requisition of fine singing.
Without it the correct expression of the feeling intended by the
composer could not be attained. She felt that the difference between the competent and incompetent Italian teachers of singing
was that the true singing masters "taught only according to a
sound and just feeling for the beautiful, guided by the faculty of
acute observation, which enabled them to distinguish what be-
longs to nature." [Few of them could put their art into words.]
Her aim and effort in life was to "obtain such a knowledge of the
human voice [physiological and acoustical] as is indispensable to
a natural and healthy development of its beautiful powers." It
was her belief that science can only furnish artistic talent with
aids—it cannot create it.

The *physiological* has to do with the quality and strength of the
organ of singing in the art of uttering sound under the variations
that take place in certain tones—the transition of registers. The
physical [the physics of sound—*acoustical* is today's word] has
to do with the airflow from the lungs bringing the vocal cords into
vibration and the vocal tract into resonation.

This review will be limited to the aspects of her work pertaining to the cultivation of the voice. She restudied Garcia's *Observations with the Laryngoscope* (1855), accepted Garcia's register
terminology of the male voice, embellished on his register terminology in the female voice, and made additional observations.
She noted that "in the falsetto register [middle voice of the
female singer] the larynx preserves its natural position, as in quiet
breathing." In the head register at f#2 in female voices there was
another action, a vibration of only a third of the whole glottis,
"immediately under the epiglottis."

Emma Seiler, in investigating the physiological nature of
larynges, believed that *cuneiform cartilages* existed in the mem-
branes of the vocal ligaments in female voices. She described
them as being "two long, slender cartilaginous laminae which

become somewhat broader at both ends. These cartilages, with their base, rest at the middle of the anterior surface of the *arytenoid cartilages,* and reach to the middle of the vocal cords, by which they are enveloped. The action of these cartilages renders possible the production of the head tones, but they are not found in every larynx.'' [They are now regarded as an articulating part of the arytenoid cartilage and are pretty much universally found in all larynges. Whether they are used by women to obtain head voice is a subject awaiting research.]

She found the head register in female voices to have the capacity of expansion to an octave or more above its inception. She states that only in entirely healthy vocal organs can the head voice be observed.

Seiler and Helmholtz felt that "the break" of both male and female voices is on the same note, f^1 or $f\#^2$. [Singers and later investigators believe this phenomenon varies according to voice classification.] A definite rule resulted from her study—*no voice can bear over-straining beyond register limits—the result is that the voice becomes unstable and weakened.*

She observed that in the year 1700 at the Paris Opera A^1 was 404 Hz [it is now 448 Hz in Vienna]. Higher orchestral pitch means that difficult high notes must frequently be sung in a higher register [or sung by a higher voice classification than the composer had intended—neither of which may be to the critics' delight]. Her observations of the female larynx indicated several mini-registers.

Female Registers

Head Register g^2-f^3
  (feels from forehead)

Second Falsetto d^2-f^2
  (as if formed above in the mouth)

First Falsetto Register g^1-c^2
  (feels like origin in throat)

Second Chest Register c^1-f^1
  (midway from pit of stomach and sternum)

First Chest Register   e -c^1
  (lower part of lungs)

She felt that the best way to teach was by imitation, and because of this men should teach men and women should teach women. Frederick Wieck had a young woman with "practised voice" sing exercises which his female students of singing could imitate. Emma Seiler's observations on the natural laws of sounds were that in beautiful musical sounds there must be movement of air in a regular manner which is sensed by the ear as purity of tone. [When irregular vibration occurs in a voice the tone has a background of fuzzy noise.] The perfection of a tone at a certain pitch depends on the resonance of the cavity of the mouth and the utterance of certain vowels, to which the parts of the mouth can be adjusted. Helmholtz (1877) describes

> the easiest and surest method of finding the tones to which the air of the oral cavity is tuned for the different shapes it assumes in the production of vowels. . . . Tuning-forks of different pitches have to be struck and held before the open mouth—and the louder the proper tone of the fork is heard, the nearer does it correspond with one of the proper tones of the included air mass.

[The resonance is weaker on either side of the proper tone; just like tuning a radio to a certain station, there is a frequency of clear and loudest sound with the signal fading away as the frequency becomes higher or lower. Both are due to the phenomenon called tuning.]
The investigation of the resonance of the cavity of the mouth is of greatest importance.

> Since the shape of the oral cavity can be altered at pleasure, it can always be made to suit the tones of any given tuning-fork, and we thus easily discover what shape [and vowel color] the mouth must assume for its included air mass of air to be tuned to a determined pitch.

[The tuning fork gives a pure tone, so does a flute, or flute-stop on any kind of an instrument. Any person with contemporary electrical equipment can reproduce Helmholtz's findings and use them in the teaching of singing. Sundberg (1973) in his study of the acoustics of singing used a vibrator against the side of the throat. I have found that a vibrator held in front of the mouth is most easily heard by the singer to "tune in" vowel pitch (Coffin). This technique can be used in the teaching of singing and shows that harmonic transitions are the bases of the register structure of the singing voice.]

It is more difficult for the ear to hear the upper partials in the human voice than in musical instruments. The use of Helmholtz resonators [turnip-shaped resonators of brass, open at both ends with one end held to the ear] is of value to assist in hearing these harmonically compound tones of the human voice. He also described what we know as "the singer's formant."

With the use of the Helmholtz resonators Seiler listed vowels of loudest resonance for female voices (again, we are at a disadvantage because International Phonetics were not used at that time.):

> . . . all tones below c^1 should take the character of o. At c^1, a, as in the English word "*hall*," sounds the best, and at $d\#^1$-e^1 passes to a, as in *man*, at f into a, as in *May*. With g^1 the a sounds again as in *man*; a^1-c^2 are favorable to all the vowels, while d^2-e^2 sound best with e. After e^2 every tone takes the coloring of a, in *father*, and sounds well only with this vowel; b^2-d^3 sound again better with e.
>
> . . . the female voice, therefore, has only a few tones more than an octave, upon which every one of the vowels can be distinctly sung; and again, all these tones do not afford an equally sonorous tone with every vowel.

[These vowels of loudest resonance are for female voices. Other vowels were to be shaded toward these for best resonance. Note that the vowel scale of Delle Sedie (1885) in the last review in this column apparently was intended for both male and female voices.]

The most important thing in this manner of training the voice "is timbre of the tones, for *here* it is our power to form out of a sharp, hard and disagreeable voice, a voice sweet and pleasing." Yet she concluded that even with greatest resonance "it is not in our power, when once the vocal organs have become fully developed, to make a strong voice out of a weak one."

The flexibility of the voice depends upon a *physiologico-physical (acoustical) process of the organ of tone*, which among the Italians goes on in their common speech, and hence is more easily transferred to them in their singing. [Were they not in actuality combining the organ tone of the voice with their language in their pedagogy?] She also observed that the windpipe expands laterally and draws the larynx down, but ". . . if pupils do not naturally move their throats correctly, the gift of flexibility is denied them." [This is adverse to those who wish to hold their throats in one particular way.] However she did *"not seek to cultivate formation of tone and fluency at the same time."*

Concerning breathing she found that

> by a too great pressure of the breath, the form of the wave sound is disturbed. One then hears the high overtones sounding up to the sixteenth, while the lower over-tones with the fundamental tone sound weak or not at all. Thus the tone takes a shrill, sharp, and disagreeable sound. . . . Too little breath deprives the tone only of its strength, but not of its agreeable sound.

In the old Italian method "if the crowding or pressure of his breathing was too great, the student was required to learn to hold it back."

> A correct touch [attack, placement?] of the voice consists in causing the air brought into vibration by the vocal ligaments, to rebound from immediately above the front teeth, where it must be concentrated as much as possible, rebounding thence to form in the mouth continuous vibrations which are at the same time communicated to the external air. . . . That the voice must be brought forward in the mouth . . . is now acknowledged as necessary and aimed at by the best teachers. But the reasons why the tones sound better are not known. [This forward sensation can be brought about by using artificial vibrators.] Only by a correct movement of this kind are those forms of the vibrations obtained in which all the harmonic over-tones belonging to a perfect tone sound together.

"The old Italian masters naturally found their beautiful *a* most favorable to the formation of good tone in singing." But the Italian *a* is different from the English and German. "The Italians form the *l* with the tip of the tongue, the Germans and English mostly with the sides of the tongue." Do-re-mi (solfeggio) assists in the forward touch. Seiler published vocalises which included those of Miksch and Mazzoni (Oliver Ditson publications). Without doubt Seiler and Helmholtz defined the *physiological-acoustical* laws of nature upon which the early vocal masters of singing based their teaching by ear, but Seiler stated that they did not know the reasons "why."

REFERENCES

Coffin, Berton (1977). *The Sounds of Singing.* Scarecrow Press, Metuchen, New Jersey.

Garcia, Manuel (1855). "Observations with the Laryngoscope." Royal Society, London.

Helmholtz, Hermann (1885). *On the Sensations of Tone,* Translation of 4th Edition of 1877 by Alexander Ellis. Reprint, Dover Publications, 1954, New York.

Seiler, Emma (1871). *The Voice in Singing.* Lippincott, Philadelphia.

Sundberg, Johan (1977). *Music Room Acoustics.* Stockholm: The Royal Swedish Academy of Music.

10

Francesco Lamperti: *A Treatise on the Art of Singing*

One of the hallowed names in the teaching of *bel canto* is Lamperti. This review will be concerned with the elder Lamperti, Francesco (1813–1892), and the next with the younger Lamperti, Giovanni Battista. Unlike the Garcias, all of whom were singers, the Lampertis were not performers. Nevertheless, their names and principles are engraved in our art of teaching. After studying singing in the Milan Conservatory, the elder Lamperti was co-director of the Teatro Filodrammatico in Lodi, where he taught many distinguished singers. Later he taught in the Milan Conservatory from 1850 to 1875. His many students included Marietta Alboni, Teresa Stolz, Maria Waldmann, Italo Campanini, and William Shakespeare. His treatise was first published in London (1877), and the revised edition in New York (1890). This review is of the revised edition.

Francesco Lamperti despaired because there had been a great decline in the art of singing. He observed that the human voice had not undergone any physical change for the worse and that there had been an intellectual development during that time. His conclusion was that singers were appearing on the stage before being thoroughly grounded in the principles of the art of singing.

His thesis could be the statement by Pacchierotti (1839), "He who knows how to breathe and pronounce well, knows how to

Reprinted from the *NATS Bulletin* [now *Journal*], November-December 1982.

sing well.'' He then relates how singers prior to his writings were developed for the stage. By singing minor roles, it was possible for a singer to develop his art by singing with the greatest singers even without regular training under the care of a master. But with vocal music of a more dramatic character, in which both agility and melody were almost excluded, such a course was no longer possible. Before this style became prevalent the best methods and masters were in the music itself. This was a slow but sure way to success. Another reason for the decline in the art of singing was the absence of the *musici* (the castrati), who left the stage and reappeared in their students.

Also, there were changes of voice classifications—*tenori seri* became baritones; mezzo-sopranos were called upon to sing contralto roles; and the sopranos had to sing to the highest notes of the *soprano sfogato* (*sfogare*–to vent one's anger) and a few strong low notes, so the medium register became weakened and assumed a character of disagreeable inequality. The destruction of the middle register was involved with the most important notes of the whole voice. Also the raising of the pitch had greatly added to the difficulties of the *prima donnas*.

Bellini was the first to add a syllable to every note, thus rendering it more fatiguing to the voice. Syllabification executed by the head voice in women's voices is "productive of much harm." [Career sopranos are quite inventive in the ways they learn to protect their head voices.] Lamperti believed the voices should be trained by singing music of the old masters.

Francesco Lamperti sets forth the Italian three-register concept for female voices: Chest, Mixed, and Head; and, Chest and Mixed for male voices, with Chest in both to f^1 [Helmholtz notation]. The first emphasis was on a posture, with the chest expanded in the position of a soldier. He desired a ringing quality of voice caused by the vibrations striking the hard palate. He taught that the muscle of the thorax should be used in singing and that in practice the singing be done on a full breath. He taught the instantaneous or catch breath for use in long passages. He stated that the *pianissimo* tone should have the same character as the *forte* so that it would carry.

Lamperti's precepts were to train *first* with full voice, *second* to train a gradual diminuendo from full voice, *third* to train the pianissimo with a crescendo to full voice, and the last a pianissimo attack swelled to full voice and returned to pianissimo. This he called *note filate*, known to us as *messa di voce*. This term also means "place the voice." [It can be observed that a well-placed voice can crescendo and diminuendo, and that a voice that can crescendo and diminuendo is well placed.]

His advice concerning the breath was to breathe in as large a quantity as the lungs could contain and sing with a pleasant smiling expression of the face, but "the voice emitted should be less in force than the force of the breath which supports it." The *appoggio*, or support of the voice, was to be gained by the action of the muscles of the chest and diaphragm upon the lungs after "opening the lower part of the throat with the vowel *a*" [X-ray photography indicates this is a vocal imagery]. If the tone on *a* is not a full tone, then begin on *la*, which will give easier emission. [Note that in Italian *l* is made with the *tip* of the tongue and not the *sides* of the tongue which makes the tone throaty.]

Agility was to be studied with *portamento, legato, staccato,* and *marcato,* with the *legato* being given first preference since it "is the predominant quality of good singing in general." *Agility* should be studied slowly and clearly and with a shock of the glottis [slight jerk] for each pitch. He recommended moderation in the study of agility "as the voice by too rapid exercises is apt to become tremulous and weak." [The standing wave of fullest resonation is possible on long notes and in slow passages—it is not in rapid exercises.] He felt that the enormous quantities of exercises in books on singing were "superfluous and more likely to injure than preserve the voice."

In the *portamento* the slurring from one note to another should be accomplished in such a manner that the intervening notes be heard as little as possible, but the type of *portamento* depends upon the passage in which it appears. A special study of the *legato* (in which there is no dwelling on intervening pitches between two notes) should be made since "he who cannot sing legato cannot sing well." The control over the breath should be maintained in the change, or the second note will be "wanting in character and color."

Lamperti recommended singing with full, clear voice, with grace and ease without forcing. Practice should cease before fatigue is felt [because our sensory feedback of fatigue of the voice is very poor]. It is best to study for moderate periods of time with a variety of exercises. The pupil should guard against using more voice than the breath will sustain, to avoid tremulousness of voice. He advised against *humming* because "wanting in support of the chest there is nothing which more fatigues the throat or renders uncertain the intonation." [Perhaps the fad of humming would not exist if this and other treatises were available to teachers of our time.] *Piano* singing should have the same character and feeling as the *forte* so that it can be heard at great distances. [Delle Sedie had another way [TNB May-June] and we will see that De Reszke had three ways of singing piano.]

In singing, pronunciation "should be emitted with full and sustained sound with care taken" not to sacrifice clear articulation of the words to mere sonority of voice. Francesco Lamperti considered the study of solfeggio to be of greatest importance in the study of articulation. [All of the consonants do,re,mi,fa,sol,la, si,do are forward in Italian pronunciation.] He carefully pointed out that the progression of sol la should be sung as a double consonant—one of his few statements on pronunciation.

In the *appoggio* [support of the breath] all notes from the lowest to the highest are produced by holding back the breath— the opposite of straining the breath which causes such defects as frowning, contraction of the tongue, and a fixed expression of the eyes. For expression, the features must be calm and natural in singing, although it is allowable to open the mouth wider for the very highest notes [and the reverse in a descending scale.]

Perhaps his most important statement was that the singer should direct his attention to the full inspiration of breath up to eighteen seconds; the sound emitted after such an inhalation would be full and stable, whereas inhalation of six, nine, or twelve seconds would result in the sound lacking in steadiness and feeling. With the full breath the diaphragm is lowered, press-

ing upon the organs below. When singing occurred, the inspiratory muscles struggled against the expiratory muscles to retain the
breath within the body. This he called the "*lutte vocale,* or vocal
struggle." True expression was dependent upon "the retention of
this equilibrium."

In regards to solfeggio he noted the difficulty in writing exercises suited for all voices, but he did include several exercises in
this text. He also published "Daily Exercises in Singing and
Vocal Studies in Bravura," available from G. Schirmer.

Lamperti advises the student to not sing on the two lowest and
two highest notes of his or her voice, but to confine the exercises
to the middle notes so that the voice will be even and agreeable in
its full extension. Syllables should be sung only on those notes
which the singer finds easy—otherwise use a "simple vowel."
The solfeggio should be sung in various sentiments—"love,
prayer, irony"—to realize the dramatic situation embodying the
feeling of poetry which the singer has read into the solfeggio. He
reminds the singer that singing must be subordinate to art because
"untutored feeling chokes the voice; let him never abandon himself to his feelings, but instead, strive always to sing with a warm
heart, yet a cool head." He warns against the teaching of dramatic operas, which he found were destructive of voice in general
and to female voices in particular; instead he recommended the
operas of Bellini, Donizetti, and especially Rossini, with the
possible exception of the baritone—"a register of voice so to
say, created by Giorgio Ronconi, by the combination of the ten-
or-serio and basso-cantante. . . . The old repertoire will always
be found more fruitful of results, and less dangerous." [It should
be noted that Domenico Barbaja commissioned Bellini, Donizetti, and Rossini not only to write operas for Teatro San Carlo,
Naples, but also to coach the singers in their roles. The latter two
were also fine singers. Is it small wonder that they knew the
capabilities of the human voice when they had been so well
prepared by the successors of the Porpora singing line?]

F. Lamperti's text is primarily based upon the study of respiration. At that time another text on pronunciation was completed
and awaiting publication. That text is not available in any of the

major libraries of the world, which leads me to suspect it was never published. Perhaps, as we have seen in recent reviews in this column, pronunciation in singing is extremely involved and very elusive to describe and use unless one has a knowledge of phonetics. At least we know Lamperti's views for half of the statement "He who knows how to breathe and pronounce well knows how to sing well."

REFERENCES

Baker's Biographical Dictionary of Musicians (1978).
Groves Dictionary, 1980 Edition.
Lamperti, Francesco. *A Treatise on the Art of Singing* (1980). G. Schirmer. Revised and translated by J.C. Griffith.

11

Giovanni Battista Lamperti:
The Technics of Bel Canto

Giovanni Battista Lamperti (1839–1910), known as the younger Lamperti, was the son of Francesco Lamperti, and was accompanist in his father's studio when only a boy. He taught twenty years in Milan, twenty years in Dresden, then later in Berlin. Among his most famous students were Sembrich, Schumann-Heink, and Stagno. His students were singers and teachers in the major music centers of the world.

The younger Lamperti was encouraged to write this volume because he noted teachers were spending far too little time in the individualization of voices. Since no two voices are alike "it does great mischief to make one shoe fit every foot." He added that this method had withstood the test of time and could be traced back to the Italian singing masters Pacchierotti, Velutti, and others.

He wrote, "The true method of singing is in harmony with nature and the rules of health," and the chief requirements of the singer are "voice, musical talent, health, power of apprehension, diligence and patience." Those of the teacher are "experience, a sensitive ear, the gift of intuition and individualization." The teacher's responsibility was to place, develop, and equalize the voice. He pointed out *"That nothing more could be made of a given voice than the given anatomical conditions permitted."*

Reprinted from the *NATS Bulletin* [now *Journal*], January-February 1983.

He stated that the manner of breathing which should be employed is "diaphragmatic" since it is the only method by which a singer can conduct sufficient air tranquilly with a minimum of exertion from the lungs to the vocal organs. Strain is placed upon the vocal organs in "clavicular" breathing.

The position of the body should be erect. The shoulder joints should be free and loose, "with the shoulders slightly thrown back to allow the chest due freedom in front, without raising it."

The singer should inhale only through the mouth, not through the nose, with the mouth being opened enough to allow the forefinger to pass between the upper and lower teeth. Expiration should be effected chiefly by the abdominal muscles in a gradual manner to spin out the tone. If the singer has a feeling of exertion "he has not acquired the right method." He believed breath control was the foundation of all vocal study.

The place to begin exercises is in the medium register "with well-opened throat on the syllable 'la', " with the tongue lying as flat as possible and not arched upward. He believed beauty and power of tone depended on a correct tone-attack and upon the resonance of the voice in both chest and head.

He wrote that "vocal registers are determined by the different points of resonance of the tones." Their location requires experience and the acute ear of the teacher.

FEMALE VOICES

He believed that in the female voice there were three registers. In training, the singer should use a mirror to observe the opening of the mouth and expression of the face, and should "sing out into the room—not against the wall."

The teacher "should neither sing with the pupil nor accompany her on the piano with the tone she is singing." The teacher should "show her the proper position of the mouth, and breathe with her, though without singing. It is remarkable what an important role suggestive action plays in vocal instruction."

The legato was one of the first things taught; there should be no interruption of the air between the tones. This was done with the syllable "la" on an alternating interval of a whole step at a dynamic of only *mf*, nearly piano. At the end of each exercise "one should be in the same physical attitude as if one intended to continue singing." Many other exercises were given.

In the soprano voice, he observed that on D flat^2 a change to head voice will usually occur, varying with individual voices. It will be noticed that the jaw sinks a bit further than in the medium register and "the resonance of the tone [will] be distinctly felt in the top of the head near the front, but not in the forehead or in the back of the head." This was made more evident by letting the pupil sing "li," with a short pause before taking the head tone. The mouth opening will be slightly rounded, the vowel shaded towards "o."

In singing the head tone of an exercise he stated that "it is also allowable to draw a little breath through the nose." This apparently enabled the resonance to be felt on the top of the head.

He felt it essential that voices be trained in agility because even heavy voices are made more mellow and beautiful by the training. "Every individual note must sound full and round." This is possible only if the singer learns how to combine the legato with the detached technic, with the tone production being both well supported and light. Coloratura passages "must be sung strictly in time, and never rapidly, but rather slowly. However, if there is no natural gift, one should not waste time on coloratura study."

In the trill, the principal note takes the accent, the auxiliary follows lightly. He believed the trill exercise to be excellent for "pure intonation." At first the trill should be practiced very slowly but strictly in time. He conceded the trill is not for all voices, and he felt that heavy voices might even be injured by purposeless practice of this technic.

One must be very cautious in staccato practice. "The tones are now executed short as indicated by dots or short dashes over the notes." In this technic, a slight extra pressure, without waste of breath, makes the tone speak easily. If the pupil shows no aptitude for this style, it should not be practiced, "since it might injure the voice."

"Not until the voice has decided agility and facility should the pupil practice sustained tones with the *messa di voce*." In the crescendo the placement is moved from the front of the mouth "further back toward the pharynx." When the piano dynamic is approached the tone "must float lightly on the lips." [Video tape study of singers shows that at the same time they are enlarging and diminishing the size of the mouth opening.] The breathing must be very elastic, since he believed the messa di voce is produced solely by breath control. "In the decrescendo the breath pressure decreases very gradually and evenly." In this study "one ought to be able to sustain a tone eighteen or twenty seconds."

Portamento signifies the gentle carrying-over of one tone to another. "The voice describes, so to speak, an upward or downward curve, while the *appoggio* (breath control) remains unmoved." He believed this technic could be properly employed only with refined taste.

The above statements apply to soprano voices in general. The coloratura soprano has a range from c^1 to e-flat^3. "The Mezzo-Soprano, also called Dramatic Soprano, is a less flexible voice with developed chest register and medium compass." [When teaching in Europe, I am constantly asked as to whether a certain voice is Mezzo-Soprano or Dramatic Soprano. It seems that the Fach system (Voice Classification) occupies about half of one's discussion. I have quoted Lamperti's statement on this many times—they are the same! Apparently, agents and managers seem to think that if a heavy voice can sing the B-flat only with the greatest effort (or miss it) the voice is Mezzo-Soprano. If they can sing the high B-flat easily, the voice is a Dramatic Soprano.] The younger Lamperti's course of study for this voice was to begin training in the medium register, adding later the higher and lower tones.

He observed that in the e^1, f^1, g^1 transition from chest voice to medium voice, "the tones should be so evenly matched that the balance of tone is held level from the lowest to the highest note of the scale,'' and that this could be gained only through correct breathing. [Subsequent reviews will indicate that the use of certain vowel colors in certain areas of the voice have much to do with equalizing the registers.] However, he did write that a feeling of 'oh' and 'li' at c^2 would assist in entering head voice. Solfeggi were used to acquire a pure pronunciation of the vowels. He observed that on ''a,e,i,'' the mouth should be open ''about a finger breadth.'' For ''o,'' the lips should assume ''an only slightly rounded form.'' ''In the medium register, tones on the vowels 'e' and 'i' should be felt near the front of the hard palate; the tones of the head-register should be felt to vibrate in the top of the skull near the front.''

The opera repertory of that time had few roles for contralto voices, so they were being converted into mezzo-sopranos. He felt the beauty of the contralto voice [of use to us in oratorio] is in the chest register, with which the development should begin, the medium registers following. ''When the chest-voice is forced up too high, the head-voice loses its mellowness and carrying power.'' The low alto may have no gift for coloratura, whereas the high one often does, hence the term ''coloratura alto,'' in contrast to ''dramatic alto.''

MALE VOICES

Basically the training for male voices is the same as for sopranos except that they have a fourth register, namely, the ''mixed voice.'' He felt the neglect of this register was the reason that there were so few eminent tenors. Few knew how to sing with the ''half breath,'' the *messa di voce* or ''an effective, buoyant piano!'' He felt the training of the tenor voice was the most difficult task for the singing teacher. ''On the tones b, c^1, d^1, and d-sharp^1 head-resonance mingles with the chest-voice carried up from below, so that the singer sings with but half the chest-resonance.'' The main point is to blend the medium register with the mixed voice so that there is an even scale from the lowest to the highest tone.

The baritone is considered the typical male voice. Its range is usually from A to f-sharp^2. The c^1, d^1 and e^1 should be sung with breadth of tone. Beginning on about c^1, the half chest resonance is reinforced by head resonance. High e^1 should be sung broadly but rather darkly.

In the high bass the tones of the medium register, e-b, are to be sung with an open, somewhat rounded "ah."

In the deep bass, care must be taken not to force the chest register up too high, so the middle voice should be carefully developed. Not too much effort should be made to develop the lowest tones, because the voice becomes fatigued in making them speak.

He indicated faults and their causes. Insufficient chest resonance produces a flat tone without carrying power. Hollow sounds are caused by a too widely opened pharynx. Choked tone is caused by rigidity of the throat muscles. Gutteral tone is caused when the tongue is held wrong. Throaty tone is caused when the larynx is held too high and unduly contracted. Nasal tone is caused by too much nasal resonance. The dental tone occurs when the mouth is not open enough, and the tremolo is caused when there is weakness of the laryngeal muscles and vocal cords.

The Technics of Speech and Song

"Language and Song rarely go hand in hand," with the Italian language being the chief exception because of "its wealth of vowels and lack of aspirates." Most Italians pronounce the open vowel "ah" correctly, whereas other nationalities have to make a special study of it. [Helmholtz observed that the Italian "ah" resonated on d^3. When this occurs the tongue is quite flat, as Lamperti desired.] He notes that "i" and the French "u" are hard to sing on high notes and that he would take no singer to task for changing the positions of such words, or for substituting others with more euphonious vowels.

Consonants present greater difficulties than vowels. The best way to overcome words filled with clusters of consonants, as in

German, "is to try to treat entire sentences like one word, to dwell on the vowels, and to glide lightly over the consonants, though without becoming indistinct."

Regarding arias, the student should first learn to sing in Italian, later in the more difficult languages. He felt the singer was a re-creator of the thoughts of the poet and composer, and should endeavor to project their conceptions "until the hearer, carried away by the artistic effect, forgets the artist in rapt comtemplation of the art-work."

One of his most interesting statements was, "We warn students against too much Lied-singing at first, the range being too limited and the numerous tone-repetitions calculated to tire the voice; coloratura sopranos, in particular, should take this warning to heart." This book was written in Germany, and he was writing from experience!

Practicing *mezza voce* fatigues beginners, so it is best to learn with the head, without using the voice.

In conclusion, the human voice is the most precious of musical instruments, and more delicate than any other. A natural method strengthens the body and vocal organ, but if you want to "keep your voice fresh and vigorous, do not ask more of it than it can bear." "The singer who is once in possession of a perfectly trained voice, will preserve this inestimable treasure till in advanced age."

REFERENCES

Baker's Biographical Dictionary of Musicians (1978).
Brown, William Earl (1931). *Vocal Wisdom*. Reprinted with supplement by Lillian Strongin. (1957) Crescendo, New York.
Grove's Dictionary, 1980 Edition.
Helmholtz, Hermann (1885). *On the Sensations of Tone*. Translation of 4th Edition by A. Ellis. (1954) Dover, New York.
Lamperti, G.B. (1905). *The Technics of Bel Canto*. Translated by Th. Baker. G. Schirmer, New York.

12

William Shakespeare:
The Art of Singing (1921), Part I

Although neither Lamperti was a singer, both taught artists who wrote of their methods. The name of William Shakespeare, a concert and oratorio tenor and teacher of singing, appears in the Translator's Preface of Francesco Lamperti's Treatise as being one of the eminent students of that master. David Bispham, the first American baritone to receive international acclaim, was a student of Lamperti in Milan. When in London he was a student of Shakespeare, who was also a scholar of the historical bases of vocal pedagogy and followed this volume with the very valuable *Plain Words on Singing* (1924). It is not surprising that he wrote more about the breath than F. Lamperti, and probably wrote many ideas concerning vowels and consonants which were to be in the promised Lamperti book on pronunciation, which was not published. The *Art of Singing,* first published in 1898, was revised several times and can be looked upon as a valid statement of many of the principles and practices of the Italian singing masters. Because of the depth of its content this text will be reviewed in two parts.

The art of singing rose to its zenith towards the middle of the eighteenth century when the development of music in other directions, "especially in relation to the orchestra, led composers to a comparative neglect of the voice as an instrument to be studied on

Reprinted from the *NATS Bulletin* [now *Journal*], March-April 1983.

its own account." With this "has likewise vanished, to a great extent, the successful cultivation of the art of singing." Little has come to us but the maxims and sayings of the great teachers of the past concerning the methods and practices of their art. Shakespeare's purpose was "to gather up these traditions and hints and weld them into a consistent whole" which would be valuable to student and teacher. [Is not a text of this kind necessary for us today when the techniques of other instruments are being more assiduously studied than ever before and the study of the voice, as an instrument, receiving less attention?]

Shakespeare said that singing is the art of combining time and speech in such a way that "the notes are started in fulness and purity exactly on the pitch intended, the words prolonged, yet sound as natural as the most expressive talking, and every tone conveys the emotion desired by the singer." To make this possible "the breath must be under perfect control; the vocal organs must be trained to act with unconscious ease." When these elements are present, "the qualities of expression and intensity will suffer no diminution even in the largest buildings."

Poor breathing can cause singing in which "the tongue is stiffened so the tone and pronunciation are impeded, the jaw, lips, and eyes are rigidly fixed, and the face assumes an unnatural expression." This makes it impossible to start any note exactly on pitch or to negotiate a scale in other than a jerky manner. He seldom heard the crescendo and diminuendo of the *messa di voce* and too often heard scooping up to notes and the emission of sounds that were painfully out of tune. "The more naturally we wish to sing, the greater is the necessity of learning how to control the breath."

He states, "*until the student has acquired a right method of controlling the breath he will not dare to sing with the throat open.*" Unless the throat is open, there will be "harsh, throaty or nasal sounds." [Perhaps it could be said, that until a singer knows how to take his breath, he cannot sing with an open throat.] Correct breathing enables the storage of a larger quantity of air. This is in contrast to the breath of speech, in which there is the larynx position of speech and an air intake so small that only the shortest phrases can be sung. Breathing concerns the study of both inspiration and expiration.

INSPIRATION

In inspiration, the diaphragm "*descends upon the organs underneath, pressing them out of the way, so that considerable abdominal expansion is felt.*" When the abdomen is thus distended, "powerful sets of muscles now contract, and by their inward pressure against the displaced viscera force the diaphragm up again" with the result that the air is expelled. This is one way the bellows can act. The singer "must have recourse to the additional aid of yet another type of respiration" in which the spreading of the ribs becomes apparent. This motion occurs when the muscles which raise the ribs are brought into action. These muscles, "by enlarging the breath cavity, are of greatest importance to the singer." The group of muscles "which join the ribs to the backbone and shoulder-blades, is that on which the singer must chiefly rely in order to raise the ribs during inspiration." But the set of muscles which raise the ribs from point of the shoulders should not be used [because they are involved with clavicular-breathing]. Thus, "*for singing purposes diaphragmatic breathing must be combined with rib-breathing.*" When this type of breathing is used, the contraction of the diaphragm causes "the abdomen to bulge higher up, at the soft place just under the breastbone." The diaphragm is materially assisted in its descent by the spreading out of the ribs to which it is attached.

EXHALATION

Opposed to these muscles are those which pull the ribs backwards and downwards to the spine and towards the pelvis. They assist in diminishing the breath cavity on exhalation. The coordination of these muscles by the singer is involved with sustained vocal "intensity which is the culmination of his art."

There must be within the body ''an opposition between the muscles which send out the breath and the muscles which draw in the breath'' [The *Lutte Vocale* (vocal struggle) of his teacher, Francesco Lamperti. *TNB*, November-December 1982]. This control is of supreme importance because it enables the singer to press out and yet hold back in such a way that ''when he sings, *he need not contract the throat.*'' The singer's art is in balancing this action so that he is able to produce ''every gradation of force with grace and [seemingly] apparent ease. In this concealment the artist himself is largely unconscious of effort.'' [Many have thought this co-ordination to be relaxation. Relaxation results in devitalized singing.] On the other hand, if there is an unnecessary or inappropriate contraction of these muscles, there can be rigidity, awkwardness and unnaturalness. The quick inhalation of breath by the raising of the chest can bring into play muscles in the back of the neck by ''the contraction of which the throat becomes narrowed, a condition the very reverse of which the singer must aim at—a loose and open throat.''

''Noiseless and imperceptible breathing was the goal which the singers of the past prided themselves on reaching.'' The singer should breathe as high as possible without disturbing the shoulders. Thus, within these limits, one should feel an ample expansion of the back, particularly under the shoulder-blades, but the chest rises very little. ''Considerable pressure and expansion should be felt at the soft place under the breastbone; below this [the belt line] we should be slightly drawn in.'' With this usage of the correct muscles, the singer never feels that he is too full of breath and ''*should always have a quantity in reserve at the close of the phrase.*'' That means the phrase should be ended before there is ''*a sense of sudden collapse of the ribs and a sudden slip upwards of the diaphragm.*''

BREATHING EXERCISE

Shakespeare's exercise for implementing this type of breathing is of great importance to us today; half fill the lungs through the mouth and then breathe in and out small amounts of air, quickly and noiselessly "until you feel yourself panting, yet doing nothing with the chest, *and without filling the lungs.*" When this is done there is a pulsation of the soft place underneath the breastbone. "The breaths must be taken with the mouth open and noiselessly." The throat should feel open and the shoulders and the chest feel free. *"Now extend this quick, noiseless panting or quivering until it is felt not only at the soft place, but at the sides and back near the shoulder blades."* Then expand from this action to a full breath and pronounce a long "ah" for ten or fifteen seconds. Stop the note with breath to spare so that *"the throat is still wide open and natural."* When this exercise is practiced one experiences fatigue in the back muscles and diaphragm but the throat, tongue and face are comfortable. He recommended that the student practice this silent breath exercise many times during the day so that the breath action would become automatic. He states that this breath will be of priceless value when the singer endeavors to compel every note of his voice to respond fully to it.

Shakespeare interprets Pacchierotti's famous statement on breath and pronunciation as follows: "He knows well how to sing, who can tune the vocal cords in fulness without losing command over the breath-pressure, and without preventing the correct formation of the vowels which enrich the voice with tone." He makes a very perceptive statement: "It is not difficult to *whisper* pure vowels with controlled breath, but it is difficult *to tune them.*" [This relates to the observation of those who teach vowel modification based on the relationship of sung pitch to vowel pitch.]

Concerning placing the voice he stated that in order to produce any note in fullness and purity of tone, it was necessary to place or balance the larynx over the breath and retain it in its appropriate position. This involves the upward, forward or backwards pulling muscles upon the tongue-bone [hyoid bone] balanced by those *"pulling the vocal instrument downwards towards the chestbone."* These pulls are described in relationship to the different registers, but "*the control over the placing, tuning and register changes should be unconscious.*"

He describes the muscles which pull upon the tongue in the various directions but does not define their relationship to singing. He suspected that the 'extrinsic' muscles of the tongue might assist those in the body of the tongue. [His comments relate to the use of varying phonetics (the alternation of front, back, neutral and umlaut vowels) in the teaching of singing.] In the absence of this knowledge he insisted "*that the body of the tongue should act in balance and unconscious freedom.*" He did observe that the use of any muscles which would cause the tongue to be *rigidly drawn back* would destroy the purity of all vowel sounds. He later clarifies this statement. "A forward position of the tongue is a proof of its freedom, hence all of the exercises such as the Italian *ah* and *lah* for producing its forward action, if rightly studied must result in the desired freedom." [He did not say to sing with the tongue forward—he gave exercises which would front the tongue unconsciously.]

Shakespeare believed that whenever the throat, tongue, and jaw were fixed the vocal cords could only be described as "displaced." That which was desired by the old masters was "independence of jaw, tongue, and freedom of the throat . . ." This principle has been disregarded by those who teach a fixed larynx, which makes impossible the tuning in the center of the note.

There were two signs that indicated to the singer that he was singing correctly. One was that the correctly produced tone gave the most sound with the least expenditure of the breath. The other sign was that the singer was unconscious of the action of the larynx, thus the quote, "The Italian singer has no throat."

Shakespeare noted, "*the higher the note in any register, the greater is the pressure of the breath required, and the greater the art in controlling this pressure.*" This was because of the increased tensing of the vocal cords in ascending; in descending there was "a comparative slackness of the vocal cords" [and less breath pressure].

"Placing [resonating] the voice so that it speaks fully to the least breath is equivalent to an increase in breath force, for now less breath produces *more sound, and he who can accomplish this can also, with practice, intensify his notes, sending them over the largest theater.''*

In Italian the control of the breath has been termed *appoggio* (or leaning on the breath). If one preserves the quality of his voice to the end of the phrase he is enabled to draw in a new breath instantly. He quotes Lamperti's ''Treatise'': ''*on the art of finishing the phrase with the breath still under control depends the calmness of the singing and consequently the career of the singer.*'' Shakespeare implemented this technique by placing a pause and a turn after each exercise (no breath to be taken during the pause prior to the turn).

REFERENCES

Lamperti, F. (1890). *A Treatise on the Art of Singing*. G. Schirmer, New York.

Luchsinger, R. and Arnold, G. E. (1965). *Voice, Speech, Language*. Wadsworth Publishing Company. Belmont, California.

Shakespeare, William (1921). *The Art of Singing*. Ditson, New York.

———, (1924). *Plain Words on Singing*. Putnam's Sons, London.

Russell, G. O. (1931). *Speech and Voice*. Macmillan, New York.

13

William Shakespeare:
The Art of Singing (Part II)

Shakespeare, in *The Art of Singing*, states that (1) *"any note that responds fully to a breath rightly controlled is rightly produced;"* that (2) in correctly produced singing *"we tire the breath muscles, but experience no sense of fatigue at the throat;"* and that (3) *"The first badly produced note in any phrase carries the control of the breath out of our power,* and until a fresh breath is taken the rest of the notes of that phrase are faulty."

Shakespeare taught that "on the freedom of the jaw depends the freedom of the larynx." The larynx will necessarily move because of certain consonants and vowels, but the movement should be unconscious. The jaw should neither be protruding nor the mouth drawn to one side. [It appears that in singing the same vowel on changing pitches, the jaw will move for vowel tunings and register changes, as is evidenced by noted singers as shown on television.] Shakespeare notes that the mouth should be open at least a thumb-width and wider in declamatory passages.

He believed that the freedom of the soft palate depended on the freedom of the throat and tongue. "Freedom of the lips is of great importance as a *sign of our singing rightly.*" He observed that the expression of the face was entirely lost if the upper lip could not be raised as in smiling, and that it was necessary to maintain the independence of the upper lip for singing in the upper, medium,

Reprinted from the *NATS Bulletin* [now *Journal*], May-June 1983.

and head registers. He felt that rigidity of the large muscle which encircles the lips was disastrous. He observed that any rigidity of the vocal organs was reflected in the eyes, whereas contentment and happiness were expressed in the freedom in them. This is coupled with a slight smile as initiated by the raising of the corner of the upper lip.

He observed that when one is singing well *"the voice passes instantaneously from one note to the other, as the will directs."* The Italians believed that a person who did not join his notes could not sing.

A musical instrument is enriched in tone, either by the sympathetic vibration of a sound board, or by that of the air in an enclosed compartment . . . "There would be little volume in the voice unless the air in certain enclosured spaces vibrated in sympathy, these being the chest, the throat and mouth, the nasal and possibly other cavities situated in the skull." [Researchers since Willis (1829) have generally believed that it is sympathetic vibration of air in the vocal pipe that pertains to resonance in the singing voice. Russell (1931) determined the other cavities are closed and non-resonating.]

While Shakespeare thought it was difficult to separate the consideration of tone from that of pronunciation, he stated that *"the looser the tongue the richer will be the "ah," and the fuller the tone; this vowel sooner than any other reveals any rigidity and consequent closure of the throat."*

In his studies he found that the old masters insisted on the student making a rapid tongue movement before singing the *ah;* the consonant *l* was believed to be best adapted to this purpose.

CHEST REGISTER

It is probably because of the pipe organ that the term "register" exists. In the *Chest Register*, there is a characteristic vibration of the chest. "The higher the note, the greater the support required from the broad muscles under the chin and the greater the necessity for control over the increased breath-pressure."

This extends to c^1 in the *bass* and d^1 in the *baritone*. When the *tenor* "carries up the chest voice to c^1, $c\#^1$, d^1, $d\#^1$, e^1 and even f^1, he is accused of singing too open." [Written by a tenor.] He thought that contraltos and mezzo-sopranos could sing in chest from their lowest notes up to d^1, or e^{b1}, but rarely e^1. "The *soprano* seldom possesses any force in the chest register; as in the case of the tenor, her instrument is generally too slight for the production of these broad tones, and while c^1, $c\#^1$, and d^1 are sometimes fairly powerful, composers seldom rely on them for any effect." [A complete voice which makes use of equalized chest, medium and head registers is required in operatic singing. In ensemble singing, a register of six or seven beautiful and unusual notes can be of great value.]

MEDIUM REGISTER

This is sometimes called *mixed voice* and was occasionally termed *falsetto* by Italian masters. This register can be carried down until it diminishes inaudibly, "but the higher notes are characterized by a silvery quality of great brilliancy." In ascending notes in this register, the upper lip will gradually rise towards a smiling expression which exposes the upper teeth more and more as the notes ascend. "This register is accompanied by a *remarkable sense of vibration in the mouth* as though *vibrating against the upper teeth*." He observed that e^{b1} or e^1 is the first note of any force in the medium register.

"The tenor, on singing this register with any force, should associate his middle A with vibration on the front teeth, B on the second and c^1 on the 3rd or eyetooth; with each ascending note he will find the sound proceeding back along the upper teeth; on singing these notes softly he will find them still farther back." "*There is undoubtedly considerable difficulty experienced in the production of the higher notes of the medium register;* so much so, that this register has been subdivided by some into upper medium and lower medium" [Some writers have called the upper medium voice "mixed voice" which utilizes close vowels to cover the voice at the transition.] The acquisition of this upper register *"forms the key, not merely to the highest notes of the tenor but especially to the head voice of women."* In the tenor voice the most difficult notes d^1, e^1, and f^1 "vibrate on the back teeth, the upper lip raised in a smile to bring these into view."

"While basses and baritones rely on the chest register up to c^1 and d^1 for forcible effects, the true artist is able to add to these, as well as to the lower notes, all the softer gradations by singing with the medium voice, as felt vibrating on the teeth." Shakespeare says that faulty intonation and the terror of high notes will disappear when the artist allows the upper lip to be independent when singing the upper medium notes.

HEAD REGISTER

"The *head* voice . . . is characterized by a fluty and bird-like quality, lovely and essentially womanly." Its use by mezzo-sopranos and sopranos in his day was highly prized, "not only by reason of the loveliness of its quality, but because of its comparative rarity." He stated that female voices until c^2, $c\#^2$, and d^2 can use the head voice as a soft effect in a large hall. He emphasized that these head notes be practised until they can be sung with an open throat. On arriving at e^2, they can produce a note of some power, especially if the singer possesses a mezzo-soprano voice. Shakespeare quotes Lamperti as saying that "the mezzo-soprano and soprano should always sing e^2 completely in head voice, and this accomplishment is the key to the high notes. . . ." He also noted that there were many who sang the e^2, f^2, and $f\#^2$ in the medium register, but these seldom revealed lovely head notes. [We still hear screeches by some international singers in the major opera houses of today; this head-voice technique should be more widely utilized.]

Although there are three registers, "when rightly produced, these so dove-tail . . . one into the other, as to form one long even voice."

Singers who desire to appear at an early age upon the concert or opera platform frequently abuse the voice. Thus basses and baritones are apt to produce the highest notes of the chest register in a manner more like a shout than a musical note. The tenor often uses the chest voice instead of the medium, and this especially at c^1, d^1, e^1, and sometimes f^1. Contraltos, mezzo-sopranos, and sopranos force upwards the resonant chest voice to f^1 or even higher . . . and in the case of mezzo-sopranos and sopranos prevent the use of head notes.

"The true artist prefers to strengthen the lower notes of each register and these he is able to intensify. . . . The bad singer, on the other hand, is compelled to rely entirely on the highest notes of the registers, with the result that his singing is characterized by a sense of strain and effort, which becomes painful to his audience as he approaches his climax." Artists should be aware that one can increase the intensity of a tone without increasing its volume, and thus can produce the softest effects in the largest theaters.

He quotes Lamperti as saying repeatedly, "*Never sing with more voice than that which you can produce when you rightly control the breath.*" Shakespeare added that "*intensity is the basis of all expression in singing,* and without it the highest effects of which the art is capable are impossible."

With the great singer a never-ceasing pressure of breath is maintained, alike when he is singing his softest notes and when he is making his most dramatic effects without the hearer being reminded of the force of breath and effort employed. [We should hear neither whisper singing, nor shouting.] He quotes Bazzini of the Milan Conservatoire as saying that "*the end of art is not to astonish, but to move.*"

"*The play of the facial organs serves to vary the expression of the sound of the voice during singing,*" and invariably brings life and brightness to the tone of the voice.

Singing consists mainly in "*the art of prolonging and sustaining vowel sounds.*" For this reason it is best to begin with the study of Italian songs, because Italian is a language of sustained vowel sounds, devoid of awkward consonant combinations. Thus there can be freedom of action of both tongue and throat. Also, the consonants must be lightly articulated and not dwelt upon except in the double consonants.

When singing English, the vowels must be prolonged although they are rapidly passed over in speaking. When the vowels are sustained, English begins to take on the sonority of the Italian language. He has many exercises to assist the English-speaking singer in joining consonants with vowels. He desired that the last note of a phrase be ended with the throat open, with no "*after cough*," and "with sufficient breath to be able, after a slight pause, to repeat in the same breath the last note . . . a turn or a trill." When a student prolongs a pause for a few seconds before singing the last test-phrase, he will "ascertain if he is holding up his ribs with the muscles near the shoulder-blades. The extra note or passage should be sung with steady breath and with fulness of tone, as shown by the richness of the vowel." His vocalises make generous use of the *la*, as do those of both of the Lampertis.

This text has many vocalises for agility, but they must be prepared by rib-diaphragmatic exercises for the correct positioning of the larynx, looseness of the tongue, and joining of the notes. Limits are given within which exercises must be sung for the different voice classifications. Also included are exercises using technics of singing music of the Bel Canto period. The exercises are on the open vowels *ah* and *eh*.

"Let the singer never permit himself to alter the pronunciation of a word in order to be able to sing with greater sonority, turning, e.g., *man into mawn*." [He was preceded and succeeded by those who believed in vowel modification.]

The singer's dramatic power is necessarily limited by the physical force, temperament, and quality of voice with which nature has endowed him. Shakespeare believes that to train a young student by the practice of dramatic music is certain to cause a rigid style of pronunciation. "The practice of the old masters was to reserve the forcible dramatic effects for a later period in the career of the artist." The attempt should be made to train the singer in such a way that his singing is "*so moving and so powerful* as to be called *dramatic*."

All teachers will agree with this quote:

Study your songs and arias until you know them by heart, and have formed a mental picture of the expression of the words and music, and feel that you are the living embodiment of what you have to sing.

Concerning the length of study, one thing is certain: ease and elegance, concealment of art, and perfection of expression, the highest attainments of the artist, can only be the result of many years of hard and assiduous study.

REFERENCES

Lamperti, F. (1890). *A Treatise on the Art of Singing.* G. Schirmer, New York.

Shakespeare, William (1921). *The Art of Singing.* Ditson, New York.

14

Herbert Witherspoon:
Singing

Coincidental with the centennial season of the Metropolitan Opera Company, it seems appropriate to review the book *Singing* by Herbert Witherspoon, who was appointed General Manager of that company in March, 1935. He had joined the company as leading bass during the first year of Gatti-Casazza's reign and was on the roster for eight years. He concertized extensively and established a studio in New York in which there were over two hundred students and eight assistant teachers, one of whom was Graham Reed, this author's mentor. Witherspoon was later President of the Chicago Musical College, Vice-President and Director of the Chicago Civic Opera Company, and Director of the Cincinnati Conservatory of Music.

In 1933 he returned to New York and resumed his teaching. He was appointed General Manager of the "Met" at a time when its survival was in jeopardy. Feeling that he had been discriminated against as an American artist, he auditioned and contracted several American singers, and formulated plans for the Metropolitan Opera Auditions. The major tragedy was that he died six weeks after his appointment, his death being announced in the New York Times of May 11, 1935, on the front page, column one. His plans were very capably carried out by his Assistant Director and successor, Edward Johnson.

Reprinted from the *NATS Bulletin* [now *Journal*], September-October 1983.

Witherspoon was at one time a student of G. B. Lamperti. He, like Shakespeare, was a member of the Lamperti line of teachers. Hence we have two singers of that school who were illustrious teachers of singing who wrote on the principles they had received in their instruction.

In addition, he was instrumental in founding the American Academy of Teachers of Singing, and with Dudley Buck formed the organization which is now known as The Chicago Singing Teachers Guild. Both of these organizations were involved in founding NATS. Our art and craft is indebted to Witherspoon for his singing, his teaching, his writing, and his great administrative abilities.

In his training, Witherspoon always asked his teachers why something was being done. Their answer was that things had always been done that way. [Perhaps that was their way of handing down tradition.] He believed the American mind was an inquisitive one and that there should be reasons why the voice worked as it did in good singing. After a career and twenty-five years of teaching he was convinced there was only one proper way to sing—according to natural laws. He wrote this book to set forth the natural laws governing the vocal organs and those which assist in their actions, and to present a system of teaching based on cause and effect. If a singer disobeyed the laws he had to pay the price. He believed that singing could be taught only by singing and adjustment made in the act, not by discussion.

ART AND TECHNIQUE

Witherspoon believed that singing is an art of expressing the melody, the text, and their emotional colorings. He was convinced that if different moods were incorporated into training, the technique would be more meaningful and lasting. The aspects of technique were (1) the physical, as related to posture, breathing, and the intrinsic and extrinsic muscles of the larynx, and (2) the acoustical, because it was necessary to obey the laws of sound regarding the primary vibration (from the larynx), resonation (from the vowel tract), and their interaction.

The Posture and Muscular Activity

This book includes the best diagrams of any teacher of the
Lamperti School, showing the posture and the act of correct
breathing in singing. He gained singing posture by use of various
arm exercises, while inhaling, to raise the chest and expand the
lower ribs in a natural manner. This also gave the posture of the
larynx which enabled its free activity. He felt that exaggerated
breathing exercises might cause gross fatigue to the breathing
organs.

He stressed that "we do not perform any physical act through
relaxation, but with correct tension and action." The newest
thing mentioned was the suspension of the breath, a momentary
pause between inhalation and singing during which the ribs remained extended. He felt this had been neglected too long.

In singing, there is a contraction of the muscles of the abdomen and the retaining action of the flattened diaphragm and
widened rib cage: ". . . a slight reflex action takes place in the
soft spot under the breast-bone which is tensed [that is what he
says] and pushes outwards, not only at the moment of attack of
the tone, but during the sustaining of the vocal act." [For an
illustration of this action, see Vennard 1967, p. 31.]

Witherspoon believed the energy of breathing should be pro-
portional in effort and time to that required in the phrase to be
sung; he meant that if there was a quick exclamation, the time of
breathing was short; if the phrase was long, the breath effort
would be slow, full and deliberate. Some of his favorite quotes of
the old school were, "Inhale from the collarbone downwards."
"Sing as if the breath remained in the body. . . ." "Attack
almost as if continuing the breath."

The Lift of the Breath

He observed that just above the speaking range of the voice
more breath effort was required and the voice took on added
brilliance. This phenomenon occurred at a similar place in all

voice classifications but could not be heard until proper breathing had been established. The location of this note, "The Lift of the Breath," could be used as an aid in voice classification. He did not use the location of the "break" for classification but the change of timbre which lies a 5th above it in female voices and a 4th below in male voices.

ORDER OF STUDY

This versatile singer/author thought the student should be trained on *mezzo forte,* but as soon as the breath was established, the crescendo and diminuendo of *messa di voce* should be practiced, and a *sotto voce* which could be gained by almost abandoning the breath support. The last thing to be worked on was power, which gives a feeling of "singing down on the breath" and also a feeling of singing a little further back in the mouth. He believed that modern declamatory music should be avoided for the first two or three years.

NATURAL LAWS AND PHONETICS

As to the nature of the vocal instrument, he believed the voice to be like a two-part trumpet in which the mouth is "the first resonator" (the "yell" of the voice) and the head cavities "the second resonator" (which takes the edge off the yell and turns vocal noise into vocal tone). The two resonators can be adjusted in proportion to each other.

Witherspoon states the law of acoustics that "two sounds of different pitch cannot be resonated in the same resonator with equal results." [The attempt to sing everything in the same space is self-defeating. Video tapes of singing show that artists are continually changing their resonance spaces whether they know it or not. Fiberscope observations prove that this is true and that the same movements occur in whistling, where the cavity of the pharynx and its members tune the sound, including the variations of vibrato in whistling. These actions are below the level of consciousness and are involved with placement of the voice.] He states, *"For, as all perfect musical sound of the human voice is the result of vibration properly reinforced and resonated, its only imperfection can result from improper vibration or reinforcement or resonation* (Reviewer's italics)."

He elaborates on Garcia's observations of actions of the throat in singing:

> We find that as pitch ascends '. . . the tongue rises coordinately upwards and forwards, changing shape of the throat and mouth; the fauces point forward and narrow, or approximate; the uvula rises and finally disappears; the soft palate rises forward, never backward [debatable]; while the epiglottis, rising up against the back of the lower tongue, seems to have a law of its own regarding quality, clear or veiled [clear and sombre timbres]. [These physical acts] form a coordinate process of adjustment, calculated to so alter the use of the resonators in proportion to each other as to form practically a new resonator for each and every pitch, which is exactly what happens.

Witherspoon thought local control was impossible, since no power of the imagination could enable a singer to move any of the organs into the correct position for the resonation of tone exactly in relation to the other organs.

His law of vowel modification was that in ascending open vowels close and close vowels open. [The reverse is true in descending scales.]

He believed that there was a law of opposites which could be used in teaching. If a pupil sang with a tight, pinched throat, he would use the phonetics which would give a lower position. For a gutteral voice he would give a phonetic which gave a more fronted position of the tongue after properly establishing the posture of the larynx by correct breathing.

His use of phonetics was largely concerned with direct or indirect effect upon laryngeal action or muscles of the vocal tract. In spite of mentioning pitches of vowels [probably based on Aikin's writings] he did not incorporate the use of vowel pitch other than to say that AH has three sounds in the extended vocal range—AH as in *hot* in the low range, AH as in *father* in the normal middle range, and AH as in *UN* in the upper range. [He did not say why!]

He states that AW and OH cause low larynx position, but, because of their reaction upon the sublingual muscles, should not be used extensively to induce darker tone. He found them to be subject to serious interference in the region of the soft palate, especially upon high notes.

The author thought the diphthong found in "*I*" has much the same action as AH, but because of its vanish and its tendency towards the wider distribution of the tongue, it induces a better concept of the real AH, what might be called the Italian AH. *I* should be avoided in "white voices."

L is the mouth consonant and brings the tongue into a forward and upward motion. When used with AH, this forms one of the best syllables for practice in middle and low voice but not for high notes because it is too "mouthy" in formation, not "heady."

RAH with rolled R causes action in the tongue and often aids in forming the vowel well forward in the mouth.

He used various hums which were not used by either of the Lampertis.

No amount of corrective phonetics alone would make a great singer. They should lead to the practice of scales upon the perfect vowels, preferably AH with its modifications, which insures the complete development of the singer's voice in instrumental tone.

One of his important statements is that the singer should be allowed one day of rest a week without singing. Some rest is necessary for everyone. [Many professional singers keep their mouths closed for one or two days after a major performance. Baseball pitchers take three between theirs.]

Since nature gives the individual voice quality, a singer may imitate another's method but not the quality of another voice; such imitation has limited the success of many singers.

When technique is established, a "mere willing of a good tone, if the concept is correct and there is no interference, will produce the correct tone."

He stressed "that no teaching of an art can be entirely mechanical, nor can it be entirely scientific. It must return again and again to the art itself for further inspiration, in order that Technique, rightly developed, may be the servant of Expression and Interpretation.''

REFERENCES

Aikin, W. A. (1927). *The Voice, An Introduction to Practical Phonology*. Longmans, Green. New York, N.Y.
Brower, H. (1920). *Vocal Mastery*. Frederick A. Stokes, New York, N.Y., pp. 238–248.
Garcia, M. (1841). *Memoire on the Human Voice*. Paris. Translated and copyrighted by Donald V. Paschke, Eastern New Mexico University, Portales, N.M. 1970.
Grove's Dictionary.
The New York Times. May 11, 1935.
Vennard, W. (1967). *Singing, the Mechanism and Technic*. C. Fischer, New York, N.Y., p. 31.
Witherspoon, H. (1925). *Singing*. G. Schirmer, New York, N.Y.

15

William Earl Brown: *Vocal Wisdom* (*Maxims of G.B. Lamperti*)

The final book in the Lamperti line of teaching is a classic by a teaching assistant of the younger Lamperti, William Earl Brown. Mr. Brown's student, Lillian Strongin, published this volume personally when it went out of print. Later, she translated several notes which Mr. Brown had taken in French when he was a student and assistant of G.B. Lamperti in Dresden (1891–1893). These and selected essays of Mr. Brown were added to the book, which is presently published by Crescendo Press.

Mr. Brown states that life is too brief to work out the problems of an art alone. The teacher should profit from the findings and research of others and, at the same time, go on his own path, not on that of another. The teacher must listen and learn. He says, "I hope my deductions and explanations may help you in finding your voice."

The introductory statement leads the reviewer to believe that many of the statements in this volume are by Mr. Brown, based upon the teachings of G.B. Lamperti. He observed that the greatest singing masters of any period and their students were guided by the ear and not the muscles, although strenuous gymnastics of the voice and the muscles were required. No definite system of exercises was used in setting up the movements of a voice, so *Bel*

Reprinted from the *NATS Bulletin* [now *Journal*], November-December 1983.

Canto [beautiful singing] was handed down by advice from singer to singer.

Breath

The teaching of breathing is a fundamental part of this treatise, as it is of others of the Lamperti School. Of greatest importance is "the diaphragmatic control of vocal emission for breath-supported legato." Without it there would be the rough release of breath and the lack of momentum which occurs in speech. Silent breathing was the rule, because when it became second nature there would not be spasmodic breathing and a shortage of air in a phrase.

He restates the phenomenon that a diaphragmatic contraction downward against the viscera *during singing* will create an appropriate compression of the breath which allows the singer to have control over his voice. He warns, "There is a great temptation to help 'tune' the voice by either a push of breath or pull of tone." Said in another way, "Trueness of pitch is but the working of the law of regular vibration, not a muscular process." [This suggests that the singer should not confuse the control of vibration above the collar-bone with the control of the breath below it.] He said that "compressed breath crowds upward toward the 'wish bone' causing the singer to feel broad shouldered and high chested—the result is that the singer is straightened up like a soldier."

Lamperti did not wish to have the singer *relaxed*. "At no time during the song or series of exercises must you relax while replenishing the breath, or you lose the feeling of suspension. Only when the song is over may you 'let go.' " Instead of relaxation he wished to have a "sustained intensity of initial vibration and the continuous release of breath-energy." He believed there was a relationship between the muscular and the acoustical phenomena of the voice. "Tone and breath 'balance' only when harmonic overtones appear in the voice, not by muscular effort and 'voice placing.' "

ACOUSTICS

Brown's report includes some very interesting acoustical insights concerning initial vibration and resonation. Two of the most revealing quotes are (1) "The singing voice is born from the overtones of regular vibration of the vocal-cords," and (2) "The motives and movements of your mind and body make only half of the proposition of singing. Natural phenomena of vibration and resonance constitute the other half."

He advised the singer, "Do not listen to yourself sing! Feel yourself sing!" This was because "phonetic vibrations felt at lips, nose, head, throat and chest, carry distinct messages in the singer's consciousness until habitual reaction takes the place of effort and thought." In other words, the mucous membrane or 'inner skin' was the monitor for the singer, and not the ear. This could direct the singer regardless of the acoustics of the hall in which he was singing. Nevertheless, "You must become familiar with the acoustics of your voice chambers and the room you sing in." A knowledge of these chambers was deemed most essential. "It is a strange fact that the throat is controlled by what happens above it, in the acoustics of the head, through word, vibration and resonance."

In speaking of covering the voice he made this astute observation, "'Covered tone' is a misleading term. 'Closed tone' should take its place." This statement is easily understood by those who deal with phonetics.

Lamperti looked upon *legato* as a continued vibration. "Until you feel the permanency of your vibration you cannot play on your resonance." This implies that there cannot be a play of resonation until the *legato* is established. How does one build a voice? The question is easily understood in the light of one of his sayings: "The energy in regular vibration [pure tone] is constructive. The violence in irregular vibration [noisy tone] is destructive." And when lethargy or violence enter singing, "the sound of the vibration changes from tone to noise." Regular vibration seems to be the key to singing; the moment it appears in the voice "it re-educates the entire process of singing because . . . memory of how it feels is your only master." He said it in still another way: "To know the result before we act is the 'golden rule' of singing." He did not like "loose, pushed out breath," which he considered to be useless and even injurious because it caused "irregular vibration and disrupted energies."

MUSCLES

Brown says quite a bit about the muscles involved in singing and their training. In learning to sing, "thought and muscle should be schooled until instinct and reaction develop and take command." He noted, "If resonance disappears, you have lost the muscular connection between head and chest."

This is one of the first texts to say that proper action of the framework muscles is vital to good singing. "The inner muscles of the larynx . . . cannot function properly and freely in producing vibration and pitch of the voice, until the outer muscles of throat and neck are busy with pronunciation of word and resonance of tone. In fact, these outside muscles are continually in a state of elastic tension (tonicity) in connection with the rest of the body. These inside muscles are compelled to do double duty if the outside muscles connecting head and torso do not know and perform their allotted work. Inner muscles act instinctively when outer muscles assist co-ordinately and continually."

Since it takes more muscle to hold breath energy back [in soft singing] than it does to let it go [in loud singing], "therefore soft singing is more difficult than loud singing, and should be studied last."

EXERCISES

More is said in this book about what not to do in the way of exercises than what to do: "DON'T 'HUM!'" Brown states that when Lamperti said, "Singing is humming with the mouth open," he did not mean that humming with the mouth closed would bring this about. Lamperti also said, "DO NOT YAWN." He never intended one to yawn while singing. He also stated that Lamperti "never intended his pupils to relax while singing or breathing, but [wanted them to] accumulate the outer-most energy and then release it, as demanded by word and tone." He stated that "'one sided' singing is the chief cause of ugly and ruined voices. If taken in time and the right exercises used, the voice will 'straighten up.'" No exercises are given in the text—just maxims.

Pronunciation and Diction

"You will know when pronunciation is adequate by the feeling on the lips (almost a tickling)." This and the following quotation suggest that Lamperti taught with the lips somewhat rounded. "Lamperti watched the 'flower of the lips' and literally kept his hand on the region of the solar plexus of the pupil until he felt the diaphragm was functioning properly while both compressing breath and singing, and was assured that the reciprocal relationship between vocal utterance and breath energy brought the 'hum' into the singing tone."

Vowels

Lamperti states that teachers should begin with syllabic exercises, solfeggio, etc., because "a forced development of vowels before consonants prevents good diction and endangers complete control of the singing tone." It was his desire that vowels dissolve into one another without mouthing so that there would be a continuing vibration. One of the most interesting maxims was that "the throat does alter its shape somewhat for vowel and volume but that diction takes care of that." [This could be interpreted that control over the spaces of the throat is below the level of consciousness, and that diction is the control. This may be true after the voice is focused but possibly not before.] His

definition of *focus:* "Focus of the voice is but the absence of
irregular vibration and violent energies." His definition of
placement: "When the voice is 'in tune' it is 'placed' and con-
trollable by musical emotion, inherent in the desire to sing."
There was a sensory feedback to the singer when placement
occurred. "A placed voice is one that is felt in the mask of the
face as well as high in the head, in the pharynx and deep in the
throat and on low tones in the chest." The important thing was
that the memory of these placement sensations in the head, nose,
mouth, throat, and chest was the controlling medium.

CONSONANTS

Brown's use of the consonants is very interesting. "The 'start'
of vibrating consonants (m,n,l,b,d,etc.) leads to a spontaneous
start of vowels—and complete control of the throat." [These
consonants are all found in the Sieber exercises.] He used an
interesting technique in curing defects of consonants. To cure the
nasality of "m" it would be crossed with "b" somewhat as
speaking an "m" with a cold in the head. In reverse, if a "b"
was too gutteral it would be combined with "m." If "n" had too
much "twang" it would be crossed with a "d." In reverse, if the
"d" was too hard it would be melted with an "n." If "ng" was
too tight it would be combined with "ig" like a cold in the head.
In reverse, if "ig" was unpleasant it could be softened with
"ing." These alterations were to be used as cures; they were not
to be used as training exercises for everyone because they might
"do more harm than good."

OVERTONES AND CARRYING POWER

When you realize that nothing leaves the throat, then there will
not be the pushing to make the voice carry. "The 'carrying
power' depends on the regularity and intensity of the vibrations,
and not on your efforts." It is an acoustical event, not a muscular
one.

One of Lamperti's fundamental statements was, "The singing voice is born from the overtones of regular vibration of the vocalcords." [Regular vibration fed back upon the vocal cords assists them in their vibrations; the voice is described by Benade as a "self-sustaining oscillatory system." When the feedback is out of phase, the vocal cords are disturbed into irregular vibration (noise). In acoustical terminology, they are "distuned."] "When a tone is pure, the lower, harmonious overtones are heard in the voice [as in female head voice]. When the voice is forced, the higher discordant harmonics predominate causing hard, metallic, sharp quality. When overtones are lacking, the voice sounds hollow, sepulchral, wooden [such as occurs when there is (continual) practice on the [u] and [o] vowels]." In his experience, "The presence of resonance in head, mouth and chest (overtones) is proof that your voice is full-grown, full fleshed."

SENSORY FEEDBACK

In recapitulation, much is said about the sensory perception of tone in singing as it relates to the feeling of vibration. [Inasmuch as it is almost impossible for singers to hear themselves on many stages, there is a tendency to over-sing in an effort to make the sound come back from auditoriums. It is quite appropriate that these sensory cues be brought to the attention and artistry of singers.]

This concludes the review of texts related to the Lamperti school, one of the most significant in the history of singing. Were its principles to be observed, there would be a greater flowering of singing.

REFERENCES

Benade, A. H. (1973). *Fundamentals of Musical Acoustics*. Oxford, London, p. 363.

Brown, W. E. (1931). *Vocal Wisdom*. Crescendo Press, Boston. Enlarged edition, 1957.

16

Margaret Chapman Byers: "Sbriglia's Method of Singing"

Giovanni Sbriglia (1832–1916), a Neapolitan tenor, made his debut at the San Carlo Theater in 1853 and in New York in 1860 at the Academy of Music with Adelina Patti in *La Sonnambula*. He toured the United States with other artists, sang in Mexico and Cuba. After a European career, he settled in Paris in 1875, where he became an historical teacher of singing. Among his students were Jean and Edoard de Reszke, Pol Plançon, Lillian Nordica, Sybil Sanderson, and NATS member Ruth Miller Chamlee. It was under his tutelage that Jean de Reszke changed from baritone to tenor. It is obvious that Sbriglia's contribution to that golden age of singing was monumental. He wrote no book, but we know of his methods through an article written by Margaret Chapman Byers.

Although Sbriglia stated that he had no method, because he treated every singer differently, there were several definite functions of the voice which he wished to establish in his singers.

BREATHING AND POSTURE

During his career all singers breathed the same way, and he believed that all great singers breathed alike—"the same natural way." He did not like what he called "the new pushing method of singing with the back of your neck, sunk in chest, and mus-

Reprinted from the *NATS Bulletin* [now *Journal*], January-February 1984.

cularly pushed out diaphragm . . . [which he believed was] a quick way to ruin a voice.''

> The foundation of my teaching is perfect breath control without tension. The foundation of this teaching is a perfect posture. Foremost is a high chest (what nature gives every great singer), held high without tension by developed abdominal and lower back muscles and a straight spine—this will give the uplift for perfect breathing. . . . Your chest literally must be held up by these abdominal and back muscles, supported from below, and your shoulder and neck will be free and loose.

Sbriglia had belts made for both male and female singers to assist in holding up the abdomen. "You must have intestinal fortitude to support your *point d'appui*, or the focal point in your chest." This was the cornerstone of his method. He considered the lungs to be two bags of air.

> Below them is a cone-shaped muscle, the diaphragm, that divides the body in half and assists in pumping breath in and out of the lungs. It is fastened to the ribs and to the back . . . [As you sing] the air is slowly pushed out of the body through the small bronchial tubes, which merge into the big bronchial tube at the focal point in the chest, [which he had been told in three languages was] the *point d'appui*—the place of support, the place where everything rests . . . This is where the breath control, or the muscular control of the voice ends. It also controls the amount of breath getting to the vocal cords which are in the big bronchial tube, besides taking away all tension from your vocal apparatus, if it is properly supported from below. Above this point, there must be no muscular effort or tension.

Ms. Byers describes a cartoon by Caruso of himself indicating how his *point d'appui* felt after having sung Don José. It looked like a cartoon of Santa Claus.

VOWELS AND TONE PLACEMENT

As with other teachers reviewed in *Vocal Pedagogy Classics,* he was concerned with placement and the formation of career singers' voices.

The most universally accepted characteristic of this method was the loose, rounded, pushed-out lips, which Nordica always used. Sbriglia used the vowels, "Te-ro," (phonetically [ti] and close [o] according to Mrs. Chamlee) more than any other vowels in vocalizing. The Italian "T" brings the voice forward, as the tongue must be pressed against the lower front teeth to sing "E" properly. The French "R" loosens the tongue because it is made by rolling the tip of the tongue, and the "O," which is held, must be the round Italian "O," which requires perfect breath support, or it will not be round; loose-out lips are always used to make a perfect "O." "Use the vowels with a loose jaw, remember," he would say, "only your lower jaw is moveable, so you open your mouth by dropping your lower jaw as you go up the scale." Think "oh," and you will have a perfect Italian "AH" in your upper voice, a sound with an overtone, your lips and your jaw always loose.

As an Italian who was an internationally famous teacher he had a very interesting comment concerning the "AH" vowel in training singers.

More American voices are ruined by being trained on the English "AH," than any other way. It gives an open flat-topped voice. Even great singers get this open voice from fatigue. Use loose protruding lips with proper breath support to cure this common fault.

Many teachers concern themselves with the positioning of the tongue in training.

Sbriglia said, "There is no way to tell people how to use their tongues, their lips, or their mouths in singing. It depends on the formation of these organs. Always keep the tongue flat, is another universal method. How stupid! The tongue usually goes up in the back just a little, but it depends on the formation of the tongue. Have proper breath support and posture, enunciate clearly, have no tension above the chest, and these things will come to each singer—differently, to different ones perhaps. Everything coordinates, always upward until the tone seems to come down from the resonance cavities of the head.

Sbriglia felt that consonants could be used in a way which would be helpful to singers.

"Proper enunciation," Sbriglia insisted, "is the difference between singing and an instrument, and helps place the voice." He
preferred French because the nasal quality puts the voice "*dans le
masque;*" Italian, to develop a voice because of the round vowels;
German is too gutteral; and the declamatory German Bayreuth
School he classed as one of the causes of the decline of singing.
"English can be as beautiful as any language if you dwell on the
vowels." He always required his pupils to sing songs on vowels
only, "to get a perfect *legato,* the fountain of all good singing."
The consonants were then slipped in their proper places without
losing the legato.

REGISTERS

What was the secret of his changing Jean de Reszke from a
baritone to a tenor?

> As for teaching high notes falsetto, that is only for tenors who
> have trouble with their upper voice. Nobody seems to realize that
> a tenor's high notes are falsetto with breath under them. Jean de
> Reszke was a baritone. I made him into the greatest tenor of his
> time.

Ruth Miller Chamlee, one of the last students of Sbriglia,
described Sbriglia's teaching and presented his basic exercises to
the members of the University of Colorado NATS Workshop in
1964. She also demonstrated his use of "the little oo" [u] in
whistle voice. This was used by Sbriglia to find and develop the
head voice of female voices.

[Fiberscope observation of the larynx in singing reveals that
the whistle voice *looks* like the male falsetto voice and vice versa.
We now know that Sbriglia used falsetto in high male voices and
in female voices. How unique! This Italian tenor who was one of
the greatest singing masters of all time used falsetto in his teaching; it is disdained in Italy today (Miller 1977). Perhaps this is an
explanation of why there are currently so few world-class Italian
singers.]

He taught low voices differently at times:

> For some low voices, thinking down, that resonance is in the
> chest, helps the phlegmatic singer with undeveloped muscles,

who tightens his neck, to get the *point d'appui* support. Of course it is wrong for normal voices, but I have made many a fine singer by using this approach.

BELLY BREATHING

Sbriglia thought that the pushing out of the stomach muscles in singing was pernicious (not to be confused with the bulge of the epigastrium, the area between the belt line and the lower part of the sternum). He thought this was one of the causes of the decline of good singing. He had an explanation:

> When people get old, they begin to stoop. Usually the chest and abdominal muscles are the first to feel the erosion of old age. Most of the famous teachers these days are singers, who do not begin to teach until they are too old to continue their careers. As their voices fail, they begin to experiment. They discover they can sing better by forcing their weakened chest and diaphragm muscles. They conscientiously believe they have found a new method. All this unnatural pushing plays havoc with proper breath support. Really great singers, having sung naturally from childhood, begin to try to find out how they sing only as they begin to lose their voices.

SBRIGLIA'S SUCCESS

In addition to the establishment of favorable body mechanics and placing the voice, Sbriglia dealt with the singer's spiritual and psychical attitude in his art:

> Sbriglia's unprecedented success came from his ability to get the simple physical foundation in singing, then added the inspirational angle. Being in good voice is having pep, the aliveness that brings the uplift required for good singing. When you are in good voice, you do not need a method. But your big engagements usually come when you are not in good voice. Then you must have a method.

He cautioned against haste in training the voice; he considered the pushed type of breathing as an attempt to get early results. He desired that there be adequate time of preparation. He said, "It takes three years to train a voice properly, with a beautiful overtone."

David Bispham relates (Shaw 1914) Cosima Wagner's reaction to a Covent Garden performance of Lohengrin: "I have tonight, for the first time in my life, heard Wagner sung from a melodious standpoint!" It was because the artists had all studied the art of singing so well and "the psychology of their complex roles stood out triumphant over the material means of expression which so often prove a hindrance to the enjoyment of modern works."

The artists were students of great teachers: Nordica (taught by Sbriglia), Schumann-Heink (G. B. Lamperti), Jean and Edoard de Reszke (Sbriglia) and Bispham (F. Lamperti and Shakespeare). Since I have been unable to find who Sbriglia's teacher was, I must conclude that Sbriglia was the origin of another line in the historical development of singing. His contribution to the bel canto age of that time has led to that which we are having today.

REFERENCES

Byers, Margaret Chapman (1942). "Sbriglia's Method of Singing." *The Etude*, May 337–338.
Greenfield, E. (1972). *Joan Sutherland*. Ian Allen, London.
Kennedy, M. (Ed.) (1980). *The Concise Oxford Dictionary of Music*. Oxford University Press, London.
Miller, R. (1977). *English, French, German and Italian Techniques of Singing*. Scarecrow Press, Metuchen, N.J.
Sadie, S. (Ed.) (1980). *The New Grove's Dictionary of Music and Musicians*. Macmillan Publishers, London.
Shaw, W. W. (1914). *The Lost Vocal Art*. Lippincott, Philadelphia and London.

17

William Johnstone-Douglas: "The Teaching of Jean de Reszke"

Jean de Reszke (1850–1925) was the principal tenor of the Golden Age of Opera at the turn of the Twentieth Century. He made his debut in 1874 as a baritone, with limited success; he traveled with his brother and sister, Edouard and Josephine de Reszke in their careers; after training with Sbriglia (*NATS Bulletin*, January-February 1984), he made his debut as a tenor in 1879. A native of Poland, he sang Italian opera better than the Italians, French opera better than the French, and German opera better than the Germans. From 1890–1902 he was the reigning tenor of the Metropolitan Opera Company. He taught in Paris and Nice from 1902 until the time of his death. W. J. Henderson wrote, "His voice was by no means incomparable, but his art was."

Jean was the only one of the family who became known as a teacher of singing. He objected to calling his approach a method since he knew that no single method of teaching could be effective for all pupils. He had "ideas about the voice" which increased in number during the nearly 25 years of his teaching career. He found it impossible to write a book on his teaching since he taught each singer differently. Because his students tended to teach as they were taught, the most complete account of his principles is by Walter Johnstone-Douglas, who was his student, accompanist, and assistant teacher for several years. Amherst

Reprinted from the *NATS Bulletin* [now *Journal*], March-April 1984.

Webber, de Reszke's associate for 30 years, said that if anyone had to write of Jean de Reszke's teaching he would have preferred no other to Johnstone-Douglas.

Since de Reszke's career was in opera his teaching was directed mainly towards training singers for the stage, although he did not confine his efforts to that. In so doing he took into account differences in voice, physique, and intelligence in his efforts to bring forth the individual vocal and artistic abilities.

Because he was basically interested in teaching for the theater he knew that there must be "all kinds of resources and colors in the voice but primarily power." He stated, "In the opera one *"has* to shout, but one must *know how* to shout." He had an uncanny power of building a voice up out of little or nothing and seemed to prefer this type of teaching to working with career artists. The increase of power was all done without encouraging his pupils to sing beyond their capabilities and without sacrificing beauty of tone.

His training divided itself into three parts: (1) breath control, (2) resonance, and (3) head sonority and overtone, the focusing and colorings of tone, and the countless details which make up the aesthetics of singing.

Breathing

In all his instruction he used a great deal of imitation since he had been taught that way by his teachers, Ciaffei and Cotogni. [In fact, some have attributed his being a baritone to his imitation of Cotogni, a baritone, who was the first teacher of Gigli.]

His first step was to secure a good foundation—the breath support which was necessary for the control and depth of tone. De Reszke would have the pupil sit down with shoulders rounded, with elbows on the knees and hands hanging down in an attitude of complete relaxation "in order to relax all the muscles of the chest and prevent the use of any others except those of the diaphragm." Following this the breath was to be taken with the lower ribs expanding without the chest rising. "Imagine yourself to be a great church bell, where all of the sonority is round the rim.'' The abdomen was to be kept up and in [not pushed out] to give support to the diaphragm. In singing, this expansion was to be kept as long as possible, and ''the lower ribs not allowed to collapse, in order that the breath might be kept under compression to the last.'' This was the basis of ''the legato style of the true Bel Canto.'' [His statement differs from Sbriglia's account only in description, *NATS Bulletin,* January-February 1984.] The trouble was that many beginners found this type of singing fatiguing. He also trained on a tone with exaggerated compression, with no added resonance, such as on the French word *puis,* with an exaggerated [p] and extremely thin [u] and [i] to develop muscles.

He thought of singing as being an athletic endeavor:

> The whole body was to be as though one was ''settling down'' on the diaphragm, relaxed but ready to spring, as in tennis, golf, boxing, etc., rather than braced up and stiff as if ''on parade.'' The effort was to come from the back as if the sound was following ''a line drawn from the small of the back to the bridge of the nose.'' This invariably added a velvety quality to the voice as it had done to his own.

He used the sigh to establish a connection between the voice and the support. This was done by breathing out, right from the bottom of the lungs, on the pure sound of Italian ''AH'' [a] with the breath coming straight up from the diaphragm and without much compression, as though breathing out on the hand to warm it. He gained complete relaxation of the throat muscles and tongue by this device. The deep breathing assisted in a lowered position of the larynx, which was necessary for all heavy singing.

Possibly due to the stress of modern-day society we are hearing so much about relaxation that before long it may become a fad. Again, his concept of singing was that it was, like any other form of athletics, ''a question of training and natural gifts combined; the amateur has the natural gifts but the professional must have both.''

Voice Placement and Diction

De Reszke had the same difficulty we have: his students wanted to know when they could make their debuts before he had "placed their tongues, much less their voices." One of the problems teachers face is the means of combining technical studies with performance, which has been called "the transfer of learning":

> . . . with him voice-production, diction and interpretation were inseparable: the very first lessons, after vowel sounds pure and simple, would be on phrases from operas in any language to exemplify the technical point that was being studied.

He had a special gift for imparting the pronunciation and accent of languages in singing, and taught most of his students in their native tongues. He had a delicate feeling for phrasing and artistic union of word and tone. But too few were able to absorb that which he gave to the extent that they could do the same thing away from him. One of his devices was to have a student use a speaker's voice and gradually merge this into the singing voice. If the cords vibrated as they should in a ". . . tense not flabby [manner], hard not unsteady and with the edges close together, kept straight, not ragged, the illusion of speaking while singing could be maintained."

Resonance and Sonority

Most present-day teachers believe in cover—others do not. The greatest tenor of his time taught that "a bass or baritone should begin to "cover" his voice on E^b or E, a tenor on F or F#, though for occasional effect he should be able to "open" his E and F# respectively."

Jean de Reszke was quite conscious of the action of the soft palate and uvula in singing. He preferred that most of this work be done only in his presence. [I feel that a description of these procedures would be non-productive in this column.]

He placed great importance on mask resonance, which was used to obtain maximum resonance and ring in the voice. This was gained by allowing "just room enough for the tone to be thrown up into the resonance spaces behind the nose, using the sound of the French *'an'* [*.ã*] in *'souffrance.'*" [I gather that he was obtaining a vibration of air in the upper turbinate of each nostril, which lies almost between the eyes.] It was not his desire to hear a sound which went into the nose and which was "almost invariably flat." He never used the "mask" tone in piano singing. He taught mask resonance in the following manner:

> Because of its numerous nasal syllables, a very effective sentence to obtain this resonance was *"Pendant que l'enfant mange son pain, le chien tremble dans le buisson,"* monotoned on each successive syllable of the scale. This mask quality he insisted on as an essential ingredient in women's chest voices, which he would rarely allow to be carried above E above middle C, never above F: if carried above F a "break" inevitably develops. In a course of purely mask singing *o* and *a* would become *on* and *an,* the open *ê* as in *être* became *ain,* and the *i* as in *si* and the closed *e* as in *été* were hardly placed in the mask at all, but were supported on the diaphragm.

The effect of such vocalization can probably be heard in the recordings of his student, John Charles Thomas, in which there seems to be a rather continuous hum in the voice. Also, the [m], [n] and [ng] sounds tend to be softened and do not have the great pressure associated with the plosives of the Teutonic languages.

He wanted to get the maximum amount of forward tone in the voice. He gained this by having the student imagine that he was drinking in the tone rather than pushing the tone out. [X-ray motion pictures indicate that the narrow passage between the tongue and the hard and soft palate are wider in singing than in speech, to allow the instrumental sound of the voice. This probably is the opening which is called "open throat" singing.] When the tone was right the tone seemed "to resonate right on the hard palate, by the front teeth." [Others have said the teeth are resonators; if the results are correct who can argue with the means?]

COLORS OF THE VOICE

Lord Weltingham has stated that de Reszke as an artist did all his wonders "without a great natural voice, by the illuminating magic of his genius, by his extraordinary magnetism, and by artistic perfection, dramatic and vocal. . . ." [Was this the reason he did not record?] It is no surprise that the art he imparted to his students was an ever-increasing range of colors and subtlety of tone.

> . . . gradually technique began to mean to them no longer the power of accomplishing their own desires in interpretation but rather the opening up of new worlds as yet undreamed of [so that there was] the constant disappearance of the horizon the nearer one approached it. . . .

He was exceptional in the way he could color his voice. His pianissimos and mezza voce singing were unique and were a part of the art he attempted to give to his students.

> His pianissimos were obtained in three ways: 1) what he called "the crushed voice" (more often applied to men's voices), sung with almost closed mouth and low palate, the larynx being rather high, but the support as deep and strong as possible. 2) Then there was the piano tone in the head, the pianissimo tone most commonly used, obtained with a very high palate and a certain breath support. 3) And lastly, the pianissimo, which seemed to come from the middle of the back without any obvious support, with the larynx low, the mouth open, and no apparent resonances, thus differing from "the crushed voice". . . . This is a wonderfully carrying tone, but can only be obtained by complete relaxation.

He wanted declamation to be as natural as speech and, as an exercise, would take a simple everyday sentence which he would repeat and repeat with the consonants supported from the diaphragm with the larynx low but the vowels remaining as in speech. (In everyday speech the larynx is high.)

POSTURE

Special attention was paid by de Reszke to the position of the head. He said, "Sing to the gallery" with the head slightly back but not stiff. [Luchsinger and Arnold, p. 76, point out that in this case the elevator muscles and depressor muscles in opposition assist in shortening the vocal cords for the higher pitches. It can also be shown that the pitch of the vocal tract is higher with the head in the "gallery" position and the pitch of the vocal tract lower when the head is down.] In singing the mask tone the head was down a bit, "you feel like you are butting your way through."

He desired that the cheeks and lips be mobile, with the cheeks rising as the pitch rises [this is used in "formant tracking" (Sundberg 1977, p. 64)]. This was essential "for men's upper open notes and all women's high notes." He called it *"la grimace de la chanteuse"* (the singer's grimace).

EPILOGUE

This renowned teacher was criticized for not producing world artists like himself, but "great singers are the combination of great voices and great brains and great instincts." [But would he have been the reigning tenor of that golden age if Sbriglia had not been successful in "putting things together" for him? It takes great teachers also.] This reviewer would like to note that several well-known singers studied with de Reszke at one time or other: John Charles Thomas, Bidu Sayao, Maggie Teyte, Carmen Melis, who taught Renata Tebaldi, and Clive Carey, who had as a student Joan Sutherland. Sutherland's accompanist, Richard Bonynge, heard most of her lessons and assisted in finding her voice, and has influenced several other major singers of our time. Great teaching is not lost, it is handed down in various forms, and the fruits may be heard afterwards for many generations.

REFERENCES

Greenfield, E. (1972). *Joan Sutherland.* Ian Allen, London.
Johnstone-Douglas, W. (1925). "The Teaching of Jean de Reszke." *Music and Letters.* July.
Kreuger, M. (1965). *John Charles Thomas.* RCA Victor Record Vintage Series LPV-515.
Kutsch, K. J. and L. Riemens (1969). *A Concise Biographical Dictionary of Singers.* Chilton Book, Philadelphia, New York.
Leiser, C. (1934). *Jean de Reszke.* Minton Balch, New York. (Includes Johnstone-Douglas article.)
Luchsinger, R. and G. Arnold (1965). *Voice-Speech-Language.* Wadsworth Publishing, Belmont, California.
Sadie, S. (Editor) (1980). *The New Grove's Dictionary of Music and Musicians.* Macmillan Publishers, London.
Sundberg, J. (1977). "Singing and Timbre." *Music Room Acoustics.* Royal Swedish Academy of Music, 17, Stockholm.

18

Lilli Lehmann:
How to Sing (1914)

Lilli Lehmann (1848–1929) was described by Jean de Reszke as "the greatest artist of the century: (Leiser 1934), and by David Bispham (1920) in this way: ". . . certainly no artist in the history of the modern lyric stage has performed so great a number of parts or performed them with such uniform distinction." She sang altogether 170 roles, ranging from coloratura to Wagner heroines. She sang at the first Bayreuth Festival and sang Isolde in Vienna as late as 1909 when she was 61. She was instrumental in establishing the Salzburg Festival and was later its artistic director. At the age of seventy she was still appearing as a *Lieder* singer.

   She was a member of the Metropolitan Opera Company during the Golden Age when Maurice Grau was using all-star casting as manager of *both* the "Met" and Covent Garden. The roster, made up of the world's leading singers, included the de Reszkes, Sembrich, Melba, and Plançon. Several times Lehmann had been the Isolde to some of de Reszke's greatest Tristans. She said that one of the great things to learn was how to hear both oneself and others, and to learn from all with whom one was associated. During these years she was writing the first edition of her book *How to Sing* (1902), in which she was, without doubt, influenced by her colleagues. At the time of publication of that edition she

Reprinted from the *NATS Bulletin* [now *Journal*], May-June 1984.

had been on the stage 34 years. Her most notable students were Geraldine Farrar and Olive Fremstad.

Lehmann wrote as a performer to bring to others what she had learned during her career. The book was based on science as it was known at that time, as well as on the sensations of tone which she felt made up the only language the singer could understand. She wanted to clarify such expressions as "full," "nasal," "singing forward," "bright," "dark," etc. which were often misunderstood, and to relate them to the exact functions of the vocal organs. She even desired that her students have notebooks in which pictures of the vocal organs could be drawn.

It is impossible to review all of the Lehmann book within the limitations of this column, so I will mention several principles which she added to the teaching of singing. She was interested primarily in teaching artistic singing rather than natural singing. To her, artistic singing consisted of

> . . . a clear understanding, first and foremost, of breathing, in and out; of an understanding of the form through which the breath has to flow, prepared by a proper position of the larynx, the tongue, and the palate, [and] of the chest-muscle tension, against which the breath is forced, and whence, under the control of the singer, after passing through the vocal cords, it [the air] beats against the resonating surfaces and vibrates in the cavities of the head.

She thought some of the terminologies should be abolished because they were false; for example:

> . . . the false idea of the breath on which for years nearly the entire attention was directed, thus diverting it from the form for the breath. The misunderstood idea of breath-restraint on the part of the pupil corresponds to the idea of a channel without outlet, in which the water collects without flowing off; whereas the breath must continually issue from the mouth. It has become the habit of considering the breath as the only cause for a bad or a good tone. This is the cause of the eternal breath pressure with which so many singers produce their tones and ruin their voices.

She believed that at first the entire attention should be directed to the form only, and that the coordination with the breath should be established later. By form she meant the relative position of nose, palate, larynx, and tongue.

BREATHING—CHEST MUSCLE TENSION

Lehmann states that all of the effort of breathing should be directed against the chest so that the throat could be free. She called this "the chest muscle tension;" it is related to what Sbriglia called *point d'appui*. She believed that as far as the senses are concerned, we do not have control over the vocal cords either as beginners or artists. Since we do not feel them,

> We first become conscious of them through the controlling apparatus of the breath, which teaches us to spare them, by emitting breath through them in the least possible quantity and of even pressure, thereby producing a steady tone. I even maintain that all is won if we regard them directly as breath regulators, and relieve them of all overwork through the controlling apparatus of the chest muscle tension.

But she did not always press the breath against the chest:

> Only when I have begun to sing—especially when singing long cantilena-like phrases—do I push the breath against the chest, thereby setting the chest muscles in action. These combined with the elastically stretched diaphragm and abdominal muscles; the abdomen is always brought back to its natural position during singing. [Some singers of the German school keep the diaphragm (abdomen) pressed out.]

Her method exerts a pressure in the form which

> . . . is the supply chamber and bed of the breath. This pressure enables us to control the breath while singing. . . . The more flexibly the breath pressure is exerted against the chest . . . the less the breath flows through the vocal cords and the less . . . are they directly burdened.

Vowels—Forms Through Which the Breath Flows

Lehmann thought that vowels were different in singing than in speech because of language height, and that sung vowels must be constructed in such a way that they are mixed. She constructed them from [i], [e], and [u]. She further states that the *ah* vowel should be forgotten in singing because of its deficiency of overtone [the 1st and 2nd formants are very close together; and the vowel is hard to tune at the register transitions]. In this she was very explicit:

> Above all strike out the so-called pure vowel *ah*—since it is the root of all evil—and also eliminate from the memory that it is a single tone. [In singing it has] nothing in common with the accustomed vowel *ah* as ordinarily spoken . . . [since] the tongue is usually pressed down—not only by false habit but often pressed down artificially with instruments. This leads to flat, ordinary, defective singing, if not often to the ruin of the voice itself. . . .

From the above it seems that Lehmann sensed that the Vowel Triangle of singing was smaller than that of speech and that the beloved [i], [a] and]u] of researchers is different in singing than in speech. This probably has to do with the vowel coupling of "in line" resonators, which amplifies sung language from 100 to 1,000 times the loudness of speech. She believed that [u] should be mixed with [e] to give it overtone, that [i] must be blended with [e] so that it would carry, and the *ah* of speech should be disregarded. Did she have some advanced knowledge of formants and harmonics or was this a revelation through the senses when singing from the stage?

Registers

This artist and teacher admits there are registers, but she wishes to do away with the terminology. She thought that vowels and registers were related, and that if the appropriate vowel mixtures were used the registers would not be heard as ugly transitions.

She was more explicit in another statement:

> Everything should be sung with a mixed voice in such a way that
> no tone is forced at the expense of any other. [The use of mixed
> vowels would also enable the artist] to avoid monotony . . . and
> place at his disposal a wealth of means of expression in all ranges
> of his voice.

She believed that voices which contain only one or two registers were called short voices, and that ". . . a singer ought always to extend the compass of his voice as far as possible, in
order to be certain of possessing the compass that he needs."

This was to be done by finding the missing register and equalizing it with those already present. In most cases she said this
development

> . . . required many years of the most patient study and observa-
> tion, often a long-continued or entire sacrifice of one or the other
> limit of a range for the benefit of the adjacent weaker one; of the
> head voice especially, which, if unmixed, sounds uneven and thin
> in comparison with the middle range until, by means of practised
> elasticity of the organs, endurance of the throat muscles, muscular
> tension of the organs in relative position, a positive equalization
> can take place.

HEAD REGISTER

Lilli Lehmann placed great emphasis on the establishment of
head voice and related it to survival in a lengthy career, and
maintained that its establishment was necessary for the rejuvena-
tion of a voice.

> The *pure* head voice (the third register) is, on account of the
> thinness that it has by nature, the neglected step-child of almost
> all singers, male and female; its step-parents, in the worst signifi-
> cance of the word, are most singing teachers, male and female
> . . . the sensation of it [is that] the larynx stands high and supple
> under the tongue.

She believed that the head voice was of greatest importance to
all vocal artists.

The head voice is the most valuable possession of all singers, male and female. Without its aid all voices lack brilliancy and carrying power. . . . By it alone can we effect a complete equalization of the whole compass of all voices, and extend that compass. . . . Without it all voices of which great exertions are demanded infallibly meet disaster.

She thought the *ah* vowel was very treacherous:

As soon as the head tones come into consideration, one should *never* attempt to sing an open *ah*, because on *ah* the tongue lies flattest. One should think of [e], and in the highest range even an [i]; should mix the [e] and [i] with [u], and thereby produce a position of the tongue and soft palate that makes the path clear for the introduction of the breath into the cavities of the head.

FALSETTO

Although Lehmann was primarily known as a teacher of female singers she had definite opinions about male voices. She knew of the teaching of Lamperti in Milan, since her husband, Paul Kalisch, was a student of his. Incidentally, he sang Manrico to Lehmann's first Leonore at the "Met." Since she also sang with virtually all of the leading male singers in the world, she should be entitled to opinions on teaching male voices.

The upper limits of a bass and baritone voice are f, f#, and possibly g where, consequently, the tones must be mixed [covered]. Pure head tones, that is, falsetto, are never demanded higher than this. I regard it, however, as absolutely necessary for the artist to give consideration to his falsetto, that he may include it among his known resources.

CONSONANTS

This matriarch of German song, taught by her mother in the Italian method of singing, had several special techniques of dealing with the German language. Although she appeared in the opening season of Bayreuth Festival, she thought singers' en-

deavors to acquire distinctness of articulation ". . . were an entire failure. Their teachers, unconscious of what they were doing
and teaching in good faith, committed a great wrong not only
toward vocal art but toward the vocal organs of the unsuspecting
singer."

She had several very interesting techniques which may have
originated with the Italian School, involving resonant consonants
which gave better line and intelligibility.

> *K, l, m, n, p, s, r, and t* at the end of a word or syllable must be
> made resonant by joining to the end of the word or syllable a
> rather audible ë (eh); for instance, Wandell(e), Gretel(e), etc.
> [This could be used by American singers to avoid the dull Ameri-
> can *l*, which we sing as [ɛəl]].

She stated:

> A thing that no one teaches any longer . . . is the dividing and
> ending of syllables that must be effected under certain conditions.
> I was taught it especially upon double consonants. When two
> come together, they must be divided; the first, as in Him-mel,
> being sounded dull, and without resonance, the syllable and tone
> being kept as nasal as possible, the lips closed, and a pause being
> made between the two syllables; not till then is the second syllable
> pronounced, with a new formation of the second consonant.
>
> And this is done, not only in case of a doubling of one conso-
> nant, but whenever two consonants come together to close the
> syllable; for instance, win-ter, dring-en, kling-en, bind-en; in
> these the nasal sound plays a specially important part. . . . The
> tediousness of singing without proper separation of the syllables is
> not appreciated till it has been learned how to divide the conso-
> nants. The nasal close of itself brings new color into the singing,
> which must be taken into account; and moreover, the word is
> much more clearly intelligible. . . .

PLACEMENT

She had a schema of voice placement sensations which appeared
in a diagram. This was a gradated method of singing the lower
notes towards the upper front teeth and the high notes towards the

soft palate (covered). She believed that when a person sang continually on one point it created registers. Her favorite exercise
was "the great scale" in which she sang every note in her voice
slowly and with varied colors.

TECHNIQUE

Her credo was that

> Technique is inseparable from art. Only by mastering the tech-
> nique of his material is the artist in a condition to mould his
> mental work of art and to give it . . . to others. Even artists
> intellectually highly gifted remain crippled without this mastery
> of the technique.

She furthermore thought that

> As beauty of tone is the foundation of vocal art, it should be the
> aim of every singer to alter it as little as possible by means of
> skillful and flexible pronunciation without endangering the dis-
> tinctness of enunciation.
>
> Consciously or unconsciously used, technique remains a ne-
> cessity to art and to the artist himself, as without it there is no art.
> Is it not a magnificent task to secure for one's self a privileged
> position in the world of art by acquiring conscious ability? By
> gaining for one's self a beautiful voice or, if such a one naturally
> exists, by preserving it to the end of one's life?

PHYSIOLOGICAL ACTIONS INVOLVED

Lehmann wanted her students to know of the physiological
events involved with singing as realized through the senses.

> . . . that all muscles contract in activity and in normal inactivity
> are relaxed; that we must strengthen them by continued vocal
> gymnastics so that they may be able to sustain long-continued
> exertion; and must keep them elastic and use them so. It includes
> also the well-controlled activity of diaphragm, chest, neck, and
> face muscles. That is all that physiology means for the vocal

organs. Since these things all operate together, one without the others can accomplish nothing; if the least is lacking, singing is quite impossible, or is entirely bad.

DIFFUSION OF TEACHING METHODS

She was critical of the manner in which the teaching of singing was being diffused through degree study in which a certificate of competence was given after a short period of study in a conservatory. She considered this to be a "factory system" in which mistakes did not show up until too late, when there was ". . . no time, no teacher, no critic and the executant has learned nothing whereby he could undertake to distinguish or correct them."

She thought the whole art of song was more and more given over as a sacrifice.

REFERENCES

Bispham, D. (1920). *A Quaker Singer's Recollections*. Macmillan, New York, p. 258.

Kutsch/Riemens (1969). *A Concise Biographical Dictionary of Singers*. Chilton Book, New York.

Lehmann, L. (1914). *How to Sing*. MacMillan, New York.

Lehmann, L. (1914). *My Path Through Life*. Putnam's Sons, New York.

Leiser, C. (1934). *Jean de Reszke*. Minton, Balch, New York, p. 213.

Seltsam, W. H. (1947). *Metropolitan Opera Annals*. H. W. Wilson, New York.

NOTE

The Editor of the *NATS Bulletin* wishes to thank Dr. Berton Coffin for his insightful reviews of eighteen important classics of vocal pedagogy. His own statement appears a fitting way to close this series of reviews:

After having written 18 reviews of the classics on which our teaching of singing is based, I have come to the conclusion that by the time of Maurice Grau's Golden Age of Singing all the principles of classical singing had been stated and that anything written since then has been either derivative, tangential, or an assimilation of principles. At that time Garcia, Marchesi, Sbriglia, G. B. Lamperti, Stockhausen, Marchesi, and Shakespeare were alive— their students and their principles dominated the stage. I believe that nothing new in the way of classical singing has occurred since that time, and most of the things which have been written are available. As a consequence this will be my last review of **Vocal Pedagogy Classics.** Much that is currently written is confusing and of questionable validity. We have much that is scientific and unrelated to the senses, to methodology, and to artistic singing. We have had much writing on registers which has been counterproductive, and much on relaxation which would not be accepted by the vocal masters of the past; they believed that singing was a form of athletics. To wit: "Before all, never neglect to practise every morning, regularly, proper singing exercises through the whole compass of the voice. Do it with painful seriousness; and never think that vocal gymnastics weary the singer. On the contrary, they bring refreshment and power of endurance to him who will become master of his vocal organs."

Appendix A: The Relationship of the Breath, Phonation, and Resonance in Singing

> It has become the habit of considering the breath as the only cause for good and bad tone. This is the cause of the eternal breath pressure with which so many singers produce their tones and ruin their voices . . . it would be advisable to leave the coaction of the diaphragm out of play at first, directing the entire attention to the form only.
>
> —Lilli Lehmann (1914, p. 280)

PREFACE

Because of the above statement I have discussed the resonance (form) and the relationship of resonance to phonation before writing on the various breaths of singing. My work was unfinished when I published *Phonetic Readings of Songs and Arias* (1964) with coauthors Delattre, Errolle, and Singer, *because spoken phonetics are **not** the same as sung phonetics*. I made a preliminary statement in the Preface of how they should be modified, based on the findings of Howie and Delattre. Since that time I have been delving into *why* they are different and *how* they can be used in the building of a singing voice and a singing diction. The statement of "pure vowels" is true and false. It is true if the vowel formation gives a pure and liquid sound; it is false if speech values are forced on most sung pitches. I described a *vowel mirror*, Echophone, by which a singer or teacher of sing-

Reprinted from the *NATS Bulletin* [now *Journal*], December 1975.

ing can find the resonant vowel colors of any note at the flick of a finger on an electric organ.

By the same process, with a Radioear Bone Vibrator used as an electric larynx, we have been able to play all kinds of sounds through the vocal tract in order to better understand the relationship of the natures of *phonation* and *resonation*. Now we should be able to safely observe the breaths of singing and the advantages that can be gained by their appropriate use.

BOX OFFICE

Singing is a matter of air space in auditoriums and of setting that space into vibration. Since 1963 my wife and I have heard 106 operas in 45 opera houses in Europe. We have also been in the prominent ones in this country. We have heard many of the same singers in different opera houses and have found that different houses have different sounds. In truth, singers play houses, and audiences listen to how they play them. Breath is air which energizes the movement of the vocal cords and resonances of the vocal tract which vibrates the air spaces of opera houses or concert halls which vibrate the air spaces in our ear canals. We will leave the physiology and psychology of hearing for others to explain. Singing is basically a manner of vibrating air spaces, by vowels and changing the vibrations of air spaces by consonants. We need to continually think of the particular air space we will be vibrating in singing. *I believe that our art of singing as we know it today can be traced back to certain air space conditions.* I believe that the Neapolitan school of singing, from which our Italianate singing derives, was an outgrowth of the air space of the San Carlo opera house. The manager, Domenico Barbaia, director from 1809–1824, had a theater with a certain air space and discovered Rossini, Bellini, and Donizetti who used it in such a way that the result was known as the "Bel Canto" period. It was this house to which the father, Manuel Garcia, was attached when Rossini wrote Almaviva (*Barber of Seville*) for him. It was a Neapolitan tenor, Caruso, whom many people consider to be the outstanding singer of our century. What was special about Naples? San Carlo was a singers' theater where vocal gymnastics and rivalry between the artists were the rule rather than the exception. It was the first of the large opera houses in Italy (1737) with 2,500 seats. Later there was La Scala in Milan (1778) with 2,289 seats and La Fenice in Venice (1792). It probably can be said that the singers who sang in those houses were the survivors of the fittest. They were the ones who had the *gifts* and the *techniques* to be heard effectively.

All the great Italian opera houses are *Box Theaters* from whence the term *Box Office* is derived. A box theater has unusual acoustical characteristics in that the sound dies away quickly; translated to musicians's terms this means that a full orchestral sound will die away to the sound of room noise in about 1.2 seconds: "In such houses the voices of singers are projected to the audience with clarity and sufficient loudness and the orchestra sounds clean and undistorted" (Beranek, 1962, p. 5). But we are a century ahead of our story because San Carlo (1737) was built a century after the first public opera house, San Cassiano, in Venice.

A TALE OF TWO CITIES

We are indebted to Winckel's "Space, Music, and Architecture" (1974) for most of the following details. There are many kinds of vocal music, small room music in which amateur singers can sing effectively for their own enjoyment, small recital halls comparable to court theaters, and large space vocal music which must be vibrated with "know-how" for the enjoyment of many people. Large space vocal music is historically bound to two churches, St. Mark's Basilica in Venice, and St. Thomas Church in Leipzig.

Let us speak first of Venice. St. Mark's was rebuilt in the form of a Greek Cross with five vaulted cupolas, in the 11th century. It became significant musically because of several very narrow galleries, 3 or 4 feet wide at a height of about 25 feet in which the choristers could stand in a single row. The galleries made possible antiphonal effects by the choirs and the words could be understood. The spoken word from the priests was not intelligible from the altar since there was a reverberation time of over 5 seconds. In this situation there was a transfer of communication from speech to music which, according to Winckel, "led to a reproach made by the Council of Trent, which was issued without a knowledge of the acoustic causes."

When Monteverdi served as *maestro di cappella* from 1613 until 1643, the architecture of St. Mark's had already created a music workshop which served as a place for the study of resonance and restated theories of music by Zarlino, and his student, Galilei, and the "spatial music" of the Gabriellis. Monteverdi meanwhile had written several operas for the court at Mantua, and according to Winckel, had initiated the construction of San Cassiano (1637), the first public opera theater which was supported by partricians and the wealthy middle class. In so doing he united himself with the young army of seekers after public applause.

Monteverdi, working in the spaces of St. Mark's and the opera theaters of Venice (there were 8 in 1630 and 16 by the end of the century) led the way from the madrigals of the court, through the declamation of the Florentines, to the bel canto arias of the Neapolitan Scarlatti. It has been stated that Baroque opera was the center of social life and also the focusing point of artistic endeavor in poetry, music, and architecture. It has not been pointed out that *architecture involves the formation of spaces which have had much to do with an evolving understanding of the structure of vocal music and its practice as an art.*

Now let us speak of Leipzig. St. Thomas Church was modified from a small Romanesque church to a Gothic church with a large nave, in 1496. The church became Lutheran in 1539 and was soon fitted with galleries in the north, south and west. In 1575 the pulpit was first used. Two second galleries were added later as were *Stübchen,* which were wooden boxes hung on the wall in imitation of the private boxes in opera houses! The result was a reduction of the low frequency echo to that of a high frequency church in which the spoken word could be understood. According to Hope Bagenal, the acoustical architect of Great Britain, it was more!

The reducing of reverberation in Lutheran churches by the inserted galleries, thus enabling string parts to be heard and distinguished and allowing a brisk tempo, was the most important single fact in the history of music because it led directly to the *St. Matthew Passion* and the *B Minor Mass* [Beranek, p. 46].

Thus when J. S. Bach served as Cantor from 1723 to 1750, St. Thomas Church, by a rather odd sequence of architectural developments, had become a "Hi-Fi" church which fitted the voice in both speech and singing, fitted the high frequencies of violins, and the fast passages on the organ, including the bass. The church seated 1800 people and, in musician's terms, the sound of a loud chord on the organ would die away to room noise in about 1.5 seconds.

This is in comparison to the large cathedrals where a loud chord on an organ can take over 7 seconds to die from forte to room noise and the characteristic sound is a booming bass. The vocal music for this space is Gregorian Chant which is in reality spoken word elevated and stabilized in pitch and given greater duration. By accident the Lutheran churches had gained the acoustic condition of the box opera houses, a situation which was necessary for Baroque music. This atmosphere was a constant one for over two centuries and one for which composers wrote and singers trained.

It is interesting to note that Tosi (1723) wrote on Italianate singing in the same year that Bach became Cantor in Leipzig. Teachers training soloists for the Bach Cantatas, Passions, and Masses know that a highly developed vocal technique is required. The voices must be able to make considerable sound if they are to approximate that required in St. Thomas Church which at Bach's time, according to Winckel, had a volume of 18,000 cubic meters (635,000 cubic feet) compared to the 397,000 cubic feet of La Scala (Beranek, 1962, p. 560). The performers of Bach's music should think of vocal sounds in terms of the space for which Bach wrote. One of the first concert halls was built at Oxford, England in 1748. It is interesting to note that it seated about 300 persons and had a reverberation time of about 1.5 seconds. One of the first concert halls on the Continent was built in Leipzig in 1780, the old Gewandhaus which seated 400 people and had a volume of 75,000 cubic feet. This is the hall in which symphony concerts were given by Mendelssohn. By means of adding a balcony, the seating was increased to about 570 as compared to Carnegie Hall in New York which seats 2,760 people and has a volume of 857,000 cubic feet. Shall we imagine that we have a vocal studio which is 18 feet long, 12 feet wide and 10 feet high? That space would be 2,160 cubic feet. Is it a wonder that our students sound so good in our studios?

We teachers of singing are frequently lulled into developing a technique of singing which will communicate only in studio space. What some teachers say concerning breathing and resonance may be correct for studio space, but only partly true for the large space where exaggeration of vibration and gesture is required. One can easily comprehend why the vocal music of concert halls, cathedrals, churches, and opera houses differs. One can also suspect that the larger the space to be vibrated the more critical becomes the proper use of the breath, and of pronunciation which especially involves vowels in Italy (since it is a more vowelized language than the northern languages) and consonants for comprehension in German and English. The Italian consonants are weaker than those in the Teutonic languages.

We will address ourselves to large hall singing since it can be modified to small hall singing whereas small hall singing is very difficult to change to large hall singing. We will observe that large hall singing is commercially more valuable from an economic standpoint. European theaters can be smaller because of governmental support of the arts. Our auditoriums are larger since the economic support must come from large audiences and we must have more seating room for comfort. (5.5 sq. ft. per seat in La Scala compared to 7.5 sq. ft. per seat in America.) It is easy to imagine that when a singer appears on the stage, he looks

towards the audience and wonders how his voice can project over
a large orchestra or a 9-foot concert grand piano, and be heard in
the far reaches of the auditorium. The answer is, *there must be a
technique.* There is one which was stated by Gasparo Pacchierotti
who began his singing as a choir-boy in the spaces of the cathedral at Forli, Italy. According to Henry Pleasants (1966, p. 84),
Pacchierotti may have been the greatest of the castrati. He sang in
San Carlo, La Scala, and at the opening of La Fenice in Venice.
He said:

> Mettete ben la voce
> Respirate bene
> Pronunciate chiaramente
> Ed il vostro canto sarà perfetto.
> *Collected by Philip A. Duey*

This means, "Place your voice well, breathe well, pronounce
clearly, and your singing will be perfect." The Lampertis based
their teaching on this statement. A better approach to singing has
yet to be found. It was developed in the spaces of an Italian
cathedral and was used in the major houses of that time. How
should we breathe to vibrate large spaces?

Italianate Singing

It is only logical that since Italy was the birthplace of opera, had
the first *public* opera theaters, and had the *largest* opera theaters
that there should develop what is known as Italianate singing. In
the 17th century, in Venice there was a great need for singers and
so the first burst of teaching singing occured there. Because the
Church viewed with disfavor the appearance of women on the
stage, and by that time the male soprano voice had been "discovered" and developed, it is not surprising that the first schools
were institutions founded for the poor and infirm. It was the poor
and not the noble who were "prepared" for careers as castrati.
The teaching of music to the convalescent and the poor came to
be so important that it overshadowed their other activities. Soon
the Venetian singers were noted far and wide. By 1702 the

Bolognese school came into eminence and soon after the Neapolitan school was dominant with Porpora being its most prominent teacher.

THE FULL BREATH

We have no description of what Porpora taught other than the music which he wrote for his singers. It would seem that there should be a great similarity between his technique of teaching singing and the vocalization of his singers in his operas. One can deduce from his music that he taught a great amount of agility, the messa di voce, a rather moderate range, and very long phrases. Certainly he taught on the full breath. Corri, his only student who wrote on singing, stated (1810, p. 11): "Take as much breath as you can, draw it in with moderate quickness, with suspiration, as if sighing, use it with economy, and at the same instant sound the letter A as pronounced in Italian or Scotch, thus "ah." (He taught for a time in Edinburgh.)

The most complete statement of breathing comes from Manuel Garcia, the son, whose father studied in Naples in 1814–1816 with the illustrious singer and teacher, Anzani. Garcia taught both the full breath (*Respiro*) and the half breath (*Mezzo Respiro*). We can understand his purpose best when his breathing exercises are analyzed according to their function. Although he said that a person should not become fatigued in the exercises, it is interesting to continue them long enough so that fatigue can tell the singer what is happening. *Exercise 1* was to draw in a complete breath through the pursed lips. This exercises the exterior costal muscles which causes the widening of the flexible ribs, the lowering of the diaphragm, and the rising of the upper ribs which are attached to the sternum. At the end of the inhalation, the floating ribs widen which cause a thinning of the waist. (Without the thinning of the waist, Garcia (1894, p. 4) considered the breath to be an incomplete one.) This fatigues the *inspiratory* muscles. After this exercise the breath was to be let out quickly. *Exercise 2* involved a rapid taking of the breath and a slow blowing of the breath through the pursed lips. This involved the strengthening of the interior costal muscles and of the contracting muscles of the abdomen. In this exercise the singer is aware of fatiguing the muscles just inside the hips—if there was an appendix on both sides these muscles would be over each of them. At the instant the blowing out begins, the distance is lengthened between the lowest part of the sternum and the backbone, and there is a further thinning of the waist. This exercise fatigues the *expiratory* muscles. *Exercise 3* concerns taking a full breath quickly and holding it for a long period of time (the vocal cords should remain apart). This exercise fatigues the *inspiratory* muscles as did exercise No. 1. (The exercises should be done independently of each other.) In *Exercise 4,* the breath was completely exhaled and the chest was held empty for an extended period of time. This exercise was omitted in *Hints on Singing* (1894). We will surmise that in the 50 years of additional experience after his first book he found this exercise to be of small value or of detriment to the art of singing. We will observe that there are two exercises to strengthen *inspiration* and one to strengthen *expiration.* Another stated purpose of the exercises was to develop the elasticity of the lungs. He called this type of breathing *thoracic* or *intercostal.* The strength of the inspiratory muscles is needed for an easy attack in which the breath is retained in the lungs. Their strength is also needed to keep the chest up for the artistic ending of phrases.

Caruso stated that (Marafiotti, 1922, p. 158) in the full breath " . . . the chest must be raised at the same time the abdomen sinks in." Anatomically the upper ribs rise on expansion and the lower ones widen. He further stated that it is "this ability to take in an adequate supply of breath and retain it until required that makes, or the contrary, mars, all singing." Caruso's statement was made 80 years after Garcia's statement and both statements were based on training in Naples!

EXHALATION

The exhalation was the reverse of inhalation. Garcia stated that it consisted " . . . simply in effecting a gentle, gradual pressure of the thorax and diaphragm on the lungs when charged with air; for if the movements of the ribs and of the diaphragm were to take place suddenly, they would cause the air to escape all at once.''

FRICATIVE INHALATION

It is a bit inconvenient to inhale through the pursed lips in performance. A technique used by my last teacher, the late Paola Novikova, was an inhalation on the sound of deep sleep (cords partially adducted) while the lips were closed, the cheeks were partially contracted, and the nostrils widened. She used this inhalation in all vocalization except when the catch-breath (half breath) was being taught, with the mouth open, during which time the chest did not drop. Her fricative inhalation was to be used in recital or opera whenever there was time, otherwise the catch-breath was to be used. Her students Nicolai Gedda, George London, and Irmgard Seefried have used this technique in their extended careers. It filled the lungs from the bottom, and the flexible ribs and diaphragm did their work before the upper ribs made their expansion. It was excellent for calming a singer before an important entrance. It protected against dryness of the throat since the breath was taken through the nose. It provided a downward movement of the larynx because of a pull by the trachea. In my judgement, some of her students went too far with the tracheal pull and had trouble with their upper notes. The larynx must be allowed to take various positions. Test this statement by octave leaps [1 to 8—8 to 1] with the upper note on or above the passaggio.

THE HALF BREATH

Garcia described the half breath (*Mezzo Respiro*) as being a ''slight and hurried inspiration which gives the lungs a slight supply, merely sufficient for a moment.'' In addition to the full breath, Jenny Lind used the half breath, according to Rockstro (1894, p. 15): '' . . . the lungs are neither completely *emptied,* nor completely *refilled*, but replenished only by means of a gentle inhalation confined to that portion of the organ which lies immediately beneath the claviculae or collar bones.'' She had great skill in using these widely different processes. They are the basis of flexible breath. F. Lamperti (1890) taught the full breath by timing the length of inhalation and the length of a tone. A preferable time for him was 18 seconds and he thought 12, 9, or 6 seconds would find the voice wanting in steadiness. He also taught the half breath.

Flexible Breath

We often hear that one should give a *deeper* support as one ascends a scale—how often do we hear that the singer should give a *shallower* support as he descends. This is a technique which is very important in descending phrases and should be taught and practiced daily. Also it is possible to give heavier support to low notes and light support to the high notes. The independence of breath effort and pitch height should be taught for colorful singing.

F. Lamperti considered his book to be largely on the breath, the most significant point being the balancing of effort between the inhaling muscles and the exhaling muscles. He calls this the vocal struggle (lutta vocale). When the lungs are full an effort must be made to retain the breath in the lungs. At the end of a long phrase the expiring muscles must contract to exhaust breath from the lungs. The balancing of effort between the inhaling muscles and exhaling muscles must be done so artfully that the voice will flow evenly. The Italians attained the balance by use of the famous *messa di voce* (crescendo and diminuendo) which also involves changes in the vocal tract and changes in pressure of the breath.

Messa Di Voce

We have spoken of the ability of the vocal tract to form resonating cavities in the pharynx and in front of the tongue hump. The

Italian *Ah* has a small space in front of the tongue hump and larger space in the pharynx than does the *AH*[ɑ]. Basic to a successful *messa di voce* is that the resonators are smaller in the *pianissimo* and larger in the *forte*, there being a gradual enlarging of the cavities as the tone becomes louder and a diminished size when the tone becomes softer. Increasing the breath pressure through the same sized vocal cavities is courting disaster and a fatigued throat. This conforms to the acoustic law of cavities. A large cavity of a given pitch will always be louder than a small cavity of that pitch. This also explains why a large-mouthed singer will be louder than a small-mouthed singer when the two are singing piano, mezzo forte, and forte respectively. This is an explanation of the large stature of singers of roles in heavily orchestrated operas. Age plays a part in this—the heavier voices are seldom at their best before 35 years of age. The *messa di voce* should be sung on the favorable vowel colors or hoarseness can ensue.

SOMBRE TIMBRE

Garcia's *Complete Treatise on the Art of Singing* was published four years after an important milestone in the history of singing which relates to the use of the breath and pronunciation. Gilbert-Louis Duprez, in 1837, sang a high C from the chest in Rossini's *William Tell* and displaced Garcia's father's student, Nourrit, from dominance at the Paris Opera. Duprez' high C eventually brought into existence the baritone and mezzo-soprano voice classifications and led to the more dramatic operas of Verdi and Wagner.

In this type of singing the mouth was opened much wider and an increased breath pressure was required. The voice moves less fast in this type of vocalization; Duprez was noted for dragging the tempo. Garcia called this type of singing *sombre timbre* in comparison with the *clear timbre* of Nourrit. A singer must give greater pressure from the area of the belt to sing in this manner. It is not just poetry to say that someone belted a high note. It happens to be a physiological truth. This also means that the 200 years

Gilbert-Louis Duprez made operatic history when he sang a sustained high C from the chest in *William Tell* in 1837. The sombre voice technique led to the baritone and mezzo-soprano voice classifications and heavier orchestration in opera.

between the first public opera theatre in Venice until *William Tell* in Paris, singers were singing with *clear timbre* which used the "smile" opening of the mouth with what is known as an Italian *Ah*. According to Garcia in *Memoire on the Human Voice* 1840, the differences of clear and sombre timbres pertain most especially to the pitches between ♯♯ whether sung by male or female voices. In two of our contemporary sopranos, Beverly Sills and Marilyn Horne, the middle voice has a metallic ring. This sound will penetrate a large concert hall and an opera house with a fair-sized orchestra. When this part of the scale is sung with a bright *Ah* or Italian [a], a small amount of breath pressure is used—a pressure from near the collar bone. When sung in *sombre timbre*, there is a dramatic character to the tone; the mouth is more open, a darker *Ah* is used and greater pressure is required from the area of the belt, a sound heard in the heavier female voices. The same thing pertains to the male voices which sing in this area, concert pitch. For basses, the interval shifts down to around 🎵 and for baritone around 🎵. Of the male voices, the tenors have the greatest facility for singing in either clear or sombre timbre. Baritones and basses are more dependent on sombre timbre for finding their upper voices. However, some of the great artists have both colors.

In 1968, Delattre and I made an X-ray motion picture study of clear and sombre timbre. In comparison with clear timbre we observed that in sombre timbre the opening between the tongue and palate was wider, that the vocal cords were lower and that the lips were rounded as if to retain the sound inside. The puckered mouth opening has the effect of increasing the pressure in the mouth which in turn requires more pressure in the trachea and lungs. Garcia (1894, p. 13) called ''pushing the lips out like a funnel'' a defect. The singers who most frequently use this mouth opening are those who have the umlauts in their language [y, ø, œ]. In fact, a case could probably be made that as long as singing was being taught by the castrati, almost always Italian, clear timbre was taught. However, when Italian singers began singing in Paris there was the influence of [œ, ø, y] which became incorporated in their technique and from it derived sombre timbre and Duprez' high notes. Let it be noted that this preceded the development of the mezzo soprano and baritone voices. All are dependent on *voix mixte* and I will conjecture that it all came from the French influence. This meant that instead of the purity of sound sought by the Italians there became a more *dense* sound in which many more overtones were present, each with its own vowel color! Consequently it became much more difficult to distinguish the vowels since they were mixed. Also, the voices sounded "rougher." Delattre found that any great amount of energy above 1500 Hz makes the voice sound scratchy. This reminds us of Resch's account (1974, p. 6) of G. B. Shaw's criticism. "He criticized German singers for coarse singing, but acknowledged that it did not seem to hurt them as they were 'as robust as dray horses' and 'sixty appears to be about their prime'."

Eric Leinsdorf considered the middle voice to be extremely important for a successful career in singing (1966, p. 84): "Most singers believe that an abundance of high notes means a heavy role; what really matters is how much middle-range singing is asked for and how heavy the texture of the accompanying instrumentation is." Since most singers and teachers of singing never see a full orchestral score, they rely on the sounds of a piano reduction and make mistakes in assigning repertoire. We hear continually that there are shortages of dramatic mezzo sopranos, lyric tenors, spinto tenors, Heldenbaritones, and serious basses. All of those voices are concerned with the scale between 𝄞 concert pitch, with a slight movement downward for the lower male voices mentioned. We will therefore surmise that there is a lack of understanding today of how to teach voices in this area. Teach sombre timbre with the darker vowels on the Vowel Color Chart with a greater pressure from the area of the belt.

BELTS

Joal stated (1895, p. 92) that in the classic Italianate singing, the singer could excite more pleasure and enthusiasm by means of trills, *messa di voce,* singing line and embellishments than by violent efforts of passion. This demanded a great art of breathing. It was based on the open Italian vowels. In dramatic singing there is more decibal output and the louder sounds take greater pressure. The perceptive eye will note that the heroic singers are frequently belted or girdled. There is an historical background to this. Dr. Joal, in his book dedicated to Jean de Reszke, has much to say about the use of belts by singers (1895, p. 126). This causes a costal or thoracic type of respiration which increases the power and solidity of the voice. One singer stated that the voice was fatigued much less after singing with a belt. Some artists used a band of flannel for purposes of slightly compressing the abdomen, the result being that their voices were better sustained. Another, after having been taught diaphragmatic breathing with poor results, constructed a belt which obliged him to enlarge the lower part of his chest [flexible ribs]. His voice had a return of strength. Joal concluded that costal breath (p. 130) " . . . is employed by the majority of singers, advised by the most renowned artists, and recommended by the old Italian masters, who have carried to such a high degree of perfection the art of singing." The teacher of Jean de Reszke, Edward de Reszke, Pol Plançon and Lillian Nordica designed a belt for singers which was on the market, The Sbriglia Belt. I have never been able to find a picture or obtain a description of its design. We know the purpose of a belt and how it assists singing. Franco Corelli uses one (*N.Y. Times,* February 8, 1970, p. 56) "for support under his chest." Plácido Domingo (*N.Y. Times,* February 27, 1972) wears a sturdy elastic supporter around his waist against which he presses all the way out for high notes, "for the middle register halfway and for pianissimo he lets it relax."

Let us say that one of the great pictures in Eisenstadt's *Witness to Our Time* is that of the heroic tenor, Lauritz Melchior, in an enormous corset that extended from his hips to halfway up on his rib cage with 5 straps that could be adjusted independently. The evenness and density of his vocal scale was no doubt related to the advantage that this device gave him.

I know of women artists who have said they have liked to sing with tight girdles, although their remarks are not in print. However, there are many pictures of the prima donnas at the turn of the century who were not only corseted but cinched to give the "wasp waist" in vogue at the time. Some singers feel that a belt reminds them of good posture and makes them "feel like a singer." A well-known American baritone who was a student of de Reszke said that he did not recommend the use of a belt to him but that several of the European singers with whom he sang used them.

In conclusion, as the diaphragm lowers on a deep breath, there is a downward pull on the trachea which lowers the larynx. It is our belief that the use of a belt or elastic band around the body reduces the trachea pull and leaves the larynx in a better position for singing middle and high notes than does a deep breath without a belt. A belt is almost a guarantee that the breath will be thoracic. It seems that there is a mechanical advantage gained from its use. Also, there is a possibility that the voice is slightly raised in tessitura.

Opening of the Mouth

Jean de Reszke's name is mentioned with the Golden Age of Singing that occurred in the 1880's. The principles of his teaching relate to both pronunciation and breath. One of the most remarkable concerns the assistance he gave to Adelina Patti, the historic coloratura soprano, through a student in 1905. Patti, then 62, wrote (Leiser, 1934, p. 275): "I certainly *do* open my mouth now and those exercises are positively excellent for avoiding the fatigue of too many scales." Without doubt, Jean de Reszke, through his student, had taught Adelina Patti the sombre timbre of singing. Our question is—why is it not wise to train both the front [a] and the back [ɑ]?

In that kind of training the singers will have both *clear* and *sombre* timbres in their voices; so their singing will be more colorful and they will also have a more evenly balanced musculature. De Reszke said (Leiser, 1934, p. 313): "The chin must be kept still and absolutely loose, the lower jaw hanging from the ears as if dislocated." This is sombre timbre.

On the other hand, Garcia (1894, p. 12) said, "The mouth should be opened by the natural fall of the jaw. This movement which separates the jaws by the thickness of a finger and leaves the lips alone, gives the mouth an easy and natural form." To a question of how the mouth opening could be regulated, he said that the opening could be found ''by placing laterally between the jaws from front to back a piece of wood no thicker than a pencil.'' This is clear timbre and the jaw is *not* dislocated. Caruso stated (Marafioti, 1922, p. 157):

> If one is well versed in the art, one can open the throat perfectly without a perceptible opening of the mouth merely by the power of respiration.
>
> It is necessary to open the sides of the mouth, at the same time dropping the chin well, to obtain a good throat opening. In taking the high notes, of course, one must open the mouth a little wider, but for the most part the position of the mouth is that assumed when smiling. [Also when coming down from a high note the mouth should return to its original position and the breath pressure should return to the original.]

SOMBRE TIMBRE THEATER

The most unique opera theater in the world is the Festspielhaus at Bayreuth. It is a house for Wagner's music only and his music is at its best only in that house. It is a coincidence that we can speak of it in its centennial year. Its uniqueness lies in the fact that the orchestra pit is covered in such a way that only the conductor can be seen by the singers on stage and yet the orchestra of over 100, seated on descending steps in the pit, can see the conductor. The sound from the pit can only be heard by reflection which according to Beranek (1962, p. 248) muffles the sound of the strings and reduces the ''brassiness'' of the dominant brasses. This means that the brilliance of the orchestra is muted and that the singers' voices can more easily penetrate the orchestral sound, even though they are singing in sombre timbre. It also means that the words can be understood at Bayreuth as in no other theater since the higher harmonics on which the voiced consonants play are more easily heard there as are the aspirate and sibilant consonants which extend to very high frequencies. Thus for his musical dramas, Wagner built a house which would play down the orchestra and play up the sung word! This means that *Parsifal* and *Der Ring des Nibelungen* played in any other house does not have the sound which Wagner had in mind for these operas. It means that singers must work much harder to sing over the orchestra in other houses since the brilliance of the orchestra masks the "Hi-Fi" of the singing voice to a greater extent. The vibrating air pressures at Bayreuth come more from the voices than the orchestra than in conventional houses. Unless voices have great brilliance, his operas are heard more as symphonic expression elsewhere. In recordings, with multiple microphones, it is possible to balance the orchestra and the sung word; to a certain extent this is possible in broadcasts. However, it is very obvious that a voice which can be heard in a moderate sized European house sounds quite different than the same voice trying to be heard in an American house which is significantly larger and has a longer reverberation time. This "attempting to be heard" frequently comes through on broadcasts as awkward vibratos and poor intonation and is less evident in recordings, or in performances in smaller houses.

The Acoustics of Posture

Corri (1810, p. 11) stated: "Keep the Head and Body upright which gives free passage to the Voice." Garcia (ab. 1855, p. 10) went further: "To insure easy inspiration, it is requisite that the head be erect, the shoulders thrown back without stiffness, and the chest expanded." F. Lamperti (1890, p. 10) said the singer "should hold himself erect, with the chest expanded and the shoulders easy—in a word, in the position of a soldier." When one observes the taking of a breath as a reflex action, the head usually tilts back, just as before a burst of laughter or just as one becomes ready to speak after a "brilliant idea." Likewise the sound comes out with the head slightly back. There is a balancing of the downward pull of the muscles on the back of the head and the downward pull on the muscles between the larynx and the sternum and the larynx and the shoulder blades. This inhaling action "opens" the throat. Pure voiced lyric sopranos, who have no *mixed voice* to speak of, frequently raise the chest on inhalation and lean back to bring the sternum and backbone closer together at the end of a phrase. The quality of tone this gives is very popular with many people although the lower voice lacks strength.

The lower female voices, which must have some of the chest quality blended into their voices to have a hearable scale, will have an outward push of the epigastrum as a preliminary part of their inhalation. This must be done so that there can be more effort from the abdomen and the area of the belt. There will also be a greater breath pressure when they sing.

We will make the statement that the heavier the voice (the greater the mass of the vocal cords and the larger the cavities of the vocal tract), the more the work is done in the abdomen and area of the belt. Nevertheless, there should at the same time be a slight raising of the chest at the end of the inhalation for there to be a complete breath. It is interesting to note that in the complete breath of many great singers the shoulders are moved up slightly; this was very observable in the case of Bjoerling.

Many singers will tilt the head back on high notes. Nathaniel Merrill, Stage Director at the "Met," has said that he stages according to singers' postures, some of them almost double over backwards on high notes. If teachers would listen and watch from side boxes, they would soon see the patterns of posture which are used for various types of singing. In a box theater in which there are many tiers, it seems perfectly natural that singers should look and extend their arms toward the second or third tier. Little do they realize that unless the head is tilted back there is not enough room for the depressor muscles to make a downward pull on the larynx, which assists in bringing about the tensing of the vocal cords necessary for high notes.

Persons who bow their heads have difficulties with high notes because there is not room enough for the depressors to work and the cavity of the throat gives a pitch which is too low. This can easily be detected by thumping the throat with vocal cords adducted while raising and lowering the head. Admittedly *covering* places a great pull on the front of the neck and is seen in basses on the back row of choruses. If basses and baritones expect to extend their voices upwards, they will need to develop the musculature on the back of the neck and the back itself which will give them the higher pitched vowels for their high notes. If more teachers would listen functionally with their eyes, when hearing operas and concerts, there would be more understanding and less fear of exploring the techniques of singing. This sometimes shows up in the statement—I don't vocalize—which means that the singers are uncertain as to the correct thing to do in vocalizing to build a voice and to prepare it for performance.

Invisible, but related to posture, Novikova taught that in sustained singing the singer should feel support from the area of the diaphragm and that in coloratura the support should be from the area of the collarbone. This shifting of the flexible breath support should eventually become automatic.

SUMMARY

Singing as we know it today developed first in the church spaces of Europe and in the opera house spaces of Venice, Bologna, and Naples. The traditions of Italianate singing have been written for over a hundred years, which included the influence of the umlaut sounds on the clear vowels of the Italian. The darker singing required a different breath mechanic which led to the heavier vocalization in later operas. Large hall singing can be adapted to small hall singing, to art song, folk singing, and pop singing. The reverse is very difficult.

Although F. Lamperti ascribed to Pacchierotti's statement (in translation), "He who knows how to breathe and pronounce well, knows how to sing well," he never got around to writing on the complexities of pronunciation (and resonation). He did conclude (1890, p. 28), "He who has the best command over his breath is the best singer." This could only occur when the pronunciation was in proper relationship to sung pitch; the relationships described in articles One and Two.

REFERENCES

Beranek, Leo. *Music, Acoustics and Architecture,* N.Y. and London. John Wiley and Sons, Inc., 1962.

Coffin, Errole, Singer, Delattre. *Phonetic Readings of Songs and Arias.* Boulder, Colorado, Pruett Press, Inc., 1964.

(Corelli) Honan, Wm. H. "A Champion Tenor Defends His Title." N.Y., *New York Times Magazine,* F. 8, 1970.

Corri, Domenico. *The Singer's Preceptor.* London, Chappell, 1810. (In The Porpora Tradition. Pro Music Press, 1968.)

(Domingo) Walker, Gerald. "The More I sing, the Better I Sound." N.Y., *New York Times Magazine,* F. 27, 1972.

Eisenstadt, Alfred. *Witness to our Time.* N.Y., Viking Press, 1966.

Garcia, Manuel (Patricio Rodriguez). *Excerpts from A Complete Treatise,* 1841 and *Memoire on the Human Voice, 1840.* Translated by Donald V. Paschke, 1970. Available through the University of Colorado Bookstore, Boulder, Colo., 1970.

Garcia, Manuel P. R. *Hints on Singing.* London, Ascherberg & Co. (Present address: 50 New Bond St., W 1, London, England). 1894.

Husler & Rodd-Marling. *Singing: The Physical Nature of the Vocal Organ.* London, Faber and Faber, 1965.

Joal, Dr. *On Respiration in Singing.* London, F. J. Rebman, 1895.

Lamperti, Francesco. *The Art of Singing.* N.Y., G. Schirmer, 1890.

Lamperti, G. B. *The Technics of Bel Canto.* N.Y., G. Schirmer, 1905.

Lehmann, Lilli. *How to Sing.* N.Y., MacMillan, 1914.

Leinsdorf, Erich. "Sound Versus Fury." *The Atlantic Monthly.* Boston, April 1966, p. 82.

Leiser, Clara. *Jean de Reszke.* N.Y., Minton, Balch and Co., 1934.

MacKinlay, M.S. *Garcia the Centenarian and His Times.* N.Y., Appleton and Co., 1908.

Mancini, Giambattista. *Practical Reflections on Figurative Singing.* Champaign, Ill., Pro Musica Press, 1967. (First published 1774 and 1777.)

Marafioti, P. Mario. *Caruso's Method of Voice Production.* N.Y., D. Appleton Co., 1922.

Pleasants, Henry. *The Great Singers.* N.Y., Simon & Schuster, 1966.

Resch, Rita. "George Bernard Shaw's Criticism of Singers and Singing." *NATS Bulletin,* Dec. 1974.

Rockstro, W. S. *Jenny Lind.* London and N.Y., Novello, 1894.

Winckel, F. *Music, Sound and Sensation.* (Berlin, 1960), trans. N.Y., Dover Publications, 1967.

Winckel, F. "Space, Music, and Architecture." *Cultures,* Vol. 1, No. 3, 1974. UNESCO and la Baconnière, Paris.

Appendix B: A Recommendation for the Correction of Pitch Involving Performances of Singers in Opera, Oratorio, and Choral Music of the Baroque-Classic Period, 1620–1820

American Academy of Teachers of Singing (Member, National Music Council)

Hermanus Baer
Clifford E. Bair
Marshall Bartholomew
Berton Coffin
Philip A. Duey
Bernard Ferguson
Donald Gage
William Gephart
Robert Grooters
Carl Gutekunst
Frederick H. Haywood
Frederick Jagel
Alexander Kipnis
Hubert Kockritz
Allan R. Lindquest
Harold C. Luckstone
Samuel Margolis

John McCollum
Homer G. Mowe
Louis Nicholas
Henry Pfohl
John B. Powell
Donald Read
E. Llewellyn Roberts
Earl Rogers
Martial Singher
Dolf Swing
Bernard Taylor
Conrad Thibault
Craig Timberlake
Henry Veld
Walter Welti
Arthur Wilson
Willard Young

Reprinted by permission of the American Academy of Teachers of Singing, New York, 1974.

In this 20th century there has been a revival of performances of the vocal music of Bach, Haydn, Handel, Mozart, Beethoven, Gluck, Lully, Rameau, Cimarosa, and others. Alexander Wood in *The Physics of Music* (London, Methuen, 1962, p. 48) states that "Praetorius (1571–1631) suggested a 'suitable pitch' of a' 424.2 in 1619. This pitch—sometimes called Mean Pitch—agrees with Handel's own fork (a' 422.5 in 1751). . . . This pitch prevailed for about two centuries—the period of Handel (1685–1759), Haydn (1732–1809), Mozart (1756–1791), and Beethoven (1770–1827). It is the pitch for which their compositions were written."

This means that singers of today with our pitch a' 440 to 443 are required to sing the music of this period almost a semitone higher (in layman's terms 70.3 percent of a half-step) than originally composed. This presents a problem for the successful performance of the vocal music of 1620–1820. There is no evidence that the physiology of the singer's vocal equipment has altered since 1820.

Referring to *On the Sensations of Music* (Helmholtz and translator-editor, Ellis[1], 1885, p. 512, art. 11, available in Dover reprint, 1954), Ellis states:

> As this was the period of the great musical masters, and as their music is still sung, and sung frequently, it is a great pity that the pitch should have been raised, and that Handel, Haydn, Mozart, Beethoven and Weber for example, should be sung at a pitch more than a Semitone higher than they intended. The high pitch strains the voices and hence deteriorates from the effect of the music, when applied to compositions not intended for it. (It is almost a semitone higher, not more than a semitone higher.)

Ellis further states, p. 544:

> Instruments can be tuned or manufactured at almost any required pitch. The human voice is born, not manufactured . . . an instrument beyond human control. The usages of Europe have, how-

[1] Ellis discusses "mean pitch" in *The History of Musical Pitch in Europe*, App. xx, Section H, pp. 495 and 496, indicating the variance between 415 and 428.7 vibrations.

ever, made it the principal instrument, and when it is present, have reduced all others to accompaniment. Hence it is necessary that these other instruments should have their compass and pitch regulated by that of the human voice . . . it is evident that Handel's sustained a'' in the Hallelujah chorus had 845 vib., but would now be sung in 904 vib.; and that Mozart's f''' in the Zauberflöte would have meant 1349 vib., but would now have to be sung at 1455 vib. The strain that this would put upon voices is evident, and no composer who wished his music to be well represented would think of making such demands on his singers.

Alexander Wood in The Physics of Music, p. 47 states:

For one thing, the musical effect of a performance depends on the pitch at which it is played. The human voice is particularly sensitive in this respect, and if the pitch demanded for a vocal piece is uncomfortably high, more effort is involved and the quality is less satisfactory . . . the effect designed by the composer is achieved only if the pitch of the instrument is that for which the music was written.

Much has been said by conductors, coaches, and musicologists about authenticity of performance. Therefore it is astounding that such a fundamental aspect of musical performance has been so overlooked as that of original pitch of performance and the consequent harm done to voices trying to adjust to modern pitch.

It is not only a question of the pitch of vocal cord vibration. Recent advances in the knowledge of vowel resonance (formants) in relationship to pitch have shown that a singer of any category, male or female, sings naturally and freely and with maximum ease and quality when the vowel formant is harmonically related to sung pitch. Just as a vibrator of a certain pitch must find the correct length and width for maximum resonance, so must the singer find a correct vowel mold which will resonate and yet not be forced beyond its elastic capability. Otherwise there is a loss of quality and a possibility of vocal injury. In the light of vowel-pitch relationships of the voice and the relationship of vowel-pitch to registers, there seems to be more involved than voices singing music almost a half-step higher than originally written.

There seems to be a "conspiracy" against the registers of the voice and the vowel-pitch relationships for which Bach, Handel, Haydn, and Mozart wrote. We may deduce that many of the difficulties of singing such arias as "Bleed and break," "Il mio tesoro intanto," "Dies Bildniss," "Un aura amorosa," "The trumpet shall sound," and roles such as Florestan in "Fidelio" are due to the fact that they are now performed almost a half-step too high for the voice classification involved. If a voice can easily sing them, it is by nature a half-step higher in its vocal form and sung pitch possibilities than the voice for which the composer wrote.

We can also state that this is one of the reasons that it is difficult to keep basses and tenors in choirs singing Bach and Handel. They are frequently singing music which is too high for them.

We must emphasize that the great composers knew the voice as a musical instrument. Handel's association with such virtuosi as Caffarelli, Farinelli, and Senesino is ample proof of his understanding the human voice. Mozart stated (The Letters of Mozart and His Family, Emily Anderson, 1966, Vol. I., p. 292): "I like an aria to fit a singer as perfectly as a well-made suit of clothes." His tuning fork was 421.6. Imagine his returning and hearing singers performing his music almost a half-step higher than he wrote!

Does it matter with the instruments—not too much, they are inanimate. But human voices can be seriously injured by singing vowels and pitches about a half-step above their tessituras.

Our Recommendation

The American Academy of Teachers of Singing recommends that in concert singers be allowed to perform in the pitch for which the music was written. We emphatically suggest that they transpose their arias down one half-step if it is to their musical-vocal advantage. We also recommend to conductors that operas and oratorios of the early composers be performed with instruments of the original pitch, even if it is a matter of securing different instruments. Where this is difficult, we urge conductors to have the scores transposed one half-step down. We recommend that Music Publishers re-issue music of this period in the original pitch. This procedure will create an authenticity of performance that will replace the false brittleness of many of the performances of music of that period.

There will be a whole new, relaxed and happy audience for this beautiful vocal music when the tension of the high pitch is removed, a new depth and warmth. In performance at the original pitch, there should be a "new," free outpouring of beautiful singing in which excellence rather than exhibition of high notes prevails.

Voices can better obey the law of Nature than the opinions of man. Welcome Beauty! Welcome Nature! Welcome voices which are unhampered in their ability to express the musical-poetic intent of the composers before 1820.

Copies of this pronouncement may be had on application to the Publications Officer, **Donald Read, 2109 Broadway, New York, New York 10023.**

Appendix C: The Tonal Art of Singing

Editorial Note: Appendix C is a preface to a series of four articles published in the *NATS Bulletin* [now *Journal*], December 1974 to February-March 1976. "The Relationship of the Breath, Phonation, and Resonance in Singing" appears in this text as Appendix A. The other three articles, "The Instrumental Resonance of the Singing Voice" (Appendix D), "The Relationship of Phonation and Resonation" (Appendix E), and "Articulation for Opera, Oratorio, and Recital" (Appendix F) had not been included originally, since Dr. Coffin felt they required a great deal of rewriting, "which I do not have the strength to do" (June 14, 1986). However, in the interest of preserving early investigations, recent studies, and conclusions, Albert W. Daub, President, The Scarecrow Press, Inc., and Mildred W. Coffin, Editorial Assistant to Berton Coffin, feel that this work should be included. Mildred Coffin has discussed this aspect of *Historical Vocal Pedagogy Classics* with several of Dr. Coffin's teaching colleagues and former students, and they concur with this opinion.

As in any work entailing the use of technology or science, one begins at the beginning, and these articles, in part, present that aspect of Coffin's findings. Research progresses, or should, as time broadens the perspectives. These findings were valid initially and still have some bearing on the present and future by showing the direction of thought and investigation. Seldom does one find the answers the first time a study is made.

Including these three articles is in no way intended to be controversial or to represent Dr. Coffin's final writings as revealed in *The Sounds of Singing* (revised and enlarged, 1987) and *The Overtones of Bel Canto*. As he continued to work with professional singers in Europe and the United States, as well as teachers

150

and university students, Coffin was ever-expanding his horizons, and theirs, vocally.

As Professor Coffin said in his article of December 1969, "our (singing) art is based on Man's hopes, aspirations, and expressions." This is all the more reason to provide a historical background, not only to the master singing teachers of past centuries, but to those of the last two decades as well.

Mildred W. Coffin
Editorial Assistant

What was the magic of the Italianate art of singing that has existed since the early 17th century? We believe that the Italianate principle "La qualità e la cosa più importante" has as its basis some very important phenomena which occur in the singer's throat. These articles are an attempt to state the phenomena involved with resonation, phonation, respiration, and articulation. The most unique aspect of the presentation involves the resonance characteristics of the vocal tract and their relationships to the other facets of singing.

"THE INSTRUMENTAL RESONANCE OF THE SINGING VOICE"

The famous singer Pacchierotti wrote in his memoirs: "He who knows how to breathe well and pronounce well, knows how to sing well." What is the secret force of pronunciation in singing? Vowels have several components of sound that are involved with pitch, since the vocal tract of the singer constitutes an air column that can have one, two, three, four, or five simultaneous modes of vibration. When some of these vibrations are harmonically related to sung pitch, the voice will "bloom." An Echophone (later termed a Vowel Resonator) is a means by which singers and teachers can explore and use the sympathetic resonance of the vocal tract. When the Echophone is used with an electric organ, the optimum resonance (best tone) for a vowel in a song can be heard and easily sung. This approach can be used for "placing" the voice. Vowel resonances have been notated in relationship to absolute pitch on vowel charts.

"The Relationship of Phonation and Resonation"

Singing is concerned with the continual interplay of frequencies from the vocal cords (which give sung pitch) and superimposed frequencies of the vocal tract (which give vowels). Sharp (ringing) voice, soft voice, and falsetto register, as well as whistle register are described. The 3,000 Hz singers' formant is discussed in relationship to the cavity of the larynx. The 19th-century description of head register, falsetto (middle in women), and chest register appear to be quite real when viewed from the perspective of vowel resonance. The whistle register appears to be above the first vowel resonance in female voices and an octave lower in male voices. The Jenny Lind scale is described from the perspective of vowel resonances. Absolute language singing is a form of self-destruction as well as a form of forcing poor intonation and weak resonation on singers. For good singing, the vowels must be allowed to function as resonators.

"The Relationship of the Breath, Phonation, and Resonance in Singing"

Singing is an art involving the vibration of air columns in the vocal instrument, the airspaces in opera houses, concert halls, or churches, and in the air chambers of the ear canals. The art of singing is traced to the airspaces of San Marco in Venice and San Carlo in Naples. The use of the breath varies with the size of airspaces in buildings, with loudness of accompanying instruments, and the dynamic change within that framework. When sombre timbre singing came into existence in 1837, the teaching of breathing changed. The traditional uses of *full breath, half breath,* and *flexible breath* are described. The underlying thesis is that the breath must be taught that will sufficiently amplify the singing voice for large hall singing, since it can be modified to small hall singing, but the latter can rarely be modified to the former without electric amplification.

"ARTICULATION FOR OPERA, ORATORIO, AND RECITAL"

The greatest influence on singing has been the teaching and writing of Manuel Garcia II, honored in this article. Articulation concerns the beginnings, connections, and endings of tones as well as those interruptions known as "consonants." The use of the hard attack, sweet attack, and aspirate attack is discussed. The action of the breath and vocal cords is described in the connections of tones—portamento, legato, marcato, and staccato. The Italianate pronunciation of consonants is given as a basis for singing in all languages, and procedures are indicated for correcting defective [r] and [l]. A chart is given by which consonants can be practiced. The Italian teachers used solfeggio to train vowels and consonants at the same time. The consonant modifications of G. B. Lamperti are given. The phonation, resonation, respiration, and articulation systems should be activated for the expressive and musical singing of our times.

Appendix D: The Instrumental Resonance of the Singing Voice

Unless the spaces of the mouth and throat vibrate in sympathy, there would be little volume in the sound of the voice.

—William Shakespeare (1924)

The modification of vowels in relationship to sung pitch has been quite widely accepted by teachers of singing since the writings of Herbert Witherspoon, internationally famous bass and teacher of singing who later was General Manager of the Metropolitan Opera Company until his death in 1935. He wrote (1925, p. 75),

> Quality is closely allied not only with vowel and consonant sound, regarding their own individual pitch, both of these phenomena being more or less radical and unchangeable. Because of pitch, which must be perfect, we shall see that vowel sounds and colors for expression are modified in relation to pitch. This is an important factor in pronunciation and expression much neglected and too often only partly understood.

This is a statement of the "fixed" pitch of vowels and *sympathetic resonance*. Concerning the effect of modification on diction he states, p. 30,

> The modification of the vowels, and the perfect action of the vocal organs for tone, does not injure or make indistinct our pronunciation, or harm our enunciation and emission. On the contrary, the obedience to the natural laws of singing, which causes the slight modification, is alone possible if we accept this doctrine, and the result will be far more natural and spontaneous

Reprinted from the *NATS Bulletin* [now *Journal*], December 1974.

and true to laws of pronunciation than if we force the vowels to
sound their "medium-normal" form. It is perhaps the latter forcing which causes many singers to sing out of tune on their higher
notes.

This is a statement of *forced resonance*. One of Witherspoon's
teachers, Giovanni Battista Lamperti, made one of the greatest
statements of them all: "The motives and movements of your
mind and body [the musicianship, the coaching, the style, the
communication, the spirit and the physiological movement in-
volved] make up only half of the proposition of singing. Natural
phenomena of vibration and resonance contributes the other
half" (1931, p. 22). We are paying less attention to this half than
did the great teaching lines of the past. William Shakespeare, a
student of the elder Lamperti, stated it this way, "He who knows
how to pronounce, and control the breath knows how to sing"
(1921, p. 30). The pronunciation control in singing plays a somewhat similar role to the singer that the slide does to the trombone player, for it controls the pitch of the "tubing" which, in
the voice, makes vowels. In the simplest of terms, vowel modification occurs so that there can be sympathetic resonance.
Let us understand this by hearing and feeling the sounds in our
throats through the use of an extremely simple artificial vibrator.

ECHOPHONE

The equipment for finding, hearing, feeling, and "singing on"
resonances we have called the Echophone. It is a 2¼ inch speaker
and a mini-plug connected by speaker-cord or electric-light wire.
(This can be assembled for less than $5.00.) The Echophone can
be plugged into a cassette tape recorder monitor or a reel tape
recorder speaker output. Any sustained tones may be recorded
from orchestral instruments or organs for use in observing instruments by means of sympathetic resonance. If a person can plug
an Echophone into an electric organ, he will have the greatest

flexibility for his observations. Some organ and tape recorder outlets which are for use with earphones have a resistance in them so that the sound is not dangerously loud. This should either be bypassed in some way, or an amplifier used. The following procedures can be used by singers, teachers, or vocal pedagogy classes for the modification of vowels in relationship to pitch. Those without Echophones should still find the observations very interesting.

INSTRUMENTAL RESONANCE

Let us explore the resonance of instruments to get some concepts of what we may find in the resonance of the human voice. We will first speak of observations of flute resonance. First record a slow scale from the lowest pitch to the highest of Fig. 1a. Second, have someone hold all of the notes down on a flute. Third, hold the Echophone near the end of the flute opposite the mouthpiece. Fourth, play the recorded pitches (or play the scale on an electric organ). What do you hear?

1. You will notice that certain pitches are louder than the others. They will be the notes in Fig. 1a.
2. The person holding the flute will notice that the fingers tingle when the resonant pitches are sounded. This is a most important observation. The tingle of the fingers is due to the vibrational pressures against the pads under the keys. The walls of singers' throats are vibrated by the same occurrence. Lilli Lehmann called them ''whirling currents'' (1914, p. 33).

Let us examine the resonance of a trumpet (or cornet). First, record a slow scale from the lowest pitch to the highest of Fig. 1b. Second, have someone hold his hand over the mouthpiece of the trumpet. Third, hold the Echophone an inch or so into the bell, and fourth, play the recorded pitches (or play the scale on an electric organ). What do you hear?

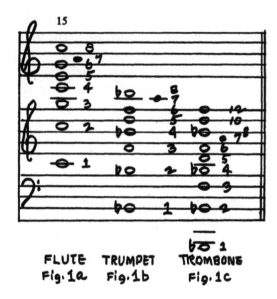

FLUTE   TRUMPET   TROMBONE
Fig.1a   Fig.1b   Fig.1c

1. You will notice that certain pitches are louder than others. They will be the notes in Fig. 1b.
2. The person with his hand over the mouthpiece will notice that the palm of the hand tingles when the resonant pitches are sounded. This is a most important point because in brass instruments there is a continual bounce-back of sound between the ends of the resonator. In brass instruments, the bounce-back of the tone largely *controls* the pitch and amplitude of the lips. In singing, the bounce-back *affects* the pitch and amplitude of the vocal cords.
3. Next play some long tones into the bell of the trumpet while fingering the valves. There will be little tone on some and large amounts on others. When the pitch of the Echophone is the same as that of the tuning, there will be *sympathetic resonance.* This is one of the reasons trumpet players play long notes as a part of their practice to tune the lips to give the same

pitch as the trumpet with consequent increase in resonance. This probably is one of the reasons for long notes in vocalization studies.

4. You will notice the increase of resonance better with changing the valves of the trumpet than with playing scales. When you find a resonant note, slowly pull out the tuning slide and see what happens to the resonance. You will notice there is an enormous change of fullness in the mere shift of a half step. From this you will know that a good trumpet player tunes his lip to the resonator to get good tone. The singer tunes the resonator to the vocal cords to get good tone.

Let us now examine the resonance of a trombone. First record a slow scale from the lowest pitch to the highest of Fig. 1c. Second, have someone hold his hand over the mouthpiece of the trombone, keeping the slide in first position. Third, hold the Echophone two inches or so into the bell, and fourth, play the recorded pitches (or play the scale of an electric organ connected with the Echophone). What do you hear?

1. You will notice that certain pitches are louder than others. They will be the notes of Fig. 1c.
2. The person holding his hand over the mouthpiece will feel a tingle on the resonant notes—again the reverberation between the bell and the mouthpiece.
3. You will notice that all of the resonant notes are not equally loud. The higher pitches are more resonant in the brass instruments as in voices.
4. You will also notice that the odd-numbered harmonics of 11, 13, 15, etc. are weak. This may be in our hearing or in the instrument. Both the instrument and the ear have a preference for harmonic overtones and tend to filter out the non-harmonic overtones.

All of the wind instruments are based on the harmonic series and all of the resonated notes in Fig. 1 for Flute, Trumpet, and Trombone form the Harmonic Series. These are known as modes of resonance. We will see them again in the singing voice but in an inversion!!!

Let us now speak of the resonance of a violin. Ellis (1877, p. 87), who translated and annotated Helmholtz' *Sensations of Tone,* made a very interesting study of violin resonances. He had a series of tuning forks each four vibrations apart with which he tested the resonance of a violin. He found that by blowing over the "f" hole next to the *G* string he could hear the natural resonance of the air column in the violin. When he took a tuning fork of that pitch and held it over the "f" hole, the violin had its greatest resonance by *sympathetic vibration*. This sounds like our experiences with the flute, trumpet, and trombone. Indeed at this point the violin acts as a *wind* instrument. When he held the rest of the series of tuning forks over the "f" hole the tuning forks were heard as being louder than when held away from the violin. The violin was forced to vibrate at the pitch of the tuning forks. This is called *forced resonance* because the air column was forced to resonate at another frequency than its own. Forced resonance in the voice occurs when the sung pitch and resonator pitch are not in harmonic relationship. This is not healthy for the singing voice although we do it frequently. One further thing about the violin, the air frequency of any viol instrument is its "wolf tone" and below that tone all sound is carried by the harmonics of those pitches.

Form and Length

Resonance control in brass instruments, in addition to embouchure, depends on length since the form was established by the manufacturer. However, the delicate hands of the craftsmen in the last century have molded the form of the instruments to give an equal reinforcement of the tone in the scale and a quality that is desirable to the ear. Paul Hindemith (1952, p. 154) states that the major difference of modern instruments is their reinforcement. Wind instruments have their form established but their length is variable by slide, piston or key. Each human voice has a basic length between the larynx and teeth, and has variable forms. Most of the tuning of the resonator is brought about by the altering of its shape by the tongue, lips, jaw, soft palate, elevation of the larynx up and down, and the narrowing or widening of the side walls of the throat just above the larynx (observable by fibre optics). As may be surmised, the movements of the articulators are so multitudinous that it would appear to be impossible to form the throat consciously for a given vowel. It is fine to say "mentally form the vowel" (Herbert-Caesari, 1951, p. 20) but the singer needs to know what he should mentally think. Sympathetic resonance allows us to have an almost miraculous shortcut, which is simple, easy, and uninvolved. It is a technique which is meaningful to all singers from the beginner to the career artist. All can maintain their voices by this approach or have a momentary check on any passage. I will write this discourse as though we were hearing the voice by this means. We will avoid a great morass of theory if we speak of what we hear and remain rather unspecific concerning what brought it about.

RESONANCE AND VOWELS

Record the pitches of Fig. 2 very slowly on a tape—perhaps 15 seconds on each note. Hold the Echophone in front of the mouth with *the vocal cords together—no air passing through them.* Pronounce the modifications of the vowels indicated in Fig. 2, Series III until they come in loud and clear, somewhat as though "tuning" in a radio. The vowel-color which resonates is the "mental color of the vowel" which you must think when you sing that vowel on that pitch. It is the mental thing which you must do in singing. It is possible that the vowel-colors given do not fit your voice. The values given happen to work for a high baritone and a contralto. You have found that these vowel-colors vary with voice classification. So you may need to record again! If you are a lyric soprano, record g^1, b^1, e^2, and a^2; if you are a coloratura soprano, record a-flat^1, c^2 f^2, and b-flat^2. For a mezzo-soprano or tenor, record f-sharp^1, a-sharp^1, d-sharp^2, and g-

æ	a	ɑ (750 cps)	roughly g^2
ɛ	œ	ɔ (600 cps)	roughly d^2
e	ø	o (456 cps)	roughly a^1
i	y	u (350 cps)	roughly f^1
I	II	III Series	

Fig. 2: The pitches of the lowest resonance of vowels. Coffin and Delattre (1964), p. v.*Phonetic Readings,* I II III Series.

$sharp^2$. For a baritone, record e-natural[1], g-sharp[1], c-sharp[2], and f-sharp[2], for a bass-baritone, record e-flat[1], g^1, c^2, and f^2. You will notice that these will work for all of the classifications. This contradicts Helmholtz's statement that men, women and children have the same pitches of vowel resonances. Your experiences will show that voice classifications differ slightly but that the vowel-colors are the same for the same classifications.

Now pronounce Series II and III on the pitches which you have recorded for your own voice. You will find their resonances after a short time.

Resonances or Formants

Fig. 2 is a notation of pitch for the lower resonances of vowels which we choose to call R^1. This is the tonal resonance of vowels. We believe that *resonance* is more meaningful to singers than the term *formant* which is used by many investigators. Chiba and Kajiyama (1958) have also used the term resonance and have given a classic explanation of how the throat operates to give the several resonances of a stopped pipe. See Fig. 3.

Several resonances occur at the same time! It is easiest to understand this by recording the lower notes of Fig. 4 with appropriate transposition for your voice classification. You can find the vowels which resonate on these pitches and in so doing define the color of vowel D. C. Miller (1916, p. 260) had in mind when he

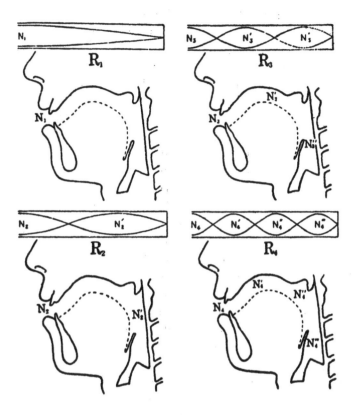

Fig. 3: The resonances which occur *simultaneously* in a stopped pipe. Chiba and Kajiyama (1958), *The Vowel, Its Nature, and Structure.*

made the notation. Again this is R^1 which extends in his observations from d-sharp[1] to b-natural[2].

Next record the high pitches where there is a double resonance. It is easier to read if we use the composer's convention of a second treble clef written at the 15th.

The resonances of Fig. 5. are much more difficult to find than the lower resonances in Fig. 4. They are the true characteristic resonances of what are known as the Front vowels, in which the

moo mow   maw   ma mot mat met mate meet
pooh poe   paw   pa pot pat pet pate peat

Fig. 4: Pitches of vowel resonances in musical notation. The upper notes are R^2; the lower notes are R^1. Miller (1916), *The Science of Musical Sounds.*

tongue lies forward in the mouth. They are made up of the second and third formants which we call R^2 and R^3. For the "forms" of vowels see Fig. 6.

The "single resonance" vowels are the Back vowels in which the tongue plays up and down the rear wall of the pharynx. The Umlaut vowels are rounded Front vowels (*Umlaut* means *round sound*). And, the Lateral vowels are modifications of [u, o, ɔ, and ɑ]. Notice the various series of vowels in the alphabet we have used from the International Phonetic Association. See Fig. 7.

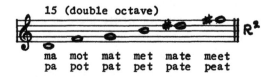

15 (double octave)

ma mot mat met mate meet
pa pot pat pet pate peat

Fig. 5: Miller's values of the high resonance of front vowels.

Fig. 6: The forms of the throat by which the simultaneous resonances are altered (Speech values). Delattre, French Review, O. 1958. Permission granted.

WRITTEN VOWEL SOUNDS

The International Phonetic Alphabet is present in wide use. It is a written system of sounds which has been used in the phonetic transcription of 53 languages by the International Phonetic Association (1972). Singers can easily acquire this language tool which can at the same time assist them in placing their voices if

VOWELS		Front	Central	Back
	Close . .	i y		ɯ u
	Half-close .	e ø		ɤ o
			ə	
	Half-open .	ɛ œ		ʌ ɔ
		æ		
	Open . .		a	ɑ ɒ

Fig. 7: Basic vowel symbols of the International Phonetic Association.

they use it acoustically. But rigid language values of vowels can uncouple a voice until there is little glory in it. Kurt Adler (1965, p. 5) conductor and former director of the Metropolitan Opera chorus has said:

> One of the most widespread errors is that spoken and sung sounds are the same. Nothing is further from the truth. To sing the way you speak may be advisable for popular music, but it would make the voice sound brittle, harsh, and uneven in opera, song, and choral music. The adjustment of phonetics to the vocal phrase is the real problem for any accompanist and coach and the solution constitutes a very real part of his art.

It is even more so for singers and teachers of singing who are forming and maintaining voices.

A Vowel Scale

If a person is fortunate enough to have an Electric Organ into which he can plug an Echophone, he will be able to hear a vowel scale. Hold down *all* the notes between e^1 and b^2 and pronounce *WOW* very slowly. The echo will be a *glide* from about the lowest pitch to the highest pitch and down, and will go through the Back and Lateral vowels [u, ɯ, o, ɤ, ɔ, ᴜ , ɒ, ɑ, ɒ, ᴜ , ɔ, ɤ, ɯ, and u]. Believe me, you say a lot when you exclaim *WOW!* You can also pronounce a glide on *YIKES* (*rhyming with Mike's*) and the vowel sequence will be [i, ɪ, e, ɛ, æ, a, æ, ɛ, ɪ, and i]. A person says a lot when he exclaims "yikes" which is not yet in dictionaries. This is a fun word. Have two or three composers listen to you when you perform this demonstration and have them tell you whether the glide goes down-up or up-down. There will be disagreement. Some will hear it one way, some the other. As you know from Fig. 4, the sound goes both was at the same time. Both glides form actual vowel scales!

WHISPERING

What you have heard so far are the actual pitches of vowels— exactly the same ones that your ear hears in whispering. The early investigations of Paget and Aikin were based on whispered resonances. Since we are singers, what happens when we sing on the same pitch as the vowel resonances? First of all, only a high female voice can sing all of the pitches of the R^1 of vowels, but when they do, they find their voices are quite resonant and that there is extreme ease in the throat. They are singing on sympathetic resonance and the vocal tract is exactly echoing every vibration of the vocal cords. But it would be a sad day when only high sopranos could sing! (*However, historically the art of singing was developed by the high voice of the castrato soprano. This might lead one to conjecture a bit!*) How can the various voice classifications sing with a resonator that is roughly 6½ inches long? Dayton Miller (1916, p. 260) states: "A vowel can also be freely intoned upon any lower note of which the characteristic note is a harmonic, such as an octave, a twelfth, or a fifteenth lower [in musical intervals] than the characteristic." We will notate this musically, slightly modifying the vowels to that which we have found in our observations. Again record the pitches with the necessary transposition for your voice classification.

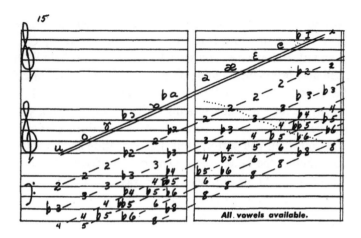

Fig. 8a: Class I Vowels and the pitches upon which they can be freely resonated with an Echophone.

Fig. 8b: Class II Vowels and the pitches upon which they can be freely resonated with an Echophone.

1. In Miller's terminology, Class I vowels have one resonance, Class II vowels have two vowel resonances.
2. The actual pitches of the characteristic vowel resonances are doubly underlined. They are sounded by their first harmonic.
3. The pitches on diagonal 2 sound the characteristic resonances of vowels by their second harmonic (at the octave).
4. The pitches on diagonal 3 sound the characteristic resonances of vowels by their third harmonic (at the 15th), etc.
5. The dotted line of Class II vowels indicates the approximate location of R^1.
6. About any vowel can be resonated on pitches below the fifth harmonic diagonal.
7. Class I vowels will reinforce on the double line.
8. Class II vowels can be coupled with a lower resonance lying on the treble clef.
9. In Helmholtz' terminology (p. 44) the harmonic diagonals

are "undertones of a resonator" and may be memorized as the inversion of the harmonic series of Fig. 1. These are modes of resonance in singing.

10. Fig. 8 is a pattern of vocal sound which helps explain why the higher one sings the more difficult it is to sing vowels because singers find there are fewer vowel resonances in the upper part of the voice. This explains why critics for a century have admired the diction of baritones and basses (about anything is possible below e^1) and why sopranos have been criticized for their poor diction. If they do pronounce distinguishable vowels above e-flat^2 they are endangered species. They are criticized for brittleness of tone because they can pronounce only by forced resonance which is brutal to the vocal cords. "She sang harshly and flat, but what a performance" is a prophecy of an early departure from the lyric stage.

There are two or three questions which can be asked about Fig. 8a and Fig. 8b.

1. What about the big distance between the First and Second Harmonics? Is there any other reinforcement within that octave? The Echophone shows that there is. While playing a pitch into the front of the mouth, a vowel whose resonance is a 5th below the vibrated pitch will reinforce the vibrated pitch.

2. While singing in the lower part of the vowel range a vowel whose resonance is a 5th above will seemingly amplify the vibrated pitch.

3. While singing in the upper part of the vowel range, a vowel whose resonance is an octave below will amplify the sung pitch.

Why is this? This brings us to a magic phenomenon of our hearing which is missing for those who count the lines of a spectrogram.

The Ear Creates

Benade (*1960, p. 67*) states that "much of what we call music is
determined for us by what goes on in the mechanical arrangement
of our ears." Let us simply state that sympathetic resonance takes
place in the ear to certain sounds it receives and that, since it is a
harp structure, the ear has a great preference for being especially
receptive to sounds which are harmonic. Not only that, it will
tend to emphasize the harmonics in random sounds and to delete
the non-harmonic overtones. Even more important, the ear can
even create pitch. The five lowest pitches of the G string of a
violin are nonexistent in air and will not show on a spectrogram,
yet the ear hears them, (*Harvard Dictionary*, p. 164). They are
heard by their harmonics. Fletcher (1953) found out that any
consecutive four harmonics would give the illusion of a fundamental even when the fundamental was missing. If this sounds
complicated, buy two Disney slide whistles. Have one maintain
its highest pitch while the slide of the other is slowly extended.
The ear will hear three tones. There will be a "subjective pitch"
ascending when the slide *lowers* the pitch of the second whistle.
This lower pitch has been called a difference tone. The difference
in frequency of neighboring overtones is always the same as the
frequency of the fundamental. In this way, the ear hears the
fundamental pitch. This phenomenon exists in the human voice
below "the break" which is concert pitch 🎼 in most
voices. All resonance in the voice is by means of vowels and all
of the lowest vowel resonances, R^1, lie roughly between f^1 and b-
flat^2. This can be confirmed by anyone using the Echophone. It is
by this phenomenon that we hear chest voice in female and male
voices. This is the only way a 6½ inch vocal tract can resonate
fundamental pitches between 🎼 and 🎼 This is the acoustical basis of the chest register.

Fig. 9 shows a part of a sonogram of Caruso's singing "Vesti
la giubba" in which the fundamental pitch is heard by difference
tone. His sung pitch is actually missing. Fig. 10 shows Alda and
Caruso in a duet. The harmonics which are widely separated are

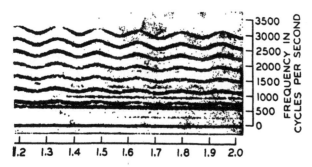

Fig. 9: Harmonics of Caruso singing with missing fundamental. Potter, Kopp, and Kopp: *Visible Speech,* Dover Publications, 1966; permission to reprint granted.

Alda's voice and the harmonics which are close together are Caruso's voice, with the sung pitch missing again.

PHONETIC SYSTEM

Witherspoon included a *phonetic system* in his book based upon his knowledge of vowels and consonants. He said that it could enable a teacher or singer to exaggerate or lessen vocal activity in any part of the mechanism and to practically "massage" any part of it. This is a concept of a doctor prescribing a cure for a patient.

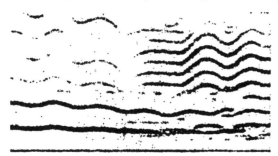

Fig. 10: Duet of Alda (*harmonics wide apart*) and Caruso (*harmonics close together and with missing fundamental*). Potter, Kopp, and Kopp: *Visible Speech,* Dover Publications, 1966; permission to reprint granted.

I am of the opinion that more effective work can be done by *constructing an acoustical instrument than by peering down a throat or by having "clinics" to cure what is wrong.* Is the forming of a vocal musical instrument a new idea? No. The Lamperti and Garcia lines of teachers have made many statements concerning sound. W. Shakespeare, a student of F. Lamperti, has written extensively on how the voice is sounded. G. B. Lamperti made a very interesting statement as quoted by Brown (1931, p. 68): "It is a strange fact that the throat is controlled by what happens above it, in the acoustics of the head, through word, vibration and resonance."

By the use of an acoustical phonetic system, singers can be taught to sing on the vowel resonances. The reverberation upon the vocal cords is such that the throat feels as though it has been massaged by the vibrating air pressures. Sympathetic resonance, besides causing an amplified emission of the voice, massages it; forced resonance over a period of time beats the voice into physiological trouble, especially in prolonged forte singing. It is a bit like a person trying to go through swinging doors out of phase. If he waits for just exactly the right time he can go through them without being scathed (or the door being scathed). He is better off going through the doors in time with their swing but he can force his way through if necessary, especially if they are not swinging very much. In forced resonance, there is physiological interference to such an extent that our throats ache when we hear much of it. One of the joys of great singing is that, in our empathy with it, our throats are given a joyous massage and our bodies feel its jubilant sensations. We conclude that the construction of an excellent vocal musical instrument is the same as forming a healthy vocal physique. In other words, the correct physics of sound in the throat will give a healthy physiological instrument. Good acoustical sounds mean good vocal health. Poor acoustical sounds lead to poor vocal health.

ACOUSTICAL-PHONETIC SYSTEM

We have presented enough background material so that we can show the R^1 harmonic patterns of Fig. 8a in relationship to a keyboard. See Fig. 11. (*Both male and female voices can hear and feel these with the Echophone.*)

Vowels of the 2nd harmonic diagonal sound the lower vowel resonance, R^1, by their 2nd harmonic. Vowels of the 3rd harmonic diagonal sound the lower vowel resonance by their 3rd harmonic, etc. The broken lines are subjective in that the resonator of the voice and vibration of the vocal cords are in a $2:3$, $3:2$ and $2:1$ ratio. We will leave a better explanation to someone else. These reinforcements are hearable with the Echophone. Several fascinating observations can be made concerning Fig. 11:

1. The human voice is unique as a musical instrument in that it can vibrate below, on, and above the actual pitch of the resonators. Wind instruments can only play on and above the pitch of their resonator, never below.
2. The "break" of the voice occurs just below the arrow, the lowest pitch of the vocal resonator, whether the voice is male or female. This is the e-flat, e-natural, f area of all classifications which must be treated very carefully in resonant voices. "Soft" voices are in less danger of breaking because their vibrating air pressures are small.
3. The first note above the 2nd harmonic diagonal has been called the lift of the breath by Witherspoon (1925, p. 90).
4. The area between the top [ɑ] of 1.5 and 1 has traditionally been called "Head Voice" in female voices.
5. The area between the top [ɑ] of 2 and 1.5 is called the "upper passaggio" by teachers of Italianate schools of singing.
6. When singing above the highest pitch of the 1st harmonic diagonal, the voice is in whistle register. Pull the upper lip forward with thumb and forefinger and sing, pronouncing [ʊ] or [o]. You are in whistle register.
7. When playing an Echophone at the top of the 4th harmonic diagonal, a person can pronounce the vowel colors of [o, ʊ (open aw) and ɑ] and find three harmonics. The harmonics can also be found by pronouncing vowels in the Front Umlaut and Neutral series. These vowels reinforce those harmonics.
8. When playing an Echophone at the top of the 2nd harmonic diagonal the vowels [o and ɑ] will select the 1st and 2nd

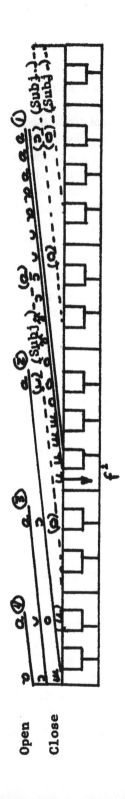

Fig. 11: The relationship of vowel color to sung pitch of Back Vowels, R[1], female voices. The above is a schematic reduction of a full scale vowel-color chart for female voices which can be used at the piano keyboard which gives the precise vowel color of back vowels on each note. In the full scale model, each harmonic diagonal has a complete vowel scale which can be used for singing vowel modifications in scale passages. The arrow of the chart should be moved to the right or left for the vowel resonances of the different voice classifications. We have found the arrow should be on f[1] for contraltos, f-sharp[1] for mezzo-sopranos, g[1] for sopranos, and a-flat[1] for coloratura sopranos (Coffin, 1973). The double line in Fig. 11 is the actual pitch of vowels from [u to a]. Again the full scale charts can be used for singing the correct vowel formation on any pitch. Echo a vowel, then sing it on that pitch or any harmonically related pitch below—octave, twelfth, double octave, etc. (Vowel charts are possible because of the logarithmic basis of frequencies which we hear as pitch and vowel colors.)

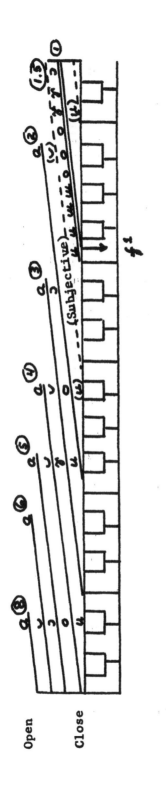

Fig. 12: The relationship of vowel colors to sung pitch of Back Vowels, R¹, male voices. The above is a schematic reduction of a full scale vowel-color chart for male voices which can be used at the piano keyboard (Coffin, 1973). The arrow of the full scale chart should be moved to the right or left for the vowel resonances of the different voice classifications. We have found the arrow should be on f-sharp¹ or g¹ for tenors, e¹ or f¹ for baritones, e-flat¹ for bass-baritones, and d¹ for bass.

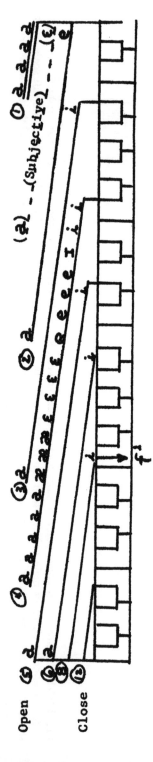

Fig. 13: The harmonic relationship of vowel color to sung pitch of Front Vowels, R², female voices.

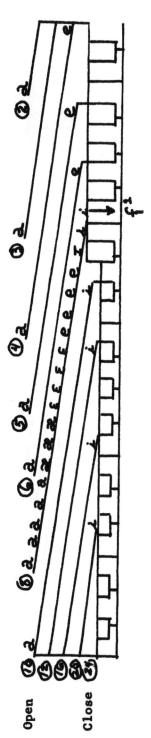

Fig. 14: The harmonic relationship of vowel color to sung pitch of Front Vowels, R², male voices.

harmonics. [ʊ] will reinforce *both* the 1st and 2nd harmonics.

9. While resonating the highest pitch of the 1st harmonic diagonal, [ɑ] can be resonated, and with considerable maneuvering [ɔ and o] can be resonated. In other words, when singing these vowels, sung pitch is going through resonators which are pitched lower than the sung pitch. This phenomenon will not show on a spectrogram. These are subjective vowel-tones but they are heard.

Fig. 12 shows the harmonic pattern of the lower vowel resonance, R^1, of the male voice. Both female and male voices can sense these with the Echophone when the arrow is placed correctly for their voice classification. Several fascinating observations can be made concerning Fig. 12.

1. The pitch of the resonators of the male voice are almost always above sung pitch. The resonators are usually energized by the harmonic over-tones of the sung pitch. Only on the double line above the arrow does it ever sing on the lower resonance of vowels.
2. The male voice has many more harmonics with which to energize the resonant cavities of the vocal tract than does the female voice.
3. On the 5th harmonic diagonal, 4 harmonics will resonate 4 Back vowels, or the vowels select the 4 harmonics; they are the same. Four harmonics will also energize four Front, Umlaut, and Neutral vowel-colors.
4. On the 8th harmonic diagonal, 5 harmonics will energize 5 Back vowels. They will also energize 5 Front, Umlaut, and Neutral vowel-colors.
5. Singing on any of these harmonic positions will give a focused rather than a mushy sound. The overtone of the voice will be heard because it has been selected and amplified by the lower vowel resonance, R^1.
6. The note just above the 3rd harmonic diagonal and below the arrow is the "break" which some persons call the cover area.

This is done by singing the vowels on the double line. It is better to sing the vowels on the dotted line since they are more resonant (but they are treacherous until well-established).

7. The first note above the 4th harmonic diagonal has been called the "lift of the breath" for male voices by Witherspoon. It is a spot where the number of available harmonics of R^1 diminishes from 3 to 2.

8. The 5 pitches (notes) above the highest [ɑ] of the 5th harmonic were called a phenomenon by Garcia (c1855, p. 11) in that there is a tendency for the larynx to render these dark rather than clear with a consequent source of trouble. There was a time when writers referred to lower chest and upper chest with the division occuring near this place.

THE UPPER RESONANCE OF VOWELS, R^2

To tell the complete story we must show the patterns of the upper resonances of vowels which we will simply call, R^2. We will show first the harmonic patterns of Fig. 8b in relationship to a keyboard. See Fig. 13. Several fascinating observations can be made as follows:

1. In ascending scales, the R^2 harmonics of vowels proceed from open to close.

2. Sensations are now felt between the tongue hump and the front of the mouth.

3. There is a hidden shift of the lower resonance, R^1, of these vowels and in some cases, no lower resonance. That is, at times there is no coupling between the upper and lower resonances. As [u o ɔ ɑ] have no evident R^2, the vowels [a æ ɛ e ɪ i] sometimes have no evident R^1.

4. Couplings are possible and can be gained by alternating the resonances in ə/i, u/i, u/e, ʌ/e, etc.

For the harmonic patterns of R^2 for male voices in keyboard notation see Fig. 14. Several observations would include the following:

1. In singing ascending passages, the R^2 harmonics of vowels proceed from open to close.
2. About any vowel is available below the 8th harmonic.
3. There is a hidden shift of R^1 in scale passages on these vowels with a better chance of coupling in the male voices than female voices.
4. Couplings are possible and can be gained by alternating the resonances ə/i, u/i, u/e, ʌ/e depending on pitch.

CONCLUSION

In wind instruments the length of the pipe controls fundamental frequency. In the voice, the vibrator and vocal pipe are independent to such an extent that about any vowel can be sung on any pitch. However, for resonant singing the fundamental frequency and the vowel resonances must be in harmonic relation to each other so that sympathetic vibration can occur. The vowel-pitch relationship runs as a thread through the classic books on vocal pedagogy. Teachers have heard these resonance relationships and have incorporated them into voices by their techniques and by an umpiring process. "That's it," or "that isn't, try it again." Resonance relationships have been notated in relationship to pitch to take a place with the agility, messa di voce, and register studies which have traditionally been a basis of the formation of the bel canto art of singing.

As a starter, record the melody of one of your songs or arias and play it into your throat with an Echophone while you silently pronounce the words, vocal cords together. You will hear the vowel colors you will need to use in your singing and get a feel of what the throat spacings should be. This is the answer to Delattre's (1958) statement that "Singing-voice quality and vowel color are in articulatory conflict. The good production of one tends to impair the good production of the other." Our statement of the law of singing would be, "He who knows how to pronounce and breathe knows how to resonate and color his voice, both of which are basic to distinguishable diction and consistently good singing."

References

Adler, Kurt. *Phonetics and Diction in Singing*. Minneapolis: University of Minnesota Press, 1967.

Apel, Willi. *Harvard Dictionary of Music*. Cambridge: Harvard University Press, 1967.

Benade, Arthur H. *Horns, Strings and Harmony*. N.Y.: Doubleday & Co., 1960.

Chiba, T. and M. Kajiyama. *The Vowel, Its Nature and Structure*. Tokyo: Phonetic Society of Japan, 1958.

Coffin, Berton. *Manual for Vowel-Color Charts, Female Voices; Manual for Vowel-Color Charts, Male Voices;* Milton Press, Box 3295, Boulder, CO 80303, 1973.

Coffin, Delattre et al. *Phonetic Readings of Songs and Arias*. Boulder: Pruett Press, 1964.

Delattre, Pierre. "Vowel Color and Voice Quality." *NATS Bulletin*. O. 1958, p. 4.

Fletcher, Harvey. *Speech and Hearing in Communication*. N.Y.: Van Nostrand, 1953.

Garcia, Manuel (translated, Beata Garcia). *Hints on Singing*. London: Ascherberg & Co., 1894 (available—Chappel, London).

Helmholtz, Hermann L. F. *On the Sensations of Tone* (fourth and last edition). N.Y.: Dover Publications, Inc., 1954 (new), 1877 and 1885 (old).

Herbert-Caesari, E. *Voice of the Mind*. London: R. Hale, 1963.

Hindemith, Paul. *A Composer's World*. Cambridge: Harvard University Press, 1952.

IPA. *The Principles of the International Phonetic Association*. University College, Gower Street, London WC1E 6BT.

(Lamperti, G. B.) Brown, William E. *Vocal Wisdom*. N.Y.: Arno Press, 1957 (available—Boston: Crescendo Press).

Miller, D. C. *The Science of Musical Sounds*. N.Y.: MacMillan, 1916.

Potter, Ralph K. et al. *Visible Speech*. N.Y.: Dover Publications, 1966.

Shakespeare, William. *The Art of Singing*. N.Y.: Oliver Ditson & Co., 1921.

Shakespeare, William. *Plain Words on Singing*. London and N.Y.: G. P. Putnam's Sons, 1924.

Witherspoon, Herbert. *Singing (A Treatise for Teachers and Students)*. N.Y.: G. Schirmer, Inc., 1925.

Appendix E: The Relationship of Phonation and Resonation

Clear-air turbulence ahead. In the first article on this series, we have written on the instrumental resonance of the voice. We wrote of this first because it is the ONLY part of the singing techniques of respiration, phonation, resonation, and articulation which can be studied *as sound* independently of the others. What is the relationship of phonation and resonation in singing? Delattre in private communication stated (1968):

> We vary our fundamental in speech completely independently of the cavities above. We make pitch by vibrating the vocal cords at different speeds by tensing the cords more or less. And we make differences between vowels and consonants by changing the volume of the cavities in relation to one another in coupling. The independence of the fundamental (spoken pitch) from the voice cavity is something that nobody has grasped.

Our observations with artificial vibrations such as those from Western Electric Larynx and all kinds of sounds played through the Radioear Bone Vibrator used as an artificial larynx, and the Echophone have led us to believe that in singing the two controls of vibration, phonation and resonation, are NEVER completely independent because of the vibrating clear-air turbulence which exists in the vocal tract. The eye has never seen this turbulence in front of an airplane or in the vocal tract. However, passengers do fasten their seat belts to keep from being buffeted about; the buffeting occurs in singing and can be felt and heard by singers

Reprinted from the *NATS Bulletin* [now *Journal*], February–March 1975.

and teachers of singing whose senses have been directed to it. Husler and Rodd-Marling state (1965, p. xiii):

> We no longer have at our disposal the acute sense of hearing once possessed by great teachers of singing. . . Our ears have lost that strange kind of intuitive, almost sonnambulistic intelligence, together with its extraordinary accurate discriminating faculty.

They believe that one reason is that studies of the singing voice have not included "the actual functional product: the tone and its character." The value of these articles is dependent on the fact that they are written from this specific vantage point in which more can be heard than by the unaided ear. I believe our attention has been diverted by looking at the voice and its patterns so that we are listening to it less.

THE CAUSE OF VIBRATION

What is the cause of vibration of the singing voice? Which of the following statements is true?

1. Pitch is decided entirely by the vibrations of the vocal cords.

I would suspect this is the usual belief.

2. "Just as the pitch of the trombone is altered by adjustment of the slide, so the fundamental vibrations produced by the vocal bands are changed by alterations in the shape and size of the resonating cavities above." William H. Saunders, M.D. (1964, p. 37).

This indicates that vocal cord vibration is under complete control of the spaces of the vocal tract. The one instrument of this type is the Krummhorn.

3. "The chief factor in producing changes of pitch in the human voice is the accurately controlled firming of the vocal cords

under the action of the thyroarytenoid [vocalis] muscle. Supplementary factors are changes in (a) the size and shape of the glottis; (b) the dimensions of the infraglottic air column; (c) the size and shape of the supraglottic air column; and (d) the tracheal air pressure.'' Chevalier Jackson (1940, p. 439).

This indicates that in addition to the primary vibration of the vocal cords there are supplementary factors of (1) the resonators above and below the vocal cords, and (2) the breath pressure. Our observations indicate that statement three is the nearest to being completely true.

The term *Hz* (named after the physicist Hertz) is a convenient term for vocal frequency since it is not necessary to state whether the vocal cords or the vocal tract cause the vibration. The term is also seen on radios, radio clocks, etc. The vocal range is very low with the significant accoustical phenomena of speech and singing occurring between 75 Hz and 8,000 Hz. They have been called cycles per second, vibrations per second, or by one of the earliest investigators, Mairan, ''quivers.''

We have spoken of the vibrating air columns of musical instruments in the first article of this series. There are two methods of setting these columns into vibration, (1) by blowing air against an *edge*, and (2) by blowing air through *reeds*. Both are used in their own peculiar way in the singing voice. Furthermore, one without the other limits the voice in certain ways. Let us first look at *edge tones*.

AN EINE AEOLSHARFE

In the songs of Brahms and Wolf to this poem by Moericke, allusion is made to the Muse's mysterious string-instrument which makes a melodic lament. The sound swells and dies away. Then suddenly it cries when the wind blows violently causing ''my soul's sudden emotion.'' What is an Aeolian harp? It is a box fitted with strings of different diameters tuned in unison on which the wind blows musical tones. It is named after Aeolus, the god having dominion over the winds. We speak of this kind of vibration first because long before man could make musical tones the winds were producing them. This kind of vibration causes the rustling of the grass, the quaking of the aspen leaf, the roar of the forest, the whistling of telephone wires in a wind and the ruffling of a flag in the breeze. The phenomenon is this: as winds flow past an object, small eddies are set up behind it with the frequency of the eddies dependent upon the thickness of the object and the speed of the air passing the object. This also occurs in fluids and can be experienced by drawing your hand quickly through the bathwater with the "fingers" loosely spread. You will find that your fingers tend to strike against one another, vibrating from side to side across the track of your hand. (Wood, 1962, p. 114).

You will notice there are small eddies behind the fingers. The same thing will occur when a small brush is drawn through the water, with eddies forming alternatively on each side of the brush. This phenomenon is the basis of sounding a flute—the breath is directed against an edge with eddies forming alternatively above and below it. The eddies forming below the edge are the vibrations which the flute resonates. When the flow of the breath is increased the frequency of the eddies will double, triple, etc., and we will hear the pitch jump an octave, twelfth, etc., because of the effect of the tubing. This is called overblowing.

This type of vibration seems to be slightly different in the voice, rather like the vibration in Fig. 1 in which the stream of air takes a sinuous course through eddies just above a slit. We may conjecture from experiencing the fluttering fingers when drawn through water that the slit in the singing voice, a vocal cord on either side, is given a slight push as each eddy is formed. We will conjecture that this alternating vibration in the voice can make a transition to the vocal cords striking each other in the reed form of vibration. This is the basis of the crescendo and diminuendo of the classic *messa di voce* called by Corri (1810, p. 14) "*the soul of music.*" This has always been considered to be one of the greatest techniques of a singer. Handel made frequent use of this

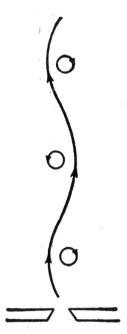

Fig. 1: Jet from a slit showing sinuous form and vortices (A. Wood, 1962). This is the basis of the "whistle" register and the flute sound in the singing voice. Eddies are formed on both sides of the moving air. The number of eddies per second gives the pitch.

device even opening the "Messiah" with it, "Comfort ye." Since half of the eddies of the flute escape above the edge against which the player is blowing, it sounds breathy when one is close to it. The flute tone in the voice uses more breath than the other kind of vibration and may also sound breathy when one is close to it. The eddy vibration has another sound which is frequently heard on children's playgrounds when they are squealing very high. It is interesting that Nathan (1836, p. 117) called this register the *voice of the child*. This is the whistle register which Calvé learned from the castrato Mustafà of the Sistine Chapel (Pleasants 1966, p. 304). More about this register later.

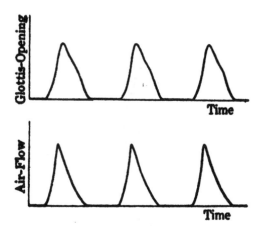

Fig. 2a: Sharp Voice

THE VOCAL CORDS AS REEDS

In the usual origination of vocal sound, the vocal cords slap each other. In such vibration, the air flow is brought to a rather gradual halt while the cords come together. There is a pause while the air

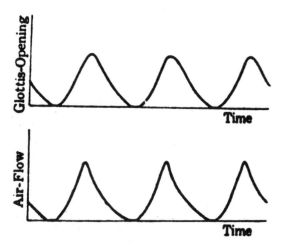

Fig. 2b: Soft Voice

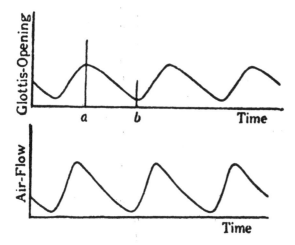

Fig. 2c: Falsetto Register

pressure builds up and then a sharp explosion. This has been called "sharp" voice by Chiba and Kajiyama (1958). Fig. 2a is a picture of the air flow and air pressure in this kind of vibration. Notice that the vocal cords are closed for a large portion of the vibration. In soft voice, Fig. 2b, the vocal cords are together much less of the vibration, and that in Fig. 2c, the vocal cords do not touch at all so there is a continual flow of air with slight alterations of air pressure. This form is almost a sine wave. Chiba and Kajiyama (1958) have referred to this as *falsetto,* the word used by Garcia to describe the middle register of female voices and the register just above the chest in male voice. This action probably pertains to the woman's head voice beginning at c^2 and to tenor voices a half or whole step lower, concert pitch. This is Garcia's definition of head voice and is almost absolute in pitch. The teachers who formed the great voices of the past were surely aware of the various sounds brought about by these types of vibrations. Garcia II, the historical teacher and researcher of the singing voice stated (1894, p. 12) that there were certain qualities in the mechanism of larynx itself. He used the terms, dull, and ringing. He further stated that the ring or dullness of sound was produced in the interior of the larynx (1855, p. 399): ". . . the

Page 186 / APPENDIX E

epiglottis also plays a very important part, for every time it lowers itself, and nearly closes the orifice of the larynx, the voice gains in brilliancy; and when, on the other hand, it is drawn up, the voice immediately becomes veiled."

Observations of X-Ray motion pictures of singing made with Delattre indicate that in the attack of a vowel the orifice of the larynx is more closed than it is after the vibration is established. Teachers and singers, who are actually specialists of sounding the human voice, can do their work more efficiently if they know what is happening. There is still enough mystery about the human voice to keep our interest for a long time.

The Singer's Formant (Resonance)

There is a vibration around and just above the highest of the vowel resonances located at e^4, f^4, f-sharp^4, which is present in good voices in *mezzo forte* to *fortissimo singing*. According to Winckel of Berlin (1971, p. 228), the vibration is in the area of 3,000 Hz. He states that it is "dependent on the shortness and sharpness of the pulse at the output of the larynx." Thus it increases with the length of closure time of the vocal cords in their vibratory cycle. When the vocal cords do not close, as at the start and end of a *messa di voce,* this vibration is not present. He further states that, "this frequency component has the function of a carrying power which is important for singing in large opera houses." He has developed a 3,000 Hz extractor by which he can measure the maximal intensity in that area in relationship to the total energy output of the voice. I have had the experience of singing into this machine in an anechoic chamber (no echo). By this device I was able to *see* the relative amount of 3,000 Hz in my voice and in some way control the amount of it. The instrument, in small form, will probably be of use in the teaching of singing. It is Dr. Winckel's belief that this device can measure the relative value of an individual voice in relationship to other voices. He states that it can also be used to estimate whether a singer is as good as his reputation. If this maximum is missing, he has found that it means the voice is malfunctioning, and can mean that there is a tumor on one or both vocal lips which prevents their tight closure and lessens the amount of 3,000 Hz available. In such cases, the voice will not carry over an orchestra and is reduced in value for singing in large auditoriums and with heavy accompaniments.

We stress that this *"fixed"* vibration is in addition to the vowel resonances which are *movable*. Helmholtz (1877), who was one of the first investigators to notice this vibration, found that it was unique to the human voice and not found in the resonance of other instruments. He further pointed out that the ear is especially sensitive to pitches between d^4 (2350 Hz) and g-sharp^4 (3322 Hz) which means that our ears are actually attuned to the "fixed" resonance. This is the "ring" to which Bartholemew referred (1942, p. 146).

> It is probably produced by a form of resonance in the laryngeal chamber itself [the cavity of the larynx as the mouthpiece of a trumpet], and is in direct proportion to the amount of "chest quality" being used . . . Speaking generally, the better the voice, or the louder the tone, the more prominent this formant becomes at least during some part of the vibrato cycle.

Bartholemew points out that the high vibration tends to drop out at some point as the pitch rises (where the vocal cords do not touch each other), and "aesthetic judgments of 'quality' tend to be made on the basis of other criteria than those used for lower voices."

WHEN IS THE 3,000 Hz USED?

We use the 3,000 Hz every day in our speech when we use chest or mixed voice. If someone is mumbling we say, "speak up," or "speak clearly." Usually there is a bit of yelling added to the voice and the coded message of language is received. Whenever we speak to someone at a distance we use it, and when someone "explodes" he literally does just that with the vocal cords. Artistically it is used in the opera house and large concert halls; it is present in the voices of successful performers. It is that curious something which choir directors wish to reduce when they attempt to "blend voices." On the other hand, it is that resonance which is needed by choirs to project over large orchestras.

The voice works efficiently when this resonance is present in the chest or mixed voice and becomes fatigued when it is played down. Nilsson stated, "A shallow theater is not good for my voice. It should be deep. Generally, though I don't like to sing in small places, because I get tired and somehow overdo something with the voice." (*Opera News*, 0.10, 1970). The chances are that she is undoing the glottal closure and running the voice at low efficiency. Choir singers frequently find they become very fatigued vocally when asked to sing continually with an open glottis without the relief of some glottal closure.

Fig. 3 shows graphs by Dr. Winckel of *messa di voce* notes of Maria Callas and Dietrich Fischer-Dieskau. The test *messa di voce* delivers the following evaluations:

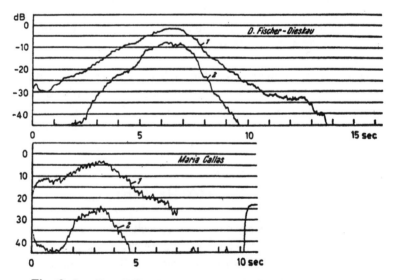

Fig. 3: Level recordings of the swell and diminuendo tone of two first class singers. *Curve 1:* Total energy of the voice. *Curve 2:* Portion in the area of 3000 Hz (Winckel, 1970).

1. "The diagram (Fig. 3) reveals the energy of the 3,000 Hz area, relatively to the total energy of the spectral sound.
2. The steady increase and decrease of the curve of *messa di voce* is a measure corresponding to the breath support (Atemstuetze). This is also to be seen in the 3,000 Hz curve which begins later and ends earlier (cf. the plotting of all overtones in Fig. 3).
3. The duration of sound *messa di voce* is a measure for the capacity of the breathing air on condition that . . . the diaphragm is fully used.
4. The level difference of the curve means the maximum level over the zero level, as a measure of the total dynamics being the control capacity of singing."

SEARING

It has been said of a certain Wagnerian singer that she uses a *searing* quality of voice in certain passages. It is always interesting to notice the stressed vowel sound in an adjective describing a voice quality because it is usually echoic (onomatopoeic) and actually describes the sound. The vowel in *searing* is [ɪ] which has the frequency of around 2489 Hz. The quality of voice described is largely made up of vibrations in that frequency area. There is a classic word *spinto* which comes from the Italian word *spingere* which means "to force." So *spinto* sopranos and *spinto* tenors are actually "forced" sopranos and tenors who are using the reed vibration which has a major resonation in the area of the vowel [i] which is very close to the "fixed" resonance of 3,000 Hz. The last evidence is not in yet as to what causes the 3,000 Hz. The triangle wave of Fig. 2a is rich in high harmonics but it does not indicate that a major part of the energy can lie in this region. Both Bartholemew and Luchsinger (private communication) believe it to be an occurrence within the collar of the larynx—the bottom of this cavity being the closed vocal cords and the top of the cavity being the aryepiglottic folds. The last publication of Russell (1959, p. 66) describes how he and Cotten

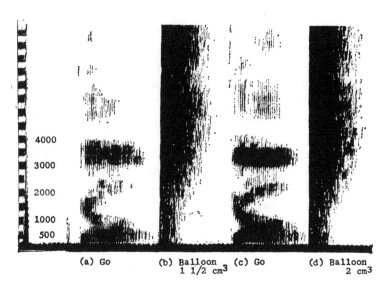

Fig. 4: Balloon bursts to find the 3000 Hz; (a) and (c) are the
spoken word "go" with 3000 Hz present. The vertical lines
are the individual explosions. The lines moving horizontally
are the resonations. The 3000 Hz is not predominant in the
single ballon bursts (b) and (d). It is *predominant* in the single
bursts of the voice.

created puffs just above the vocal cords by bursting small balloons on the end of a length of glass tubing. This experiment was
performed three times and they found that the characteristic frequencies were 2720, 2800, and 2820 Hz. They broke balloons in
other resonators and found that *all resonators* amplified this high
frequency component with slight shifts upward and downwards
according to the resonator used.

I have duplicated part of the experiment with balloon bursts
without a resonating body other than the room which was eleven
feet wide, Fig. 4. To assist in clipping the tape, I said, "go" just
before each balloon was punctured. The contrasts of my vocal
explosions and the balloon explosions are illuminating. Several
interesting observations can be made:

1. No extremely high energy of 3,000 Hz is seen in the balloon bursts but is seen in the word ''go.'' Our deduction is that the air is as elastic in the open air as in my throat. The 3,000 Hz must be due to some other factor or resonance phenomenon.
2. A small balloon burst had more energy in the high frequencies. Clapping two fingers into the palm of the hand sounds high.
3. A large balloon burst had more energy in the low frequencies, just as clapping four fingers into the palm of the hand sounds lower. Clapping with two fingers can be likened to thin mechanism and clapping with four fingers likened to thick mechanism.
4. There is no evidence of overtones in the balloon bursts whereas there is in the voice! **All** frequencies are present in a membranic burst from which a resonator may select or suppress frequencies.
5. *Pitch is based on the number of explosions per second* (the vertical lines). *Quality is based on which frequencies in the bursts are resonated and which are suppressed* (the horizontal lines). Fig. 4.

THE CAVITY OF THE LARYNX

There has been much conjecture that the cavity of the larynx is very similar in function to the mouthpiece of a trumpet (Appelman, 1967, p. 77). To that end we made the following vibrations.

First we made a whistling sound by blowing across the end of a trumpet mouthpiece while the thumb closed the lip end. This was followed by buzzing the mouthpiece in a rising pitch pattern. The two sounds are compared in Fig. 5.

1. The pitch of the whistle is e-flat⁴ (2488) and shows clearly. Its second resonance (4976) shows faintly, and its third resonance (7464) shows clearly and with significant energy. In the

Fig. 5: The resonances of a trumpet mouthpiece used as a whistle showing R¹, R², and R³. This is followed by a sonogram of buzzing the mouthpiece which shows the harmonics of the buzzed pitch with a predominance of energy at R¹. 2488 Hz.

voice, no vowel sounds exist above 3,200 Hz although there is significant energy in this region in the consonants.

2. A glide played by buzzing the mouthpiece with no trumpet attached shows greatest energy in the 2488 region whether the frequency of bursts, created by the embouchure is high or low. This is the first resonance of the whistle.

3. The 2nd and 3rd resonances of the whistle are almost completely wiped out by the vibrating pressures in the mouthpiece. There would seem to be a significant similarity between this and the action of the 3,000 Hz in the voice.

We will leave further exploration and explanation to others. We will simply say that the 3,000 Hz goes through the vocal tract, over a large orchestra and chorus, through auditoriums, and through the ear canal with great penetration and is an essential part of the singer's tonal art.

HEAD VOICE

Nellie Melba (1926), the greatest soprano from the studio of Mathilde Marchesi, stated that Marchesi insisted that she sang pure head voice from f-sharp^2 upwards. Head voice is probably the flute of the voice in which the vocal cords do not touch in their vibration. Stratton (1966) has said that Marchesi students used "*blown tone*" for their high notes. All of a sudden we return to the Aeolian tones of which we wrote earlier. The Aeolian tones of a slit, Fig. 1, raise their pitch by a greater velocity of air—and this is gained by *blowing*. Stratton further stated that the Marchesi students sang so long that they did not have enough time left to learn how to teach. There was one, Estelle Liebling, who passed along the art to Beverly Sills.

CHEST VOICE

Melba (1926) stated that she was allowed to carry her chest voice to f^1 because of her high voice. Chest is the reed vibration of the voice. Many singers want to know what to do with chest voice after they have it. Marchesi (1890, p. V) states that the singer should slightly close the last two notes of a register in ascending and open them in descending. She taught this at the Chest-Middle voice transition and at the Middle-Head voice transition. It will be seen from the harmonic diagonals in our first article that this brings about a harmonic shift which allows the voice to continually sing on its resonance. The harmonic shift of the chest voice, middle voice transition of female voices has been extensively studied by Large (1974, p. 20).

Let us say that the chest register, when blended into the middle and high voice, allows for dramatic singing. Historically the first dramatic soprano was Falcon who had a mezzo soprano voice with an extended top. (G. B. Lamperti, 1905, p. 22, discusses the mezzo soprano and dramatic soprano under the same heading.) Falcon had her vocal problems and had a career of only 7 years. Contemporary dramatic sopranos know how to develop and maintain their voices for longer careers. The blending of registers is an art which must be continually practiced. Lilli Lehmann (1914, p. 136) spoke to this point and practiced what she preached—her career extended into her 70's.

VOCAL FATIGUE

The great teachers of singing have clearly stated that singing should be restricted to two or three short periods a day of not more than 30 minutes at a time. Garcia (1894, p. 15) said that beginners could sing for four or five minutes at a time "but this may be repeated three times a day. If it causes the slightest fatigue it must be stopped at once for the rest of the day."

Chevalier Jackson (1940, p. 463), the great American specialist on diseases of the throat stated:

> About 95 percent of the aspirants for a career in vocal music are compelled to give up because of myasthenia laryngis. [The muscular disability of the vocalis muscles which is evident in a chronic hoarseness.] The damage is usually done by the training necessary to increase the range upward.

We will speak later on the upward increase of range. He believed prevention of this chronic hoarseness was better than cure, and that treatment was absolute rest of the singing voice for three to six months with only a limited use of the conversational voice, say 500 words a day. He found that under all lies the fundamental fact that almost all persons who have myasthenia laryngis are incessant conversationalists!

The singer should avoid long practice sessions, choral singing of one or two hours (be silent some of the time), opera performances on consecutive nights, and talking in such places as on airplanes, subways or at parties where the decibel level is high. At the height of a career when the voice is mature, schedules rarely call for even three performances a week and there are "covers" when the singer is indisposed. When one fatigues or loses his voice, the vocal cords change their mass and the muscles within the vocal cords must do extra work to maintain the height of pitch. Eventually they lose their ability to contract the cords to the required vibrating pitch of the voice. If these muscles are overworked, they permanently lose some of their ability to contract. There is also the possibility that the vocal cords have their mass permanently enlarged. Thick vibrators give lower pitch than thin—look at strings and reeds.

The thickening of the cords may also be due to misuse in speaking, allergies, abnormal thyroid activity (either hyperthyroid or hypothyroid), or hormonal changes (including "the pill" which is suspect by many teachers of singing and related to difficult high notes). The thickness may also be due to improper diet or related to smoking, excessive drinking, venereal disease or drug use. The voice should never be taught when the vocal cords are edematous.

High voices are built by the correct register adjustment to the upper notes.

Those who attempt to sing a fundamental pitch continually at the top of a register or above the limits of a register are courting disaster. Furthermore, the "gear shift" of registers must be automated and hidden for a prolonged career.

All of this pertains to one thing, the primary vibrator and the muscles within the vocal cords themselves. Transplants are unavailable, the cords with which a singer is born are his only ones. If conductors, opera directors or accompanists think the singer is egocentric for his care of his voice, so be it. One thing for sure, whether taken away by someone else or given away by the singer, they nor anyone else will be able to restore the voice by exercises or medication. "No training or special exercises can be carried out without working the already jaded muscles . . . the muscles must be allowed to recover from the damage previously done" (Jackson, 1940). Be careful of how much you sing even if it is great singing. This advice even applies to the most healthy of voices and the best singers with the best techniques. When Jenny Lind came to Garcia he heard that her voice was chronically hoarse. He recommended that she give her voice six weeks of perfect rest—not to sing a single note and to speak as little as possible (McKinlay, 1908, p. 145). Her voice recovered so that she could study and continue her career, but it never completely recovered from the injury she had sustained. At that time she was but twenty-one years of age!

FEMALE VOICES

Let us study the scale of that great singer, Jenny Lind (Rockstro 1894, p. 10).

> (a) was described as being the veiled notes of the middle register. These notes were more seriously injured by her early singing than the other notes of her voice. (b) was the brilliant head voice. (c) was the brilliant f-sharp which was so greatly admired by Mendelssohn that he constantly used it in *Hear Ye, Israel* (with [ɪ] vowel) and other parts of "Elijah." Besides having the notes between f-sharp^2 and c^3 in full voice, she had a pianissimo which was described by Chopin as having a "charm which was indescribable." The f^3 was the high note of the *Queen of the Night* aria which according to the American Academy pronouncement on pitch is presently being sung 100 vibrations higher than the f^3 which was the pitch for which Mozart wrote (NATS *Bulletin*, O. 1974). (g) the notes c^2 to a^2 were noticed by Mlle. Lind as the best notes of her voice. Most female voices are similar to this scale but are usually lower.

EQUALIZATION OF THE SINGING SCALE

In the development of the singing voice it is necessary to extend the range of the voice by using different types of vibrations from the vocal cords and to equalize them in a scale. According to Garcia's terminology of registers, the chest voice existed below f^1, and the middle voice extended from d^1 to c-sharp^2 (he called it falsetto). The head voice extended from c-sharp^2 to g-sharp^2. Above that was the whistle register of which Garcia spoke. From this we can gather how to proceed in the construction and equalization of female voices. Naturally there will ge great differences in the amount of each register in individual voices.

Fig. 6: The Jenny Lind Scale (Rockstro, 1894).

MALE VOICES

The history of our art of singing is related to that of the male soprano voice—the castrato. The natural male voice was trained by castrati so it followed that their techniques of agility, messa di voce, extended ranges, etc., should be passed along to their students. The Rossini, Donizetti, and Bellini operas called for tenor voices which were florid and had extremely high notes. Rubini, for whom Bellini wrote, sang to f^2. Garcia's father trained Nourrit, who had a voice which was capable of agility and broad coloring. In this type of voice it is necessary to establish the ability to phonate c^2, c-sharp^2, d^2, e-flat^2, etc. This is the pure head of the tenor voice and is probably a use of the "slit tone" shown in Fig. 1. When the resonators are correct (vowel modification) the sound can be quite loud. Many of the tenors of today will only sing to the b-natural[1] in public and will not chance a c^2 because they say it comes out thin. Indeed such is the case because they do not blend the pure head c^2 and above in Garcia's terminology into the mixed and chest voice. Contemporary tenors are much more concerned with dramatic effects than coloratura over the top of their range. So the upper notes are unavailable to them in many cases. On the other hand, the tenors who do have the upper extension are criticized for not having enough fulness in their voices. The motto is for the tenor to sing the repertoire for his voice and to ignore the writing of unenlightened critics.

The baritone voice came into prominence after Duprez began singing high notes in chest voice in 1837. The high baritone will find it helpful to blend pure head, blown tone into his upper notes. Without this blend, his upper notes will be insecure. Garcia wrote on this technique before the high baritone existed (Garcia ca. 1855, p. 7). This is the whistle technique we have referred to previously.

> It sometimes happens that when the female voice attempts to sound the notes b^2 and c^2, it unconsciously rises to d^3 and e^3, in a thin but pure tone and with much less effort than would be required for trying the notes below. [He surmised what occurs.] The process just described, and which is successfully employed by some female voices, is equally capable of application by the male; in which case it will serve to give clearness to high notes of the bass, and will enable tenor voices to extend the compass of their chest register, and sing high notes in *mezzo voce*.

Today, the opera literature is such that most voices must have the use of this form of vibration for the maintenance of the upper voice for its subtle use. This thin, head register can be found by blowing an [u] through a pencil sharpener sized opening of the mouth. And there must be such a velocity of air that it can be felt by the hand held about 12 inches in front of the mouth. This should be attempted on notes higher than can be gained by mixed register in men and head voice in women. This can be brought down and blended. The *two forms of vibration,* flute and reed, are the bases of the two register approach as I understand it. I personally believe that registers are involved with hidden "bugle tones" in the voice which I notated by means of an Echophone described in the article on resonance. Our observations more than support the statement on registers by Garcia that male voices are made up of *chest voice* and *falsetto* [*mixed*] *voice*—in the case of tenors there can be a *head voice* extension of a third or so above the mixed. We will state that the same extension exists in Verdi baritones, Heldentenors who are sometimes baritones with an added high register, and in Heldenbaritones who are sometimes bass-baritones with an added high register. This extension can be gained in some voices by blending in the whistle technique.

THE VOCAL CORDS

Vibrations originate at the vocal folds very much in the manner of a "raspberry" (Saunders, 1964, p. 37), the vibration made by fluttering the lips. If the lips are pursed, the vibration is of a low pitch, whereas when the lips are drawn from that position to vibrate thinly across the teeth, the pitch raises. This likeness has been extensively described by Jackson (1940, p. 452). The change of vibration is more easily observed with the use of a trumpet or trombone mouthpiece. Thickening the lips lowers the pitch, and thinning the lips gives higher pitch. Another visual vibration which is helpful is that of porpoises "singing" in their act at a Marineland show. There is another vibrational phenomenon observable at Marineland. There is a rainbow when the porpoises sing if the day is sunny. This type of membranic vibration can only take place in a moist condition Van den Berg (1968, p. 18) found that the vibration of an excised larynx would cease unless the air was saturated at 37°C (98.6 F). Most singers have had the experience of being so dry that the voice will tend to crackle. This may be due to low humidity or to a medication which reduces "throat congestions" to an extent that the voice works only with difficulty or will not work. The voice simply will not vibrate well if it is dry. Neither will the lips of a brass player, hence a spit valve on the instrument. The condensation of moisture is a factor of changing air pressures just as the best ski slopes are on the up slope sides of mountains where there is a reduction of air pressure.

PRESSURE SYSTEM

The voice is actually a pressure system which varies atmospheric pressure. Roughly, it can be said that the number of pressure changes per second gives us a psychological sense of pitch. This is an oversimplification but it will serve our purposes (Wightman and Green, 1974). Roughly the larger the deviations from atmospheric pressure, the louder the sound is to our ears.

Radioear Bone Vibrator

In the first article, we spoke of artificial resonation of the vocal tract with an Echophone. Another device, a Radioear Bone Vibrator, has enabled us to study the nature of vibration in the human throat. This is actually an extension of the Western Electric Larynx which was developed for the use of persons who had had their larynges removed. By the artificial vibrators we can learn a great deal by sight and sound. There are some aspects of vibration which have not been sufficiently clarified. We are dealing with *vibrator* and *resonator* also known as *source* and *system*. The vibrator always influences the resonator and the resonator always influences the vibrator. Source and system are coupled as surely as Siamese twins and an understanding of their phenomena will help us as sound technicians of the voice.

Values of Studying Artificial Vibration in the Vocal Tract

The advantages of using the Radioear Bone Vibrator as an artificial larynx is that all kinds of vibration can be played into the throat and the treatment of all types of vibration by the throat can be better understood.

1. A "raspberry" vibration slower than pitch played into the throat will give vowel pitch without harmonics.
2. When there is a "raspberry" of sufficient frequency to make a pitch, the vowels will be heard on harmonics.
3. A pure tone will reverberate harmonics even though it is basically all fundamental.
4. A balloon burst played into the throat will show vowel pitch of all vowels and, on the open vowels especially, the 3,000 Hz.
5. Esophageal vibration by a person with a larynx played into the throat will show vowel pitch and 3,000 Hz on the open vowels. It remains to be seen if this is also true of a person who has had his larynx removed.

6. Brass vibration, flute vibration, and reed vibrations or mixtures can be studied by the stops of an electric organ or by the real instruments. *The immediate feedback of sound is of great value in learning.*
7. Singing on any of the vowel colors which reinforce fundamental vibration will give the loudest resonance, liquid vibrato, and focus.

After our observations of the vocal tract by artificial vibration, we will state that the extension of range in the singing voice is made possible by the development of registers, and that registers are due to the *effect* of the vibrating air mass in the resonating vocal tract upon the vibration of the vocal cords. (The effect of the *secondary* vibration of the vocal tract upon the *primary* vibration of the vocal cords.) It is similar to the trumpet player who can buzz his mouthpiece alone in a glissando from a very low pitch to a very high one. When the mouthpiece is inserted into a trumpet, the length of the pipe causes various modes of vibration to occur which in reality are the trumpet's registers. Incidentally, the trumpet player has a kind of whistle register above his high c. These are called *sonics.* Is there a law of vibration in air that a phenomenon of this type must occur at this place? In the singing voice there is an upper cutoff of R^1, the lower resonance of vowels, at about 1,000 Hz, roughly c^3. There is a lower cutoff at about 300 Hz roughly, sometimes known as the break. There is high cutoff of all vowel resonances around 3,000 Hz. The rainbow of vowel colors exists from 300 Hz to 3,000 Hz and of consonants from 300 Hz to around 8,000 Hz, just as visible color exists between 7,400 and 4,000 Angstroms (wavelength).

The Opening of the Mouth

Registers are related to the tunings of the vocal tract which are accomplished by the openings of the mouth with the raising or lowering of the larynx. One of the basic principles of the great teachers of singing was that the mouth be opened in a certain way. Anna Maria Pellegrini Celoni (1817), quoted by both Garcia and Lamperti, said:

> Many blessed with a good *metallo* of the voice, are mediocre through not knowing how to open the mouth; others with bad voices make them good by singing with good styles and by knowing how to open the mouth. Not opening enough makes the voice obscure, opening too much makes it throaty; those who sing with the mouth too open on "ah" have the voice of an old person.

The *metallo* pertains to "sharp explosions" and the "ring" of the voice. The opening was usually described as being that of a "smile." Garcia (1872, p. 7) stated that a common fault was a certain stiffness in the action of the lifting muscles of the jaw, and that if the lips are flattened against the teeth, the voice will be better and the words more clear. The only vowels which he thought required the rounding of the lips were [o],[ø], [u], and [y]. We observe that many times the upper notes are not available in their potential quality simply because the openings of the vocal tract are incapable of attaining the high resonator pitch desired. A resonator pitch which is too high will sharp the voice. A resonator pitch which is too low will flat the voice. Extensive practice of preparing the resonators to receive the vibrated cord sound is *very valuable*. Also, the closed vocal cords necessary for studying resonation with an Echophone is effective in building the strength of the adducting muscles. This pinch of the glottis is very important for the whistle in which a small aperture of the vocal cords allows the whistle phenomenon to occur.

Conclusion

Ours is an art of sound vibration in which the two arts of language and music are combined. Frequently they are called upon to exist at high dynamic levels and on high pitches at which time they are often incompatible. This is especially true in the female voice because of the limited number of harmonics available to it for vowel differentiation. At this time language must give way to the pitch established by the composer or there will be distuning of the phonation (vibrator) by the vowel (resonator). Languages which are unspecific in the close vowels are easier to sing. English has two colors of EE (feel, fill) and two colors of U (fool, full).

Vowel modification came from Italy and according to Tosi (1723) I and U were forbidden in vocalization as well as the close forms of E and O. We should keep this in mind in our coaching. Absolute language coaching in singing is a form of vocal destruction as well as a form of forcing poor intonation and weak resonation on singers. The vowels must be given their freedom to change slightly. Vibrator and resonator are source and system which have an interrelationship which cannot be disregarded, especially in prolonged high dynamics and in the high registers of voices. The best vowel color can easily be found by the Echophone or Radioear Bone Vibrator used as an artificial larynx. Vowel colors of the various notes are available for scoring a singer's song before he sings so that the vibrator and resonator of the voice will be in agreement (Coffin, 1974).

REFERENCES

Appleman, D. Ralph, *The Science of Vocal Pedagogy*, Bloomington, Indiana, University Press, 1967.

Bartholemew, Wilmer T., *Acoustics of Music*, New York, Prentice-Hall Inc., 1942.

Chiba, T. and M. Kajiyama,*The Vowel, Its Nature and Structure*, Tokyo: Phonetic Society of Japan, 1958.

Coffin, Berton, *Favorable Vowel-Color Charts, Male and Female Voices*, Boulder, Colorado: Milton Press, 1974.

Corri, Domenico, *The Singer's Preceptor* (1810) in The Porpora Tradition (E. Foreman, editor). Urbana, Illinois, Pro Musica Press, 1968.

Garcia, Manuel, *The Art of Singing*, Pt. I, Boston: O. Ditson, ab 1855.

Garcia, Manuel, *The Art of Singing*, Pt. II, 1872. Tr. Donald V. Paschke. N.Y.: Da Capo Press, 1975.

Garcia, Manuel, *Hints on Singing*, London: Ascherberg and Co., 1894, 50 New Bond St., London W 1.

Garcia, Manuel, "Observations on the Human Voice," *Proceedings of the Royal Society of London*, London: 1854–55, p. 399–410.

Helmholtz, Herman L. F., *On the Sensations of Tone* (fourth and last edition), N.Y.: Dover Publications, Inc., 1954 (new), 1877 and 1885 (old).

Husler, F. and Y. Rodd-Marling, *Singing: The Physical Nature of the Organ*, London: Faber and Faber, 1965.

Jackson, Chevalier, "Myasthenia laryngis observations on the larynx as an air column instrument," *Archives Otolaryngology*, Vol. 32, p. 434, 1940.

Lamperti, G. B., *The Technics of Bel Canto*, New York: G. Schirmer, 1905.

Large, John, "Acoustic-Perceptual Evaluation of Register Equalization," *NATS Bulletin*, O. 1974.

Lehmann, Lilli, *How To Sing*, New York: Macmillan, 1914.

Luchsinger, R. and G. L. Arnold, *Voice-Speech-Language*, Belmont, California: Wadsowrth Publishing Co., 1965.

McKinlay, M. S., *Garcia the Centenarian*, New York: D. Appleton and Co., 1908.

Marchesi, Mathilde, *The Art of Singing*, Opus 21, Book I & II, N.Y.: G. Schirmer, 1890.

Melba, Nellie, *Melba Method*, New York: Chappell and Co., 1926.

Nathan, Issac, *Musurgia Vocalis* (1836) in The Porpora Tradition (E. Foreman, editor), Urbana, Illinois, Pro Musica Press, 1968.

Nilsson, Birgit, *Opera News*, New York: 0.10, 1970.

Pellegrini Celoni, Anna Maria, *Grammatica o Siano Regole per Ben Cantare*, Rome: 1817. (tr. E. Foreman)

Pleasants, Henry, *The Great Singers*, N.Y.: Simon and Schuster, 1966.

Rockstro, W. S., *Jenny Lind*, London: Novello, Ewer and Co., 1894.

Russell, G. O. and J. C. Cotton, *Causes of Good and Bad Voices*. Washington, D.C.: National Research Foundation and Carneige Institute of Washington, catalogued, 1959.

Saunders, William H., *The Larynx*, Summit, N.J., CIBA, 1964.

Stratton, John, *Operatic Singing Style and the Gramophone*, Recorded Sound, #22–23, April–July, 1966.

Tosi, Pier Francesco, *Observations on the Florid Song*, London: J. Wilcox, 1743.

Van den Berg, J. W., "Sound Production in Isolated Human Larynges." *Annual*, New York: *Academy of Sciences*, No. 155, p. 18, 1968.

Wightman, F. L. and D. M. Green, "The Perception of Pitch," *American Scientist*, Vol. 62, p. 208, 1974.

Winckel, F., "How to Measure the Effectiveness of Stage Singers' Voices," *Folia Phoniat*, No. 23, p. 229, 1971.

Wood, Alexander, *The Physics of Music*, London: University Paperbacks, Methuen. 1962.

Appendix F: Articulation for Opera, Oratorio, and Recital

We honor Manuel Garcia II with this article since 150 years ago, on November 29, 1825, he made his operatic debut as Figaro in Rossini's *Barber of Seville* in the Park Theater in New York City. This opened the first Italian opera season in the U.S.A. His father, Manuel Garcia I sang the role of *Almaviva* which was written for him by Rossini. Manuel Garcia II sang that season in New York, a season in Mexico, but made his debut in Naples without success. He abandoned the lyric stage for teaching at 24 years of age and became the Leonardo da Vinci of the art of singing because he was concerned with the sounds of the art, their anatomical basis, and their expression.

His observations were based on 87 years of activity in the art of singing! At 10 years of age he studied with Ansani in Naples, at 20 years of age he sang with his father's company in New York. At 25, after his appointment to the French army, he served in military hospitals where he studied "the exact anatomy of the human vocal cords [and] . . . 'the throttles of all kinds of animals—chickens, sheep, and cows' " (McKinlay, 1908, p. 100). At 35, he presented his MEMOIRE ON THE HUMAN VOICE to the French Academy, and published Part I of the ART OF SINGING at 36 in which he cleared up the confusion which had hitherto existed between "timbre" and "register." When 42, he published Part II of the ART OF SINGING which was dedicated to the King of Sweden in honor of Jenny Lind, his most famous student. He was 55 years old when his paper *Observations of the*

Reprinted from the *NATS Bulletin* [now *Journal*], February–March 1976.

Human Voice, was read to the Royal Academy of London which was made possible by his invention of the laryngoscope nine months earlier (and which he was never to use again. He was interested only in confirming his theories.) He was 89 years of age when his HINTS ON SINGING was written. He was 97 years of age when he wrote his letter to Charles Lunn in explanation of the "stroke of the glottis." On the occasion of the 100th birthday (March 17, 1905), it was written that "musical and medical sciences are in the present day brought very much together, so that it is often difficult to guess whether some learned expatiator on the last method of producing the voice is a singer who dabbles in surgery or a surgeon who has a taste for singing."

In 1922 the Spanish Medical Society placed a plaque on the house in Madrid in which he was born commemorating his contribution to medicine and noted that over 50 societies had come into existence because of his invention, the laryngoscope.

We take the position that *what* Garcia *heard* was *more important* to the teacher of singing than what he *saw.* We are grateful that Da Capo Press has published the Paschke translation of Garcia's 6th edition of the *Complete Treatise on the Art of Singing* (1872), Part II. This is a monument of the use of pronunciation in musical expression and of the authentic performance styles of that period.

The teaching of singing has suffered unnecessary mischief because his statement of basic principles of the Italian School is all but unknown. There is no better understanding of the bel canto school than through Garcia. No doubt he heard his father coached in the role of *Almaviva* by Rossini himself, for Rossini, Bellini, and Donizetti were hired by the Italian impressario Barbaia to compose for, coach, and conduct the singers at San Carlo in Naples. Thus, Garcia was there when the "bel canto" operas were coming into existence.

What is the relationship of the Garcia School to Lieder? His sister, Pauline Viardot, taught by his mother, gave the first performance of the Brahms "Alto Rhapsody." His student, Julius Stockhausen, *baritone,* concertized with Clara Schumann, Joachim, and Brahms. Stockhausen exerted a strong influence on the

Manuel Patricio Rodriguez Garcia (March 17, 1805–July 1, 1906). It is thought that the above portrait was painted by John Singer Sargent in Garcia's 100th year, and subsequently presented to him on the occasion of his 101st birthday celebration. Twenty learned societies and 800 individuals shared in the expense. The most famous singing teacher of his day, Garcia was the first to link the art with scientific investigation through his discovery and use of the laryngoscope (1854).

style of Brahms' songs and Brahms dedicated the Romances from "Magelone" to him. It may surprise many that Dietrich Fischer-Dieskau was taught by two of Stockhausen's students and says that his technique and interpretation come from Garcia's School of Singing and "Gesangs-Technik of Stockhausen" (Sugg, 1973, p. 40). Marilyn Horne attributes much of her success to Garcia's *Hints on Singing* (*N.Y. Times Magazine,* January 17, 1971), and Beverly Sills attributes her vocal background to Estelle Liebling, a student of Marchesi (Garcia's student) who taught in Paris at the same time Stockhausen was teaching in Frankfurt and Garcia in London.

Garcia (McKinlay, 1908, p. 165) taught Wagner's niece, Johanna Wagner, and was invited to train singers who were to take part in the first Bayreuth Festival in 1876. He did not accept the invitation which has been a detriment to the singing art ever since. Lilli Lehmann, who took part in the first performance at Bayreuth stated (1914, p. 297),

> Even though distinctness of articulation is necessary and desirable, the methods of the Bayreuth School were an entire failure. Their teachers, unconscious of what they were doing and teaching in good faith, committed a great wrong not only toward vocal art but toward the vocal organs of the unsuspecting singer.

The fact of the matter is that the voices of many singers have been devastated by it. The singer must keep the tone continually flowing; upon this tone the movements (transients) of the consonants can be engraved.

STAGE SINGING

The Art of Singing heard today in opera, professional recitals, and records is that which evolved on the stages of Italy. The phenomenon is that of the human voice being transformed from a non-harmonic instrument to an harmonic instrument. This was necessary because of the large opera houses of Bologna, Naples, Milan, and Venice. It first came about through the castrati who were trained to vibrate the large spaces of the cathedrals in Italy. Eventually the art was passed on to the female and natural male singers.

Today we find singing in many different acoustical environments. In Europe, most of the opera houses and concert halls seat less than 2,000 people. World famed singers can be employed in casts because of state and city subsidies. Some halls are larger and some, such as the Royal Festival Hall in London, have had to resort to assisted resonance in which weak parts of the tonal spectrum—high or low—have been amplified electronically so that the sound is well balanced.

In this country, it is unjustly expected that performances should pay for themselves, so opera houses and concert halls have been built much larger to accommodate the paying public. At the same time, the audiences have required more comfort and leg room, so that the space per person here is much larger than in Europe. This means that the same sound source will make weaker waves here than in Europe. As a consequence, the orchestra instruments and pianos have been reinforced to better vibrate the spaces in these halls. What has happened to the singer? He/she is larger than ever before with several towering over 6 feet. The larger the cavities in the vocal tract to be vibrated by the vocal cords, the louder the sound. It is said that the sound level of cities is going up 10 decibels each decade. Surely the decibel level from the stage has gone up in parallel fashion. If Mozart should come back he would wonder why his music is being performed so loudly and at such high pitches.

On the other hand, the cost of erecting small houses for chamber music has increased so much that they have been cancelled, as in Berlin. Choral music is thriving on the amateur level but without clarity of phonation. Solo singing is also thriving at the amateur level but with much of it without clarity of phonation—the non-harmonic sounds have not been completely transformed to harmonic sounds. A dichotomy exists. A small, breathy voice sounds good in a small resonant auditorium whereas the resonant voice sounds driven. When the small, breathy voice sings in a large auditorium, it sounds like nothing, whereas the well-placed resonant voice carries well.

NATS members have wondered why weak, breathy singers frequently make the finals in large auditions. My conjecture is that the preliminaries were held in small rooms where the ratings were invalid because of room acoustics. Auditions would be more successful if they were held in the halls where opera, oratorio or song recitals are given.

The problem of our times is that singers need clear, resonant tones with higher decibel levels than ever before. The conductor, in the spotlight, seems to be making greater demands on singers than ever before without the realization that the singer's sound is coming from elastic human flesh which has its limits as does that of a professional athlete. He/she is also subject to injury. The best that can be done is to evolve a technique which will be the most efficient and long lasting. *We believe this is as much concerned with consonants as with vowels.*

Richard Strauss (1924) stated, "I, myself, have witnessed especially in Wagnerian music-dramas . . . singers with big voices but with poor enunciation have been swallowed up in the orchestra waves, while artists with smaller voices but with sharp enunciation and with distinct phrasing were able without difficulty to uphold the author's words against the tonal floods of the symphony orchestra."

Spoken Language and Sung Language

Speech is a series of phonetical inflections and colors which determine the words and meanings of a language. Uris (1971, p. 54) states that these linked syllables in chains of articulation are called *smear*. There are continual blends and inflections of vowels and consonants in speech. In singing *pure vowels* there is a moment, the length of the note, in which there is a steady state long enough for a standing wave and optimum resonance to occur, but the changes which are the consonants have traditionally been taught to occur quickly so that there will be little disruption of the reverberation of the vowels. Singing, because of its steady states of vowels and raised pitches, is a departure from the true

ó	680	u̅	310	ch	42	k	13
a	600	i	260	n	36	v	12
o	510	e̅	220	j	23	th	11
á	490	r	210	zh	20	b̲	7
o̅	470	l	200	z	16	d	7
u	460	sh	80	s	16	p	6
a̅	370	ng	73	t	15	f	5
e	350	m	52	g	15	th	1

Fig. 1: Relative phonetic powers of fundamental speech sounds as produced by an average speaker. From Fletcher (1953), *Speech and Hearing.*

nature of a language. This is one of the reasons that sung language is difficult to understand except in recitative which allows language to appear nearest to the usual *smear* form of speech. In cases where there is raised speech in singing lengthy passages with orchestra or piano, the listener may need a libretto for full comprehension of what is being sung. There is another reason. Fletcher (1953, p. 86) has indicated the uneven phonetic powers of the basic speech sounds of an average American speaker. See Fig. 1. The open vowels as in *awl, top, ton* and *tap* he found to be about 3 times as loud as the vowels in *tip* and *team*. But *aw* was 680 times as loud as th (*thin*). (The decibel level expressed in the Figure is 28.) How is it possible to hear a sung language in a large auditorium over a heavy accompaniment? We must use all of the techniques possible. The main two are vowel and consonant modification.

Vowels can rather easily be handled with the approach described in the *NATS Bulletin* (December 1974). There are those teachers who say that one should sing as one speaks. This is possible if a person is willing to accept a whisper in the voice.

> Without tune, breath-pressure and pronunciation can only result in speech, or a mere whisper, the addition of tune is imperative before we can be said to be singing. It is not difficult to whisper pure vowels with controlled breath, but it is difficult to tune them. *Shakespeare* (1921), p. 19.

We will say that when where is a breathy quality in the singing voice, it is less subject to the laws of vowel modification than when it is clear.

ENUNCIATION IN SINGING

Husler and Rodd-Marling (1965, p. xiv) have said,

> What scientists tend to dismiss as 'singer's jargon' is in reality the language of the ear. With it, the vocal organ itself tells us through the singer, at some time or another and in a thousand different ways, everything worth knowing about the laws that govern its functioning. True, these statements are of things unseen and unobservable [except by the ear]; it is a vegetative knowledge devoid of thought or consciousness.

We have presented several observations which were made possible by a better way of *hearing* and *feeling*. This was done with the use of a Vowel Mirror (Echophone) which has been previously described (D. 1974). Practice with the device will reveal the optimum resonance of the voice to singers and teachers of singing. Husler and Rodd-Marling state that our ears have lost that strange kind of intuitive, almost somnambulistic intelligence, together with its extraordinarily accurate discriminative faculty. We believe that singers and teachers of singing are using the thought processes more and the subconscious less than did singers in the past. How can the lower levels of conscious be trained? The classic formula was to train the breath and the pronunciation. Let us address ourselves to how we can automate the system which forms consonants. We will include in this discussion how we start and stop tones, and how we go from one tone to another.

TYPES OF ATTACKS

Every story should have a good beginning and a good ending. So should a singing phrase. The phrase will begin with either a consonant or a vowel and on the quality of the *beginning* depends the vocal quality of the phrase. Hislop, in a paper read at the University of Colorado NATS Workshop in 1964, referred to the *sweet attack* which he used in his teaching. He was a student of Dr. Giles Bratt, a famed singer, and the last teacher of Björling. The *sweet attack* can best be established and understood by pronouncing very lightly [b b b] with the upper and lower lips, and imitating the sound very lightly with the vocal lips (vocal cords), [b b b | | |]. This is exactly the beginning of phonation desired by Garcia II in a letter dated October 28, 1902, when he was 97 years of age (Lunn, 1904, p. 21):

> In the series of explosions constituting a sound, the *initial explosion,* the first one is the one I designated by the 'stroke of the glottis' . . . . it must be the delicate action of the glottis, not the brutal pushing of the breath that goes by that name, fit only to tear the glottis, not to rectify and regulate its movements . . . . I distinguish the first explosion from the others because, as *it starts the sound,* its qualities or defects are impressed upon the emission.

It is refreshing to be in Italy and hear an Italian practicing his English. *How hard* comes out as being [| a o | a d] and the tone is clear and loud. We recommend a couple of light [b b b | | |] sequences daily to find the feeling of starting the tone. Surely this action occurred with Flagstad when she was studying with Dr. Bratt (Flagstad, 1952, p. 22).

> Dr. Bratt told me that my vocal cords did not close and that was the reason for my small voice. Air went through between the vocal cords. What he did was to close my vocal cords. By this means, my voice grew in three months to three times its size.

There are three attacks, 1) the *sweet attack,* 2) the *aspirated attack* (the tone begins with an [h], and 3) the *stroke of the glottis,* which is notated in IPA as [ʔ]; this also is known as a *hard attack.* We believe the latter attack should be used only for extreme emphasis.

CONNECTION OF TONES

Let us first speak of tone connections because there are five articulations other than consonants. These techniques are needed in agility, cantabile, and declamatory passages. Garcia has best described them (ab 1855, p. 12),

1. *Legato* ⌐⌐ two adjunct notes in which there is *equal* and continued pressure of air with sudden changes in the tension of the vocal cords. The change is made without gliding or without aspiration. This is the basic characteristic of good vocalization.

2. *Gliding or slurring* ⌐⌐ in which there is equal and continued pressure of the air with gradual changes in the tension of the vocal cords. This is heard in appoggiaturas, portamentos, swooping, and dragging. Corri (1810, p. 3), a student of Porpora, said that the

> *portamenti di voce* is the perfection of vocal music. It consists in the swelling and the dying of the voice, the sliding and blending of one note into another with delicacy and expression. . . .*Portamento di voce* may justly be compared to the highest degree of refinement in pronunciation in speaking. . . . It was the particular excellence of Farinelli, Pacchiarotti, Raaff and others of the first eminence.

All were Italians! It is particularly useful in singing Italian since the language has few consonants which end syllables. However, it can also be used effectively in other languages. Sir George Henschel (1926, p. 49) founder of the Boston Symphony Orchestra and successor to Jenny Lind as teacher of singing at the Royal College of Music in London, describes the *portamento of the soul.* "Just at the moment when you wish to make the portamento, *relax* the hold on the note you are on, and on the little thread that's left of the note gently glide down or rise upward" where the same strength may be given as on the previous note where you had relaxed the hold on it. The taste of the singer is revealed in this type of connection.

3. *Marcato* is described as *continued* and *accented* pressure of the air with sudden changes in the tension of the vocal cords. Garcia illustrated that one could also think a repeated vowel on each note. He states that, "It is a principal resource for giving color and effect to florid passages."
4. *Staccato* is a detached vocalization in which the lungs are alternately pressed and in repose with alternating and sudden tensions of the vocal cords.
5. *Aspirated* vocalization occurs when there is a continuous breath pressure with alternate contractions and distension of the vocal cords. There is an escape of air [h] before the sounds. It is used in laughter and has no other use in classical music. *Its use makes the voice dull and whispery.*

CONSONANTAL CONNECTIONS

G. B. Lamperti (Brown, 1931, p. 7) said, "The language best suited for the study of singing is Italian, because it is the only one without aspirates." There is no [h] and the [p, t, k] have no puffs of air after them. The statement was written when he was teaching in Germany. His father, F. Lamperti (1890, p. 20) stated that the consonant and vowel should begin together—the singer should voice the consonant. He continually used [1] in his vocalises which was sufficient to gain good diction from Italians. Shakespeare, his English student, said (1921, p. 23), "A forward position of the tongue should be the goal of the master and pupil, affording a proof that the note is placed without any interference with the tongue." 200 years earlier Tosi made a related statement (1723, p. 28): "Let the Master never tire in making the Scholar *Sol-Fa*, as long as he finds it necessary, for if he should let him sing upon the Vowels too soon, he knows not how to instruct." The values of *Sol-Fa* were the establishment of good intonation, the elasticity of the vocal organs, the connecting of consonants and vowels, and the ability to sing in the Italian language.

According to Mancini (1777, p. 170), the Tuscan dialect should be used because it was the most suitable for the theater since the other dialects lacked "accent and melodic sweetness." This standard of the Italian language may have been formed in the Palace of the Medici Princes in Florence. Perhaps the most beautiful language was formed at the time the most beautiful arts were again given to the world. The Tuscan dialect was not only the clearest dialect of the Italian language but its formations enable other languages to be sung clearly. Delattre stated (1958, p. 7),

> The best conditions for speaking vowels require the presence of constrictions along the vocal tract: the best conditions for singing require the absence of such constriction in order to allow the high frequency overtones that characterize voice quality to be passed by the resonating cavities.

Let us simply say that of the 24 consonants that we count in the Italian language, 14 have different formations that we give them in English! Their use gives clearer vowels to all languages. Heretofore, most singers and teachers of singing have thought that the magic was in the vowels. We believe that a great secret lies in the consonants which allow the tone to continue with a minimum of interference. We have found that after having gained optimum resonance on vowels many of the problems which arose turned out to be involved with consonants. The first thing is to be sure that the pitches of sustained consonants be easily maintained. Know what the vowel will be (*easily done with the Vowel Mirror*), take a breath, form the consonant and then go quickly to the vowel. The sustained ring and resonance of phrases will soon tell whether the vowel/consonant drills are effective. Is this new? No, Mancini (1777, p. 167) spoke of "the diligence of the celebrated Pistocchi of Bologna, who taught pupils such clear enunciation, that they conveyed every word so distinctly that their audiences could even hear the details of the consonants as 'tt,' 'rr,' and 'ss.'" Marafioti (1922, p. 228) states it clearly:

Pupils must attach the greatest importance to the correct formation of the consonants, which in connection with the vowels constitute the corner stone of correct and beautiful talking and singing.

This has been known by many great singers. Lilli Lehmann (1914, p. 279) said:

> . . . the singer must concentrate his entire attention on the form-modifications or form preservation while articulating every letter so that he may remain master of the beauty of his voice.

Singing is a symphony of many systems—the breathing system, the vibrating system, the resonance system, the articulation system, the conscious systems, and the subconscious systems. Anything of an athletic nature must be drilled so that the various actions can be automated. This is most true of the systems involved with forming consonants. We naturally use those consonant forms given to us by our ancestors and by the people with whom we associate. For singing, it is necessary to form consonants with which we can sing clearly in the main singing languages.

In Fig. 2 we have shown the Italian consonants and unusual consonants in French, German, and British English. The underlined consonants are those which have a different formation or action than those in American English; the heavily boxed consonants are those which do not exist in our language. They should be practiced while singing on the Favorable Vowels. Garcia, Pt. II., p. 15 stated that "The pupil should learn the points at which these organs are placed in contact and the mode of action which serves to form each consonant." This is shown on the left side of the Chart. This is especially important to the singer since Delattre observed that perception extends beyond acoustical occurrences and that consonants are partly perceived by the point of contact and by aural recognition of motor action. It is interesting to note that the deaf have great trouble in lip reading speakers who do not show their teeth. Showing the teeth gives clarity to diction and gives an easier observation of how speech elements are formed both aurally and visually.

Fig. 2: PRACTICE CHART OF CONSONANTS FOR STAGE SINGING

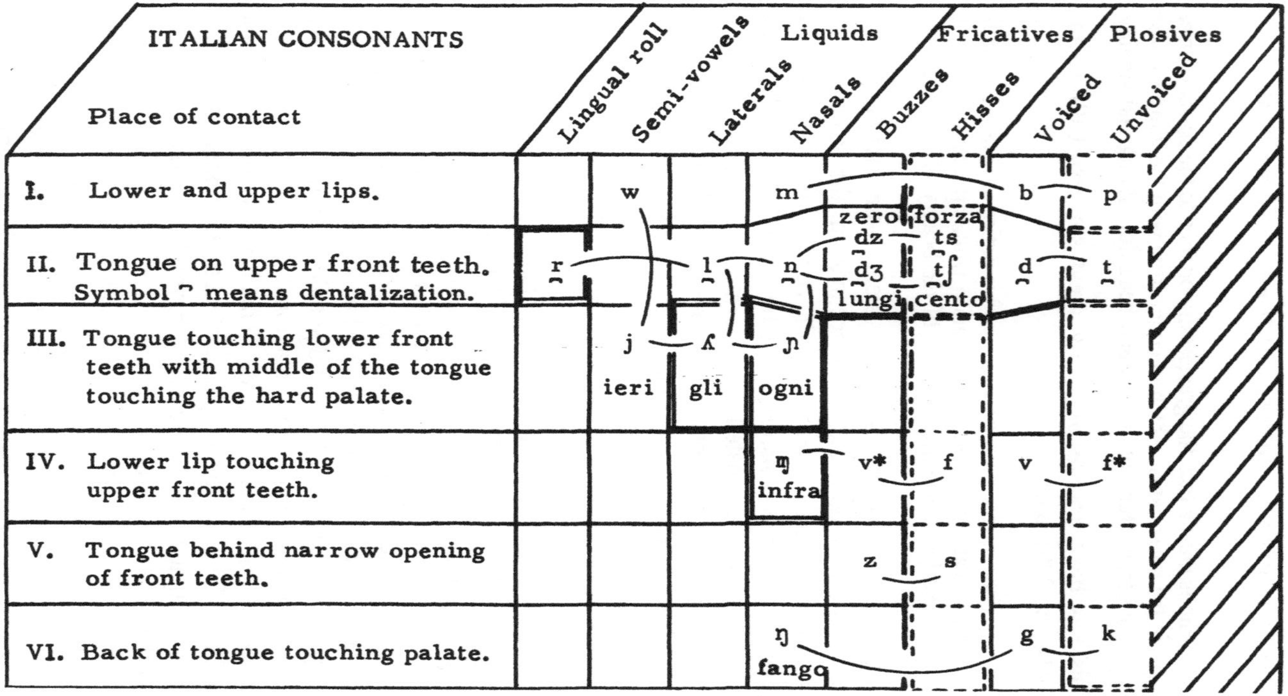

ITALIAN CONSONANTS — Place of contact	Lingual roll	Semi-vowels	Liquids — Laterals	Liquids — Nasals	Fricatives — Buzzes	Fricatives — Hisses	Plosives — Voiced	Plosives — Unvoiced
I. Lower and upper lips.		w		m			b	p
II. Tongue on upper front teeth. Symbol ^ means dentalization.	r, r̯		l, l̯	n, n̯	dz, dʒ (zero forza, lungi cento)	ts, tʃ	d, d̯	t, t̯
III. Tongue touching lower front teeth with middle of the tongue touching the hard palate.		j (ieri)	ʎ (gli)	ɲ (ogni)				
IV. Lower lip touching upper front teeth.				ɱ (infra)	v*	f	v	f*
V. Tongue behind narrow opening of front teeth.					z	s		
VI. Back of tongue touching palate.				ŋ (fango)			g	k

OTHER CONSONANTS

For FRENCH add	r, r / nuit (ɥ)	ʒ / je — chez
For ENGLISH add (p, t, k are aspirated; d, n, t and l are aveolar. r is a single flip.	r / very	θ / thin — ð / the
For GERMAN add.. (Stressed p, t, k are aspirated. l is very clear. Glottal start [ʔ] before vowel beginning an accented word or for clarification of meaning. The symbol [ǀ] represents the sweet attack or soft glottal start. (Based on IPA 1970)	(j) — ç / ich (k) — x / ach	(p̄) — pf / Pfad (b) — ǀ (h) — ʔ

*Garcia (Pt. II p. 13.) preferred the buzzed [v] and plosive [f].

• Consonants within solid lines are voiced and should be practiced daily for vocal line.

• Consonants within dotted lines are unvoiced. [p, t, k] should be unaspirated.

• Underlined consonants have different formations in Italian than in English.

• Boxed consonants do not exist in English and should be correctly established.

• Arrows indicate contrasting consonants which should be practiced daily.

There is also a fundamental phonetic principle: *a person must be able to make a sound before he can recognize it.* Black and Singh (1968, p. 125) believe that speech may be received in part as an auditory "reflection of one's talking." Consequently one must learn to make the sounds as they occur in the different languages. Waengler (1966, p. 2) suggests watching oneself frequently in a mirror so that one can *see* the differences in articulation which cause the different phonetic sounds. Otherwise, he will hear foreign sounds as being those nearest to the sounds in his own language. We will also use the sounds of our own language in speaking a foreign language which results in an American accent. Foreign-born persons do the same in speaking our language. The only solution is to learn how the foreign sounds are made, what they look like and, finally, what they sound like.

Types of Consonants

The *liquid* consonants are smooth, flowing, and vowel like. They should be practiced daily so that a flow of tone can exist between vowels and give singers a much better cantilena.

The *plosive* consonants are explosive. However, the puffs of air which occur after [p, t, k] in English and German do not occur in Italian and French. These explosions are not heard beyond a few rows. Plosive consonants in singing are mainly perceived by what they do to the vowels which follow them. In English and German if the plosive consonants are not modified, the vowels which follow them will be dulled because the velocity of the puff of air is more than the vocal cords can accommodate in the singing of the vowel.

The *fricative* consonants are characterized by a frictional rustling of the breath as they are emitted. The buzzes and hisses can be easily built into the singers' diction by alternating the pairs of consonants in the following relationships: [v f v f] as in have *fun*; [z s z s] as in hi*s s*on; [ʒ ʃ ʒ ʃ] as in pleasure *sh*all and [ð θ ð θ] as in wi*th th*em.

Shakespeare (1921, p. 170) says when the buzzes

are sufficiently sustained, the singing is warmed and illuminated with a glow, for their euphony is not only a source of charm, but their presence ensures great freedom in the production of the voice. . . . Only a good singer can sustain this buzz [v]. The fact that any stiffness of the tongue and lip hinders the pronunciation of the buzzes makes them the best of practice for the student.

CONSONANTS BETWEEN VOWELS

F. Lamperti (1890, p. 19) stated that bad articulation in singing is apt to produce hardness and harshness. He believed the study of solfeggio could not be overrated in establishing good pronunciation. His main concern, with Italian, was that the singer should not pronounce the consonants double when they were single. It may be of interest to Americans to know that when Italians hear Americans singing the Italian language, *all consonants* sound as though they are being doubled because of the great stress on consonants. Why is this a problem to singers? Good singing is a matter of vocal line—and continual double consonants play havoc with *cantilena*. The Yersin sisters (1924, p. 95) have observed that foreigners exaggerate French consonants whereas the French exaggerate the vowels. The authors give a visual representation. The foreigners say o P é R a. The French say O p E r A. When they sing, the vowels are on the beat, and the consonants are as small grace notes before the beat.

In stage singing the vowel is raised acoustically in all languages, and the consonant is made to become the partner of the vowel. If this does not occur, the voice becomes impure with a breathy, husky sound, and does not travel well. Waengler (1966, p. 2) has noted that a "certain hollowing of the front of the tongue is typical of the America. . . . It has a *concave* contour. A "German" tongue is never concave! Its basic position is just the opposite, characterized by a pronounced convex arch. . . . When one speaks German properly, therefore, the tongue remains farther forward than in American English." The tongue is also farther forward in French than in English. See Fig. 3. Dentalization in some way reduces the compression of the breath and fast airflow which causes huskiness and breathiness.

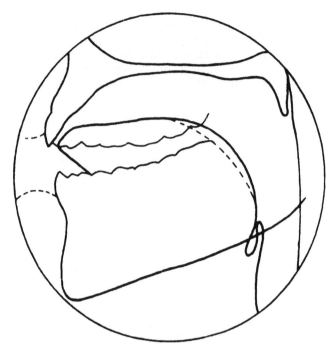

Fig. 3a: A French dentalized 1. Delattre (1965), *Comparing Phonetic Features.*

Marchesi (Opus 31, p. 6) stated that she composed vocalises with words for blending pronunciation with vocalization, that is, she wrote studies for accustoming the pupil to pronounce the words distinctly in such a way that they would not adversely affect the voice. She wrote the words in Italian because it is free of the gutteral sounds of the Teutonic languages (she was born in Frankfurt, Germany) and to keep from using the closed and nasal sounds, and the uvular *r* of the French language (she was then teaching in Paris).

How does the Italian language differ from others and why is it that Italian singers have unsurmountable difficulties in singing French, German and English? Languages other than Italian have certain constrictions which interfere with free vocalization unless certain consonants are modified. Is this a subjective statement or

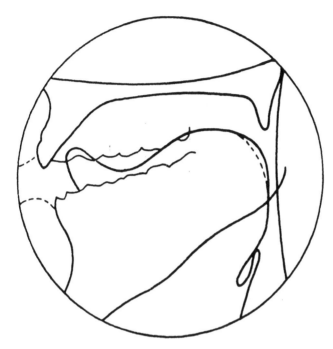

Fig. 3b: An American retroflexed 1. Delattre
(1965), *Comparing Phonetic Features.*

is it based on the nature of sound in the human throat? It is the
latter. (A simple test will suffice. Hold a tuning fork in front of
the mouth, vocal cords closed as in a grunt, and play with the
mouth and lips until resonance is heard. Holding the mouth in
that shape, strike the tuning fork again and insert it into the mouth
about an inch. The sound of the tuning fork will fade away to
resonation. When it is withdrawn it will again resonate.) There
happens to be a dead spot in the mouth! When [d, n, t, and l] are
dentalized, a standing wave is established in the mouth. When [d,
n, t, l] are pronounced on the gum ridge, as in English, the
standing wave is reduced and the resonation of the voice is weakened. How is an American to overcome this resonance reduction
in his and other languages? Simply move the tongue forward to
touch the upper front teeth when pronouncing [d, n, t, l] in

singing. Carl Heinrich Graun, the Kapellmeister of Frederick the Great, invented a method of solfeggio in which the syllables *da, me, ni, po, tu, la, be* were used. Let us say that his training was largely influenced by Italian singers and that Frederick's chief ambition was to found a first-rate Italian opera company in Berlin. Graun was sent to Italy to engage singers, much as Handel had done a few years earlier. It so happened that Ferdinand Sieber realized a value in these syllables and utilized them in his series of vocalises and solfeggios for the different voice classifications. Whereas he used the *do re mi's* for pitch interval and tonality identification, he used the 7 Graun syllables in rotation for linguistic reasons. The advantage of these syllables is that they alternate lip and lingual-dental consonants. When the tongue touches the teeth, it is brought forward out of the throat allowing a better use of the resonances for singing. Curiously the order of the lingual dentals and consonants in Graun's syllables spell [d, n, t, l] which outline the word *dental*. Phonetically, dentalization of consonants is indicated by [⌐]. These consonants can be sung on any song or aria in rotation while keeping in mind the Italian pronunciation which can be indicated as [da me ni po tu la be]. The throatiness with which so many American singers are troubled is related to the backward posture of the tongue which can be largely overcome by the dentalized consonants.

The *rogue* of all consonants is the American r. In its inverted form, Fig. 4., there is a constriction at the tip and another at the base of the tongue. It is twice as bad as has been thought! Let us remind ourselves that it appears in the code word, *Roger,* of World War II. It contained a consonant by which Americans could identify Americans. No other nationality could speak it so it was a code which was seldom broken. It is exclusively ours but it is a vocal sin since the vowels following it or proceeding it become gutteral and have weak resonation. This consonant should be modified to the rolled or flipped [r] if preceding a vowel when singing with orchestra and in the classical song literature. In such a word as *bird,* the [ø] or [œ] are resonant modifications. The inverted or bunched *r* should still be used to make American folk song authentic. This type of singing is inti-

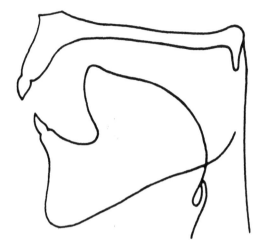

Fig. 4: An American retroflexed r. Delattre (1965), *Comparing Phonetic Features.*

mate, and the sound is not loud so there is little danger of vibrational reaction in the throat while using it. The phonetic symbol is [ɹ]. It is psychologically used in our language in such words as murder, devour, constrict, and throaty. What a sound and what meanings!

Other consonants which bring the tongue upward out of the throat are the Italian sounds [ʎ] as ciglio and [ɲ] as in signor. In these sounds the tip of the tongue touches behind the lower front teeth while the mid-tongue makes contact with the palate. As the contact is left, the sound goes directly to the [o] in ciglio and [ɔ] in signor. No [i] sound is heard between the consonant and vowel unless an [i] stands alone as in gli [ʎi]. Drills can be made which utilize [ʎ,ɲ] and rolled [r]. They can be used for overcoming the curled up tongue which comes from the American use of gum ridge contacts in the [d, n, t, and l].

Marafioti (1922, p. 255) describes the dentals [d] and [t] as being formed much differently in Italian than in English . . . . "they are formed by leaving the tongue between the teeth and pressing it very gently . . . with the [t] produced by

using a little more pressure of the teeth on the tongue than the [d],
which is softer and quite similar to the English *Th* (they)."

There is a nasal consonant used by the Italians in which the
lower lip is pressed against the upper front teeth. Its IPA symbol
is [ɱ]. It is used when [n] appears before [v] or [f] as in *invidia* [i
ɱ v i d j a] and *trionfo* [t r i o ɱ f o]. Errolle (1963, p. 46) states
that in practice the singer's tongue tip is against the lower front
teeth for the preceding vowel and remaining there when the [n]
proceeds to the [f] instead of rising to the alveolar ridge. It is our
observation that the Italian singers also use this vowel when an
[n] precedes a [d or t] as in *quando* [k w a ɱ d o] or vento [v e ɱ t
o]. It is *not* a form of [m] since the upper front teeth are showing.
It is a valuable consonant for fronting the American tongue. We
believe in exaggerating the [l] by placing it between the teeth. It
is a sure way to avoid stiff and dull "l's" of American English.
They and the American "r's" are out of place in continental
languages including British English. See IPA, p. 11.

ENDING CONSONANTS

Much of what we understand depends on the endings of
words. They vary surprisingly from language to language.

1. In *Italian* all words end on vowels or the consonants found in
   the word *mineral*. All of the sounds are liquid, have pitch, can
   be pronounced without difficulty and can be sung through
   most of the range of the voice. Garcia (Pt. II, Paschke, ed.
   1872, p. 11) stated concerning [m] and [n]:

   It is necessary first to pronounce the vowel purely and simply, to
   continue the same sound during the entire passage, and to give
   only on the last note, or at the end of the passage, that touch of the
   nose which makes the [m] and [n] heard.

   Delattre found that he could cause a nasalized sound in syn-
   thesized speech by reducing the lower vowel resonance which
   takes place in the mouth and pharynx. The prolongued m's

and n's in singing are an outgrowth of the use of the microphone.

2. *French* words end on vowels or on the consonant sounds [k, r, f, and l] in the word *careful*. Thus with two added sounds, both Italian and French words can be perceptably ended. The [f] is articulated as in English but the [k] has no puff of air following it.

3. *German* words end on the liquids [m, n, r, l, and ŋ (ng)] and on most of the unvoiced consonants—never on the voiced fricatives and plosives.

4. *English* is the only principal singing language to end on buzzes and voiced plosives. These should be practiced daily in the middle voice.

AIRFLOW

After several years of teaching the favorable vowels, it has become more and more apparent that most of the problems which have showed up in the songs or arias are involved with the consonants. The students have had little difficulty in singing resonant vowels but many times interferences occur when going to or away from the vowel sound. Sometimes the troublesome consonant is before a vowel; sometimes it is after the vowel. We have observed a priniple: *the problem can be solved if the velocity of the airflow in the consonant is made to approximate the airflow in the vowel which follows or precedes* it. This means that the unvoiced plosives can soften towards their voiced partners and the unvoiced fricatives can modify towards their buzzed partner. This is actually what exists in the classical Italian language.

CONSONANT MODIFICATIONS

Adler (1965, p. 5) has said:

> One of the most widespread errors is that spoken and sung sounds are the same. Nothing is further from the truth. To sing the way

you speak may be advisable for popular music, but it would make the voice sound brittle, harsh, and uneven in opera, song, and choral music. The adjustment of phonetics to the vocal phrase is the real problem for any accompanist and coach and the solution constitutes a very important part of his art.

In our book *Phonetic Reading of Songs and Arias* (1964, p. v), we made a guarded statement as to the use of the IPA in singing because of the above problematic results. Our December 1974 article describes how singing sound occurs in the human throat and its relation to vowels. How does it relate to consonants? Most modifications are involved with compression and velocity of air-flow. Lamperti (Brown, 1931, p. 86) said:

> To cure the "nasality" of the consonant [m] cross it with [b], as if you had a "cold in the head."
> The guttural quality of [b] disappears when combined with [m]. It then vibrates more on the lips.
> Think [d] while pronouncing [n], and the "twang" disappears, also like one with a "cold."
> The "hardness" of [d] melts if buckled with [n]. The noise seems than to come from the tip of the tongue.
> The tightness of [ng] is lessened when united to [ig]—again as a "stopped up head."
> [Ig] ceases to be unpleasant if softened by [ing]. The sound then appears to start in the head.

REGISTERS AND CONSONANTS

The middle register of the female voice tends to be breathy. When practicing this and the low register more "bite" may be given to the vocal cords by using consonants which give higher compression—b, d, v, r, and g. G. B. Lamperti (1905, p. 15) speaking of the head voice stated that on the 4th line, d♭, of female voices it is "allowable to draw a little breath through the nose." The nasal consonants [m, n, etc.] can be used before vowels to get the voice to speak a little better. Since there is more airflow in the head voice in women, the voiced plosive conso-nants should be softened towards their unvoiced partner and the unvoiced plosives because of the velocity of air, should be modified towards their voiced partner especially within a phrase. The same phenomenon exists in male voices approximately an octave lower.

SYLLABLE STRUCTURE

Garcia (Paschke, trans, and edition of 1872, p. 17) recommended that vowels always begin the syllable and the consonants finish it. "This method could lead to the doubling of all consonants but the correction of that fault is always easy." This means that the musical element of singing should begin on the beat and the noise or transitional element always appears slightly before it.

Vowel and consonant practice on the rhythms of Fig. 5. will result in the clear enunciation of 1) a consonant between vowels, 2) a final consonant, 3) a beginning consonant, and 4) a sustained consonant. Simply choose a vowel and a consonant and sing them on the same pitch in the middle voice. We would say that the singer should be able to close syllables on the sustained consonants up to the top of the *passaggio* or slightly above. Practice on such combinations should give great elasticity and projection to the voice and create clarity of diction. Practice with

The various consonants and vowels should be practiced on pitches of the singing voice. Vowels should be sung on the dotted quarter notes and consonants on the sixthteenths.
1. is an intervocalic consonants, 2. is an ending consonant and 3. is a beginning consonants. Tie 2. and 3. for a lengthened consonant.

Fig. 5: Patterns for practice of vowels and consonants

varying compressions of the consonants. It will be found that lyric singing is more a matter of liquid pronunciation and dramatic singing is a matter of more incisive pronunciation. (Paola Novikova)

CONSONANT

We have spoken of the relation of consonants to vowels and that they should be soft and quick so that there can be a vocal line. Duval (1958, p. 105) said, *"Put the words in the voice"* which we would interpret as painting the consonants on the vocalization. The consonant glides on the vowel tells us more of the consonants than do the consonantal sounds themselves. The whispers and aspirates which occur in [s, θ, ʃ, f, p, k, t, and h] are heard more by what they do to the vowel line than by the hissing sounds which carry only a few rows into an auditorium.

TEMPO AND CONSONANTS

More time must be given to consonants in German and English than in the Romance languages. This required time is necessary for the perception of the consonants and must be taken from the time preceding the vowel which should be sung on the beat since it is the tone part of the singer's instrument. Henschel (1926, p. 40) has indicated the time allotment for the consonant in a familiar passage of "Messiah," Fig. 6. Definite time is necessary for voiced and unvoiced consonants. Their emphasis derives from the breath pressure given to them. Outstanding German singers likewise use time, especially of the dot to articulate consonants at the end of a syllable.

TRANSLATIONS; CONTEMPORARY VOCAL WORKS

Rossini, in a letter to Marchesi (1898, p. 112) stated that "in order to compose for the voice, one must either sing one's self or

Fig. 6: The timing of consonants and consonant clusters. Henschel (1926), *Articulation in Singing.*

have sung. If one does not know from experience the capabilities of the vocal cords and the larynx, it is impossible to write passages that will not ruin the voice." I am just as sure that it is possible to make translations of songs and opera roles that can ruin voices. This leads us to look upon contemporary music very carefully and to not attempt it until one has developed a singing technique which is compatible with that required by the composition. If a flute player or a horn player has great difficulty in playing low notes after high notes, or vice versa, are we not aware that the laryngeal muscles and vibrating flesh of the singer may have the same characteristics of those of the instrumentalists? Mozart wrote his music to fit the voices of those who would be performing it (Anderson, 1966, Vol. I, p. 292). The singer should always think, "Do the music and the words fit my voice?" Geniuses such as Mozart, Rossini, Bellini and Donizetti knew what they were doing with language and music. Their tonal-vowel combinations are usually right if one has a good technique. Also their language settings will be understood. Translators have had some success in using the same vowels on extreme notes which were used in the original language. Very frequently the translations made are so poor in vowel and consonant values that the translation is made to be misunderstood. No singer, I repeat, no singer should be criticized for poor diction when a writer with little knowledge of the voice has made a translation. We must say that in translation a singer has the license to change the words to those which can be both sung and understood. We quote Duval's statement. "If the pronunciation is both quick and supple, the result will be clear enunciation and mellow tone." This occurs only if the vowels are available and this varies with height of pitch; the 16 English vowels cannot be sung at the top of the soprano voice. This we have explained (Coffin, 1964, p. v.). If they are sung, they are not loud enough to be heard. This is probably the basis of the statement by Sir Thomas Beecham that English could not be sung loud enough to be heard at the Royal Opera (Covent Garden) quoted by Kay (1963, p. 95).

HIGH NOTES AND ARTICULATION

Garcia (1894, p. 50) said, "When high notes have to be sung on unfavourable vowels or articulations, or when too many words embarrass the swift flow of vocalization, the singer is at liberty to displace and even suppress certain words, provided he does not distort the sense." He demonstrates this with an example of Rossini *who knew how to write for the voice.* What of the modern composer *who does not know how to write for the voice?* The subject of ethics is involved at this point. Is it ethical for a composer to ask a singer to perform music which will shorten his career? This may occur because of physical disruptions of the vocal cords or because of psychological pressures created by conductors, teachers, or critics who criticize a singer for not being able to sing music (or a translation) which cannot be sung. How often a singer is poorly evaluated when the criticism should be laid at the doorstep of the composer who wrote unvocal music.

The singer survives in his profession by the exceptional use of his body, very much as the athlete and ballet dancer. When his body is injured, his career is in danger. There are influences growing today which makes the professional singer an endangered species.

The conductors are definitely to blame for allowing the pitch of today's orchestras to climb higher and higher. They are also to blame for playing at dynamics never intended by the composers.

The most recent opera in the standard opera repertoire is "Rosen-kavalier," 1911. What has happened to orchestras since that time? Steel strings are being used in virtually all orchestras. The fingerboards of old stringed instruments has been lengthened to obtain more sound. The baseboard has been lengthened to with-stand the additional pressure caused by the higher tension of the strings. And the number of string players in an orchestra has been increased for the older operas. Winckel (1974, p. 40), quotes the Kinsky catalogue concerning a full strength performance of Bee-thoven's symphonies in his time—two violins, two violas, two cellos, a double bass, two flutes, a piccolo, two oboes, two clarinets, two bassons, a double bassoon, two horns, two trum-pets, a pair of tympani, and three trombones; whereas today, many groups are necessarily represented by several desks be-cause of the larger volumes of auditoriums. This has also hap-pened in the pits of opera houses. Would the role of Leonore in " Fidelio" be entrusted to a 17-year old soprano as it was to Schröder-Devrient in 1822? Today the role is sung by a singer about twice that age and of larger stature. While we are dwelling on increased loudness, let us state that the woodwinds have changed from a soft tone quality to one of much greater intensity through improved systems. The brass has had a great increase in resonance through optimum use of values, bores, mouthpieces, and tunings.

What developments have occurred in the human voice since that time? Singers are larger today and must wait until they are older to begin a career. Loudness and higher pitch can only be gained by greater breath compression, greater contraction of muscles which can only be gained when the cartilages have been significantly firmed and the muscles involved with singing devel-oped beyond the strength of youth. There must also be the most favorable use of resonation and consonants.

CONSONANTS AND MEANINGS

Very simply, the intensity of the consonants is directly related to the emotional utterance of the singer. This means that in expressions of anger, great joy, etc., the consonants impede the air longer so that there is greater compression. Upon release of the consonant the vocal cords and resonator are vigorously vibrated. In moments of tenderness, the compression is much less. The consonants in Fig. 2. should be practiced with various degrees of compression to enable expressive singing. Garcia states (1894, p. 48) that "the energy of consonants gives travelling power to the words in a large locale. . . . But it must be said that no jerks, no force of voice can be substituted for the clearness, precision, and energy of articulation which alone can carry the words to a distance. Violence would cause singing to resemble barking. The best method is to prolong each consonant as much as is consistent with the character of the piece."

CONCLUSION

Today's singer must be both musically and dramatically communicative, but he must first be heard to be musically effective or to be understood. There must be power which exists in the vowels; there must be messages which exist in the consonants and in the inflections. However, the consonants must be formed in such a way that the vowels become more powerful since the sound levels of today's music are very high, and because of the large auditoriums. These conditions require highly developed usages of the vibratory, resonating, breathing and articulation systems of the singing voice which we have described in a series of four articles. Like other systems of the body there are many coordinations—none are entirely independent. *All systems should be activated for the expressive and emotional singing of our time.*

REFERENCES

Adler, Kurt. *Phonetics and Diction in Singing.* Minneapolis: University of Minnesota Press, 1967.

Anderson, Emily. *The Letters of Mozart and His Family.* London: Macmillan. New York: St. Martin's Press, 1966.

Black and Singh in Malmberg, Bertil, *Manual of Phonetics*. Amsterdam, North Holland: American Elsevier Publishing Co., 1968.

Coffin, Berton. "The Instrumental Resonance of the Singing Voice." Chicago: *NATS Bulletin*, D. 1974.

Coffin, Berton. *Manual for Vowel-Color Charts, Female Voices; Manual for Vowel-Color Charts, Male Voices*. Boulder, Colorado: Milton Press, Box 3295, Boulder, CO 80303, 1976.

Coffin, Singer, Delattre and Errolle. *Phonetic Readings of Songs and Arias*. Boulder, Colorado, Pruett Press, 1964.

Colorni, Evelina. *Singers' Italian*. New York: G. Schirmer, 1970.

Corri, Domenico. *The Singer's Preceptor* (1810) in The Porpora Tradition (E. Foreman, editor). Urbana, Illinois: Pro Musica Press, 1968.

Delattre, Pierre. *Comparing the Phonetic Features of English, French, German and Spanish*. Heidelberg, Germany: Julius Groos Verlag, 1965.

Delattre, Pierre. "Vowel Color and Voice Quality." Chicago: *NATS Bulletin*, O. 1958.

(Delattre) Valdman, Albert. *Papers in Linguistics and Phonetics to the Memory of Pierre Delattre*. The Hague and Paris: Mouton and Co., 1973.

Duval, J. H. *Svengali's Secrets and Memoirs of the Golden Age*, New York: Speller and Sons, 1958.

Enciclopedia Universal Ilustrada. Madrid, Barcelona: Hijos de J. Espasa, 1924.

Errolle, Ralph. *Italian Diction for Singers*. Boulder, Colorado: Pruett Press, 1963.

(Flagstad) Biancoli, Louis. *The Flagstad Manuscript*. New York: G. P. Putnam's Sons, 1952.

Fletcher, Harvey. *Speech and Hearing in Communication*. New York: Van Nostrand, 1953.

Garcia, Manuel. *The Art of Singing*, Pt. I. Boston: O. Ditson, ab, 1855.

Garcia, Manuel. *The Art of Singing*, Pt. II, 1872. Tr. Donald V. Paschke. New York: Da Capo Press, 1975.

Garcia, Manuel. *Excerpts from A Complete Treatise*, 1841, and *Memoire on the Human Voice*, 1840. Tr. Donald V. Paschke, 1970. Available through University of Colorado Bookstore, Boulder, Colorado 80309.

Garcia, Manuel. *Hints on Singing*. London: Ascherberg and Co., 1894, 50 New Bond St., London W 1.

Garcia, Manuel, "Observations on the Human Voice." *Proceedings of the Royal Society of London*. London: 1854–55 (p. 399–410).

Henschel, George. *Articulation in Singing.* Boston, New York, and London: John Church, 1926.

(Horne) Mayer, Martin. "Marilyn Horne Becomes a Prima Donna." *New York Times Magazine.* Jan. 17, 1971.

Husler, F. and Y. Rodd-Marling. *Singing: The Physical Nature of the Organ.* London: Faber and Faber, 1965.

IPA. *The Principles of the International Phonetic Association.* London: University College, Gower Street, London WC1E 6BT.

Kay, Elster. *Bel Canto.* London: Dennis Dobson, 1963.

Lamperti, F. *The Art of Singing.* New York: G. Schirmer, 1890.

Lamperti, G. B. *The Technics of Bel Canto.* New York: G. Schirmer, 1905.

(Lamperti, G. B.) Brown, William E. *Vocal Wisdom.* New York: Arno Press, 1957 (available—Boston: Crescendo Press).

Lehmann, Lilli. *How to Sing.* New York: Macmillan, 1914.

Lunn, Charles. *The Voice.* London: Reynolds and Co., 1904.

McKinlay, M. S. *Garcia the Centenarian.* New York: D. Appleton and Co., 1908.

Mancini, Giambattista. *Practical Reflections on the Figurative Art of Singing.* Boston: Gorham Press, 1912.

Marafioti, P. Mario. *Caruso's Method of Voice Production.* New York: D. Appleton Co., 1922.

Marchesi, Mathilde. *The Art of Singing,* Opus 31, p. 6. New York: G. Schirmer, 1890.

Marchesi, Mathilde. *Marchesi and Music.* New York: Harper, 1869.

Marshall, Madeleine. *The Singer's Manual of English Diction.* New York: G. Schirmer, 1953.

Shakespeare, William. *The Art of Singing.* New York: O. Ditson & Co., 1921.

Strauss, Richard. *Intermezzo* (Foreword). 1924.

Sugg, James Ferrell. *Comparisons in Historical and Contemporary Viewpoints Concerning Vocal Techniques* (Thesis). Waco, Texas: Baylor University, 1973.

Tosi, Pier Francesco. *Observations on the Florid Song.* London: J. Wilcox, 1743.

Uris, Dorothy. *To Sing in English.* New York and London: Boosey and Hawkes, 1971.

(Viardot) Fitzlyon, April. *The Price of Genius.* New York: Appleton-Century, 1964.

Waengler, Hans-Heinrich. *Instruction in German Pronunciation.* St. Paul, Minnesota: EMC Corporation, 1966.

Wilcke, Eva. *German Diction in Singing.* New York: E. P. Dutton, 1930.

Winckel, F. "Space, Music, and Architecture." *Cultures,* Vol. 1, No. 3. Paris: UNESCO and la Baconnière, 1974.

Yersin, Marie and Jeanne. *The Yersin Phono-Rhythmic Method of French Pronunciation.* Philadelphia: Lippincott Co., 1924.

Appendix G: From the President

Editorial Note: The following constitute a series of nine articles published in the *NATS Bulletin* during Berton Coffin's tenure as President of the National Association of Teachers of Singing, 1968–1970. Whereas they were intended for the membership of this large organization of singing teachers, there are some very pertinent points brought out that will be of interest to the readers of this volume who may not be members of NATS. (The *Bulletin* is now known as the *NATS Journal.*) I hope they will provide further insight into the man's thinking and a look into the future. They are still valid twenty years later. (*Mildred W. Coffin*)

A MESSAGE FROM YOU: YOUR IDENTITY*

Socrates said there are no absolutes save one—the duty to inquire. Hence all else is relative. We are more aware than ever before that customs, tastes, societies, times and economies change. With those changes there are alterations in the quantity and quality of the singing art, and the profession of teaching which nurtures it.

We must inquire. Your new administration needs to know many things about the teaching community it endeavors to serve. Who are you? What are the professional conditions of the unaffiliated studio teacher, the affiliated studio teacher and all categories of our members?

We must therefore ask each of you many questions—a set of which you will be asked to answer anonymously and in such a

---

NATS Bulletin, February 1968.

way that your locale remains unknown. These questions will be formulated so that the answers can be evaluated through the use of modern data processing machines.

Another set of questions which will require considerable thought, and possibly a movie's worth of time to answer, will also be sent to you. We need to explore your attitudes, your evaluations, and new ideas concerning the many faceted activities of NATS. What are the meanings of these various offerings to you? How can they be of greater benefit? Activate your imaginations! You are a creative people—without doubt some of you will form ideas which will change the history of NATS as a professional organization. We need your evaluations in all perspectives—those of the first year members to those of the 24-year members. We as a national organization should have something of value for all. Maybe you have wanted to get something off of your chest; please proceed—we want your ideas!

This is a time of change for NATS. In the new administration there are eight newly elected persons on the 18-member Board of Directors and there are eight new Regional Governors compared with January 1, 1967 But we must always remember that the make-up of our organization is quite similar to the plant of a prize rose. The basis of the rose is a sturdy stock upon which carefully cultivated buds can be implanted—the result can be a sturdy, multicolored bush. With NATS, the sturdy stock is that which has been passed down to us from the administrations of the past. The buds are the many activities, some of which are a part of the organization and flourishing. From your suggestions we will select many ideas to implant in the organizational structure. It has been my privilege to have known all of the past presidents and many of their fellow officers. They have all been dedicated persons. We must say in all honesty that NATS is a miracle—a product of dedicated leaders and members who have given of their overtime, their means, and in some cases [several believe] their lives towards the solution of the enigma, the continued development of a great vocal art in a period when there is little time for reflection and other basic artistic processes. I am sure that the new administration and present NATS members will be as dedicated to our art as those in the past. I am confident that all of you will want to make your contribution in defining things as you presently see them.

The overwhelming support for establishing the office of Executive Secretary at the National Convention, under the direction of the productive 1966–68 administration, indicated that NATS members felt that something should be done to establish the organization as a more important voice for our profession. Now we have identity. We will have a telephone number for the first time! Now we can be in touch with other music agencies through a closer liaison with the National Music Council. Now we are in a position where we can pursue findings of NATS projects. We are also in a position where we can have a flow of communications to our membership to supplement those that appear in the *NATS Bulletin*. Soon we will be able to process the mountain of information that is anticipated from this questionnaire.

The National Survey will be a way of establishing a reference by which our organization can be measured in the future. As we approach our 25th anniversary, we will have a good idea of where we are now. We will have only a subjective idea of where we have been. For the future, we hope we will be able to select from your ideas several short and long term goals which are attainable with our resources. Yes there will be changes, but we must remember—to quote one of our esteemed members, "I felt a new impulse of great import at the Chicago meeting—the beginning of a new era which I hope will not lose sight of our original objective—the teaching of singing in its best form!" Thank you, Grace Leslie. All members will soon be given an opportunity for individual expression. Perhaps a copy of the *National Survey* is on your desk now. If you have not yet seen it, please await it, professionally.

How can your administrators most effectively proceed to build a better organization without knowing the strengths, weaknesses, thoughts and ideas of the membership? We believe that you will be the direct recipients of your own composite energies and ideas.

Of Gods and of Men*

"Muse"—one of the nine goddesses of song and poetry, and also the arts and sciences. "Music"—any art over which the Muses presided, especially music, lyric poetry set and sung to music [Webster]. This word relationship has carried over into the Latin word *musica* which was used to denote melody. The other components of music were *harmonia* and *mensura* [harmony and rhythm] according to *Encomium Musices* published in Antwerp in 1590.

We occasionally hear the derisive statement, "musicians and singers." We must emphatically state that we are the true musicians if we are artistically dealing with lyric poetry. Perhaps we should share the title of "musician" with any instrumentalist who performs with the effect of lyric poetry. Should we disallow the term to others in the field? Anyway, we should reemphasize our rights to the privilege of forming the voice as a musical instrument. Instrumentalists develop their craft through playing music, singers only partially so through singing it. The individual differences of students is such that there are always those who desire and need "instant" singing. This we must accept to some extent. But in the highest interests of our art there should be a return to the precepts and practices of the vocal art which have established great singing in the past centuries. And, there should be a better understanding of those precepts through the revelations of contemporary research.

Since the mythology of the Muses, the teaching of singing has been related to the work of the Gods, it is spiritual and is above the mundane. Too frequently the formation of voices and the teaching of techniques is such that little of spiritual value exists. This is not necessary. If we know how to form the vocal instrument then we can have unusual voices in our community. If, in addition, we are poetic, know how to teach lyric poetry, and know how to illumine the human spirit, then we can again and again give the thrill of song to the world.

NATS Bulletin, May 1968.

In most ages, it is the arts which are creative—and it is incumbent upon all of us to increase the creativeness in our individual arts and sciences of vocal pedagogy. It is too much for us to play "God" in making singing voices, but we can assist in forming and shaping them. Stradivarius took inanimate materials and made enduring instruments for his time and posterity. Master teachers of singing have taken animate vocal material and have formed instruments for singers whose art gave the illusion of being superhuman. [Such singers are sometimes referred to as being gods or goddesses.] But, being animate, those instruments were nevertheless mortal and could last only as long as the health of the human bodies in which they existed.

DeLuca, one of the greatest singers of them all, wrote after his concert commemorating the 50th anniversary of his debut, that a singer should see his teacher at least once every two weeks [*Etude*, November 1950]. We must realize that singers have little more perspective of their art than do dancers who seldom practice away from a person who can observe their work. Sometimes their "maestro" has a stick which he uses to touch a particular muscle which needs contraction, or a specific line which needs to be modified. The singer has need of a trained observer of his work, one who has a vocalization knowledge of his voice over a period of time, who has a functional knowledge of vocal acoustics, and one who can study his voice in a hall as it is heard over a piano or an orchestral accompaniment. This person is a partner in maintaining the artist's voice as an instrument of spiritual expression.

For centuries the art of great singing has been nurtured by great teaching. Some teachers have not been great until they had a great voice with which to work. In their continued formation of this voice a more penetrating understanding of the vocal instrument has come to both the singer and his teacher. Great artistry may be the reward to both. One of our members has been the teacher of a great singer for over 30 years! That instrument, being animate, needs continual formation whereas Anton Stradivarius during the same length of time formed about 450 instruments, which have remained formed to this day.

The eminent teacher of singing, Mathilde Marchesi, took a

soprano voice of a quality which was judged to be unworthy of singing in the Gilbert and Sullivan chorus at the Savoy Theater in London and formed an instrument known as a Melba. That singer was a goddess of song for 30 years. Melba was conscious of her art; she knew her voice—witness her book, *Melba Method* (Chappell, 1926). Many similar situations have existed but are less thoroughly chronicled.

Currently the idea is abroad that one can sing without study. The idea is a very limited truth—one may sing within certain vocal limits for a short time without study. To become a diva or a god of song, one must continuously study. The private studio teacher is a necessary element of this art. What school could afford to have a student for 30 years? What administrator would not eventually ask the teacher, "when will you finally teach this particular singer to sing?" In great singing there is no time of graduation and living off the fat of the land. Harold Schonberg in the November 5, 1967 *New York Times* lists eight and one-half column inches of great voices which sang between 1915 and 1935. He then numbers the present singers whom he considers as being comparable—possibly 12. The evidence is on the records. What happened?

My answer would be that teachers of singing, through various factors, were given less opportunity to form and maintain voices. Possibly academic degrees with a built-in concept that four years "does the job," may be a part of the dilemma. Great vocal art needs prolonged nurturing before and during the time of great singing. There should be many times the number of private vocal studios which exist today. They should be esteemed and should be very active. In turn, this activity should be increasing the greatness and abilities of the teachers of singing. We know more about the physical nature of the vocal instrument than ever before and, because of the tape recorder, singers know more about how they sound than 30 years ago. These factors have not led to a plethora of vocal riches although American singers are adjudged to be the best prepared singers in the world.

One of the great purposes of the National Association of Teachers of Singing is to establish and maintain the highest standards of practice in the profession of teaching singing. Ours is truly the most unusual art—it is mortal, intellectual, and spiritual. Too frequently the latter is missing.

Since earliest history, singing has been associated with divine services in many religions. Singing has much to offer today to the beginning student, to the advanced student, to the professional, and to society, if we fully realize what our art is about. We must dedicate ourselves to its sublime effects. In English, we may state its purpose as being, "Music for awhile shall all your cares beguile," or in German we can say, "Hast mich in eine bess're Welt entrückt" [have lifted me into a better world]. Ours is a transporting art. We must have great courage in these times to practice our art with our eyes upon the stars as well as upon the clay. We can and must minister to the greatest force of all—the spirit of man.

The Boat, the Oar, the Tides*

The boat of NATS is presently in motion with more than 200 people pulling at the oars! There soon should be a surge of energy and power which will be felt not only by our members but by those with whom our members are associated. Our 25th year must be a year of rededication, of exceptional progress, and of ever higher status for our organization and for each of its members.

It is our belief that the affairs of NATS should be treated as a whole—we must be concerned with ALL members in ALL regions and in ALL areas of our art. Only in this way can we have the greatest strength. It is my hope that all members at the oars and at the helm will work together as we navigate the ever changing tides which lie before us.

With the whole of NATS in mind, the President with the Board has formed an extensive committee structure to attain many short range goals and to stimulate thinking and action on long range goals. We will be exploring and possibly implement-

*NATS Bulletin, October 1968.

ing many of the ideas received in the replies to the membership-wide National Survey.

Thirty-four committees have been formed and 157 appointments have been made in an effort to make use of as many of our talented and energetic members as possible. Many of the younger generations have been added to the crew. We are attempting an endeavor not unlike the scientists' Geophysical Year in which all aspects of the globe were studied—we will have a 25th year in which we survey the various areas of the teaching of singing, and in which we endeavor to update our thinking, our activities, our statements, and our repertoire lists.

I would hesitate to say that any committee is more important than another but will discuss, at this time, four committees which are all encompassing to our members—all of whom are teaching in either the private studio, the public [or private] schools, or in conservatories, colleges and universities. There were many indications that NATS, as an organization, should study the professional conditions in each of the settings of the teaching of singing.

The Chairman of Vocal Affairs in the Private Studio is Miss Jessie M. Perry, 1819 Gunderson Lane, Salt Lake City, Utah 84117. This 8-member committee is formed of private teachers from the Atlantic to the Pacific, and from Canada to Texas. What are the problems of the private studio today? What NATS activities would be valuable for our teachers in this setting? We hope that you will take the time to bring your ideas to the attention of Miss Perry. Many ideas expressed in the National Survey are already in the hands of this committee. Significantly, this is the one setting for the teaching of singing which is not partially subsidized. Are any subsidies possible for projects in this area?

The Chairman of Vocal Affairs in the Public Schools [and private schools] committee is Earl William Jones, 1404 Palm Drive, Burlingame, California 94010. This committee is composed of a single representative from each of the eight regions. What are the possible NATS activities which can be undertaken at this time which will stimulate the art of solo singing in the public schools—primarily the high schools? How can NATS assist in establishing a closer rapport between the teacher of singing and the public school teacher? Several members of the committee have had most unusual experiences in this particular area. One of the most interesting was the exploratory project on pre-college voice instruction undertaken by the private voice teachers and vocal instructors of the public schools in Buffalo, N.Y. as reported in the September, 1968 Newsletter. The first word is *exploration*. There are many positive and beneficial things which can be done. Ideas related to this area should be directed to Mr. Jones.

The Chairman of Vocal Affairs in the Conservatories, Colleges, and Universities is Dale K. Moore, Southern Illinois University, Fine Arts' Division, Edwardsville, Illinois 62025. Can the diploma, bachelor, master, and doctor's degree structure be more favorable to the art of singing? If so, how can such changes be brought about? Several problems were defined in the National Survey and have been brought to the attention of this committee. Questions or ideas related to this area should be directed to Mr. Moore.

The above chairmen, with other members, will form a super-committee entitled *Singing in Our Contemporary Society*. We hope that this committee will present its findings in a valuable publication defining the value of the art of singing in this period of the 20th century. These values are basic for our individual teaching efforts. They must be communicated to present students, to future students, to educational institutions, and to society at large.

Nine months were taken to form the National Survey, to obtain replies, to read the replies, and to form, modify, and appoint the committee structure. We hope that much of the work of several committees can be accomplished in time for separate publications for our 25th National Convention in 1969. Of course, the extent of our publications will be dependent not only upon their quality and timeliness but upon monies which will be available for this purpose.

NATS is an educational institution for the teaching of singing. All educational institutions are presently concerned with fundings because none are self-supporting. NATS, if it fulfills its purposes, is no exception. I believe that NATS in its 24 years of growth has attained such *strength* and such *status* that a Gifts and Bequests Campaign can be successfully implemented. We have big plans—we know what we want to do during this administration and will be considering a total program for the next five or ten years. I believe that money will be received because many people are impressed by the good that NATS has already accomplished and by what it can do. I sense that many people will believe NATS is more important or equally important to causes which they are supporting. I believe that many individual altruistic impulses will be stimulated by the extensive NATS activities and that several people will give large gifts and many others will give smaller gifts to NATS. More information about tax deductible gifts will be given later.

Do people love the Art of Singing? Is there any national institution which can or will do more to foster it?

THE AGONY, WHEN THE ECSTASY?*

Instant results can infrequently be realized in any field of endeavor and many times there is an agony when plans are not readily attained. Fortunately, there is always a tomorrow towards which we may plan. These plans based on the experiences of the past can lead us to the ecstasy of attained dreams.

This administration has probed many areas of NATS through the National Survey which was sent to all NATS members and through frequent letters to the Board, to the Regional Governors and to the Past Presidents.

We are basically concerned with the teaching of the ART OF SINGING but there are many administrative factors which must exist to foster and stimulate its growth. Just as in other educational institutions, such as a university, the administration is a big part of any organization which exists primarily for education and research. Also, money plays a large part in the effectiveness of such institutions; many administrations are greatly concerned

*NATS Bulletin, December 1968.

with raising funds—*again, our organization is no exception.* We must think in new dimensions if NATS is going to be the strong institution that our profession and our American society needs.

I had planned to write primarily about tax deductible gifts in this Presidential Message. I will discuss this and other problems with which our organization is faced. Many NATS members have indicated they would like to be better informed on the issues of NATS and would like to take part in the discussions and decisions. It is to this end that these issues are brought to your attention, for they must be evaluated and plans made at the Portland Convention for 1969 and the foreseeable future.

TAX DEDUCTIBLE GIFTS AND BEQUESTS

A source of income, studied before the Detroit Convention, was that of Gifts and Bequests. Such a structure to be *at all effective* would need to be qualified under IRS Code 501 C 3 to receive tax deductible monies. It seems impossible that any organization can give more service for dollars budgeted than ours— this has been made possible by the dedication, overtime work, and economies in the 24-year history of NATS. But, we need to do more and this is dependent upon added monies. In a personal interview with the Internal Revenue Service administrator in Denver working in the tax deductible area, I have found that the only way this can be done is to have a structure incorporated, or unincorporated, which exists *solely* for educational purposes. [It may come as a shock to you, but the IRS would classify our organization as a Business League, and although we are tax exempt under IRS Code 501 C 6, we are not qualified to accept tax deductible gifts and bequests.] The advantage of incorporation is the protection of the officers. Of course, anybody can give money to any project of NATS, but unless that project is qualified under IRS Code 501 C 3, the gift is not tax deductible. A law firm in Chicago has drawn up papers of incorporation of a subsidiary organization structure to be under the power structure of

NATS, the Board of Directors. Payment for these legal services has been guaranteed by your President from sources outside the NATS budget. Such a new concept needs thorough discussion before it is submitted to the membership for vote, possibly during the year of 1969. We need as many members as possible at Portland to assist in these discussions.

INCREASED MEMBERSHIP

It was felt that the new office of Executive Secretary could by a membership campaign increase the total influence of NATS and increase the financial base for NATS projects. Such a campaign was carried on with around 1,000 mailings to non-NATS teachers of singing in this country, based on the directory of the College Music Society. The campaign, near the end of the academic year, did not result in a membership increase, but assisted in keeping the membership level of NATS in 1968 parallel to that of 1967. When the membership did not increase, ways were studied by the Board which might extend our influence and give us a larger financial base by other categories of NATS membership. Such ideas have been discussed as to, [a] whether we should have Student Guilds [which could prepare our students for *affiliate* membership in NATS—currently there are only 121 *affiliate* members]; [b] whether we should open *affiliate* membership to persons who were voice majors in their collegiate work but who are at present working in other fields of musical endeavor; [c] whether we should open the *affiliate* category to coaches and choral directors; or [d] whether we should open our membership to all those who are interested in the art of teaching singing. The correspondence related to this has been a veritable roll-call of the Board of Directors, Past Presidents, and Regional Governors. The "final" decision can not be made on this at Portland according to the procedures defined by the By-Laws, but the issue must be thoroughly discussed so that no miscalculations can occur when a vote is finally taken, possibly by mail, or at the Cleveland Convention, in 1969.

ARTS COUNCILS AND FOUNDATIONS

The National Office was located in New York because there was a feeling that we would be more effective there in relationship to the Arts Councils and Foundations than we would be in Washington, near to government monies. It was felt that an organization of our size would not have sufficient voice to be heard in Washington. Conclusion—to date no monies have been forthcoming from either source. In fact they can not be expected until we have defined worthy projects, their professional need and how they will be implemented. The 26 Educational and Research Committees have been asked to define any possible fundable projects in their areas. Several of these committees will be meeting in Portland.

EXECUTIVE SECRETARY

At the 1967 National Convention the members in the business meeting duly assembled voted to enable the establishment of the Office of Executive Secretary for the National Association of Teachers of Singing. This step had been dreamed of for a long time and plans were laid by some of the very best minds in NATS. James Browning of the National Music Council addressed the Convention on what he felt could be accomplished by an Executive Secretary. To establish this office, additional monies were necessary, so the dues were raised. Both issues were passed with few dissenting votes.

In January, the President and the Advisors met in New York in the office of Mr. Browning, Executive Secretary of the NMC and again discussed the activities of this office. It was felt by those present that the establishment of the office was justified, so office space was secured on 57th Street and a part-time Executive Secretary was employed. The action was duly approved by the Board.

Then began the creation of a new office. Duties assigned were publicity and public relations [various music agencies were informed of the opening of the newly created National Office of NATS], membership drive, working with officers, assisting with Foundation work, formation of a Newsletter, and collecting materials for an Officers' Handbook.

In January the Advisors had proposed to evaluate the National Office by October or November of this year so that future guidelines might be proposed.

One of the most difficult tasks is to perform work without supervision. In fact, a national firm which offers secretarial services will not send their employees to work in a situation that is unsupervised. In all probability, our situation was not right. The Executive Secretary was terminated as of October 31, 1968, because the office was not being conducted as previously requested. [The office is being temporarily maintained until reevaluation occurs in Portland.]

NATS has had deficit budgets in the past, but this year with the new office there is a larger deficit than usual. The organization *does* have money for a rainy day, but there must be considerable restudy to see how the office of an Executive Secretary can be successfully reestablished with current financing.

Several new NATS activities have been probed. Now we must very carefully select those which can be implemented with present methods of funding. These must be selected in relationship to both short and long term goals. Already we have an enlarged committee structure using many new and well-qualified people—we have more teachers working in NATS than ever before.

In much of this work we are on uncharted seas and some of the tides are acting as a restraint to our progress. Nevertheless, we are on our way to making NATS the strongest organization it can be for our profession. These are the things that will be under discussion at Portland.

I think that most of us believe in one of the Great Ideas of Western Man voiced by Bernard Berenson, "All of the Arts, poetry, music, ritual, the visible arts, the theatre must *singly* and *together* create the most comprehensive art of all, a *humanized* society, and its masterpiece, free man."

Surely the teaching of the expressive human vocal instrument must result in one of those arts. We too have our great contribution to make. How can we best do it? I'll see you in Portland!

A New Frontier*

Now that man has reached the Moon, now that man has reached an age which is as yet unnamed, we have before us another frontier which Alexis Carrel has entitled in his book of 1935, *Man, the Unknown*. It takes no imagination to look at our society and realize that in its moment of greatest triumph it is having some of its most dismal failures. How is such a dichotomy possible? How can the wounds of our society be healed?

The name of Galileo is known to all. A peculiar relationship existed between father and son, because the father, Vincenzo Galilei, was a member of the Camerata which gave to the world the greatest musical form of the Renaissance, opera, which in its development gave to the world the Art of Singing. On the other hand, the beginning of modern science is associated with the son, Galileo Galilei and the Leaning Tower of Pisa, where he studied the acceleration of heavy and light falling bodies. He later invented the telescope and supported the theory of Copernicus, the Polish priest, who stated that the stars did not revolve around the earth, but that the earth revolved around the sun and now [December 29, 1968] we can say that Man has revolved around the moon!

According to Dr. Carrel, Galileo in his studies began the separation of the measurable from the unmeasurable, the objective from the subjective and for over 300 years the division has been broadening between the sciences of man and his arts. You and I know that more people are aware of this great disparity than ever before yet there is the greatest confidence that if man can conquer space, he can surely solve the problems of his living. There are many who believe the wounds of man can be healed only through the humanization of a technological society. This is the place of the Arts.

NATS Bulletin, February 1969.

The voyage to the moon must surely hasten a Renaissance of the Arts. Man more than ever before realizes his needs, and he also realizes the nature of his great powers. Not to be overlooked in the flight of Apollo 8 was the enormous synchronization of effort of many men, for the aerospace management groups were without parallel anywhere in the world. An American trademark is teamwork be it in athletic events, in the sciences, or in business. It must also be so in the Arts. Americans have learned that more can be gained by teamwork than by individual effort. This law seems to be more apparent than ever before—work together and the rewards will be more than the sum of the efforts. The year of 1968 in NATS can be considered as being one in which we were tooling up to make our art of singing more important to a technological society through the multiplied efforts of more and more NATS members.

THE NATIONAL CONVENTION

I am sure that we are finding the Portland National Convention on the northwestern frontier of our country to be one of the most exciting of all conventions. This was a result of countless meetings of the convention committees, headed by Robert B. Walls and Melvin Geist, *General Chairmen,* and Clorinda Topping, *Program Chairman.* Incidentally, the administrative careers of Mr. Walls and Mr. Geist total 51 years! These people with all the other chairmen, and their committees, have labored long and diligently. We are deeply indebted to them for this memorable event which they have formed. I am sure all of us have also appreciated the excellent facilities afforded us by the Hilton Hotel here in Portland.

THE BOARD

The **Advisory Committee,** made up of the four Vice Presidents, Secretary, and Treasurer, has been a source of strength to the President as he has attempted to form new procedures concomittant with the implementation of an Executive Secretary, a National Office, and *some* policy changes.

John Thut, *Secretary,* and Chairman of the Committee on Admissions, has been a tower of strength, has always been diligent and punctual in processing new membership applications, in keeping the mailing list up to date, and in the reports prepared by that office.

We have had two treasurers during this year. **Paul Engelstad** handled the finances in a meticulous manner. The fiscal records were so well organized that when he left for service in Vietnam, he was able to transfer the records over to the new treasurer, **Eugene Pence,** in such a manner that the financial affairs of this Association were always operational. Mr. Pence has carried on the work in a highly efficient and business like manner.

Karl Trump, the *Vice President* appointed to act in the absence of the President, has served as his representative at the Music Educators National Conference, and at the International Music Congress. Mr. Trump has stimulated and facilitated the activities of the chapters and through his efforts the number of our chapters has increased to 31, with the newest one being the Champlain Chapter of Upper New York state.

Gean Greenwell, *Coordinator of the NATS Artist Awards,* has, in consultation with the Board, modified the *Singer-of-the Year* contest into the *NATS Artist Awards Auditions.* Much background work has gone into the modifications utilized in these auditions. He has been in communication with the Regional Governors and his contributions have been most effective.

Jean Ludman, *Vice President for Foundations and Arts Councils,* was most active in preparation for the International Music Congress. She is our representative to the National Music Council. She has ably defined for us guidelines which we should use in fundings for NATS projects from the Foundations and Arts Councils.

Vice President **Thomas Abbott** has been in charge of publications and to date the major work has been done on the revision of the NATS Brochure and the Membership Application Form. There may be much more activity in this office related to the 25th Annivrsary Publications.

Hadley Crawford, *Archivist,* has endeavored to begin the

collection of NATS pictures, stories, etc. in the National Office.
He has been diligent in his work as a member of the Admissions
Committee.

Philip A. Duey, *Past President,* has been most helpful in his
knowledgeable letters and perceptive judgement in reply to the
many issues before us. I am deeply indebted to Past President
Duey for penetrating discussions in August, 1967 on the affairs
of NATS so that procedures and approaches could be formulated
for this administration. We all look forward to a *History of Singing* which he will be writing upon his retirement this year. His
administration enabled this administration to take several steps
forward.

The **Regional Representatives** on the Board have been
*William A. Eberl, Victor A. Fields, Eugene Fulton, Stanley John
Hoban, Grace Leslie, Vera Redgrove Neilson, George Newton,
Ohm W. Pauli,* and *Paul W. Peterson.* These persons, with the
officers, have done *yeoman* work in the guidance and legislation
of this administration. They as well as the officers have been
called upon to do heavy work and they have responded with a
remarkable amount of correspondence.

EXECUTIVE SECRETARY

This administration heard the mandate at the 1967 Convention
in Chicago and moved early to establish the office of *Executive
Secretary.* Mrs. Ludman was of great assistance in establishing
the Executive Secretary Office in New York City. From October
16 to the present time, she has most generously given of her time
to go into the New York office several times a week and to
maintain and supervise the activity there. We extend to her our
deepest thanks.

Our efforts to establish this office during the past year have
been quite frustrating, but in the process there is a probability that
we had a certain success in that we had a soul-searching definition of what the office should be—*that a truly national office*
would need a person who had extensive professional experience
in New York and elsewhere in our country. In a rather remark-

able sequence of events we have found and acquired the services of **Martha Moore Smith,** who for the past two years has been the Executive Secretary of the American Harp Society and press officer of the Lake George Festival. As of December 26, she has been in our employ as the Executive Secretary of NATS. This is a part-time position. She is also the press officer of the Saratoga Festival, which you may know is the new Tanglewood of the Philadelphia Orchestra at Saratoga in New York state. Miss Smith has an academic and professional background in American History and Diplomacy, has been press relations officer of the Cincinnati Summer Festival, has worked with NCAC, was its director in the Central Region for two years, and directed its press relations for several years. She was personal representative for Eleanor Steber and at present has several well-known artists for whom she is personal manager. We believe we have in Miss Smith, a person who can be an outstanding Executive Secretary for us. There will be peak seasons of NATS activity and there will be peak seasons of the Saratoga Festival which we hope will synchronize so that work can be performed to everyone's satisfaction.

REGIONAL GOVERNORS

The 1968 administration was unique in that all Regional Governors were different from those in 1966. The Regional Governors have been interested in the action which has taken place at the national level, and the national organization has been interested in the action which has taken place on the regional level. But with our present bylaws, there was not enough liaison between the national and the regional officers. The 1967 Board voted to have the Regional Governors sit in on the 1968 Board meetings so that there could be a better mutual understanding of national and regional activities. Because of this action, Board letters have been sent to the Regional Governors since the first of the year and they are more knowledgeable of the issues before NATS as a national organization. I should like to thank the Regional Governors for their work. They are, *Oliver A. Mogck,*

Gail A. Gingery, Bruce Lunkley, Margaret Souders Enrico, Annemarie Gerts, Paul R. Zeller, Lawrence G. Rickert, and *Ruth Miller Chamlee.* Mr. Rickert replaced Charles Wade Nelson who moved from the Southern Region to the Southwestern Region this fall.

LIEUTENANT GOVERNORS

The lieutenant governors also deserve our sincere thanks and appreciation for their work in assisting the governors and the national organization in keeping in closer touch with the membership, at the local level.

PAST PRESIDENTS

I should also like to commend our **Past Presidents** for their valuable assistance and wise counsel when called upon for an overview of new policies and suggested implementations of ideas for the ongoing of NATS.

COUNCILS AND COMMITTEES

In an endeavor to better know the talent, ideas, and needs of our membership, a National Survey was sent to our members. A total of 672 answers were received to this questionnaire which had a few *quantitative* questions which could be dealt with statistically, and a large number of questions concerning basic ideas related to NATS. It is interesting to note that the percentage return on this Survey was larger than that, to a much simpler survey, sent out by the Music Teachers National Association. This speaks highly of the interest of our members.

From this questionnaire, which was designed as a *"personal interview"* to better know the personnel resources in our organization, an extensive committee structure was built and staffed with the assistance and guidance of the Board of Directors. We hear much about the generation gap. Such does not exist in

NATS since the committee structure bridges all generations from those in the 20's to those in the 80's. The committees are task forces of exploration and there are few areas related to our art which are not being explored at the present time. The committees have been charged with forming statements, possibly bibliographies and procedures related to their areas in vocal education and in vocal research. They have been assigned a date of completion of June 1, 1969. Possibly this is a beginning because further ideas and procedures in vocal education and research should evolve from these initial explorations by the committees. It is hoped that fundable projects can be defined through their efforts.

The research committees will be a part of the Council on Research with **Arthur Schoep,** *coordinator,* and the vocal education committees are a part of the Council on Vocal Education, with **Oren Brown,** *coordinator.* **Victor A. Fields** is editorial consultant of both councils. The administrative committees will act as sub-committees of the Board of Directors.

AD HOC COMMITTEES

Our special thanks go to the members of the **Nominating Committee** headed by *Louis Nicholas,* which nominated the Regional Representatives who will begin their service in 1969; to the **Resolutions Committee,** with *Annemarie Gerts, Chairman;* and to the **Ad Hoc Committee** to study the Fellowship in NATS program, *Oren Brown, Chairman.*

MEMBERSHIP

The dues increase voted in 1967 to allow the implementation of a National Office and an Executive Secretary was well accepted by the membership. It is reflected in an increase of 45 full members, and an increase of 44 affiliate members during the year of 1968. A membership campaign by the National Office is chronicled under Section T of the annual report.

FINANCES

The fiscal year has been changed from the period November 1–October 31 to the period of July 1–June 30, hence our financial report must be in two parts. The July accounting shown in your annual reports indicated a net profit of $3,634.89. The assets in cash funds, bonds and certificates on deposit in savings and loan associations were $30,474.98.

This was rather early in the year and many bills have come in since that time. Recently we have closed out two accounts, totalling $2,456.02 to meet our commitments this year. Dues notices are being mailed within the week and we soon expect to be operating on current finances.

One of the big expenses in 1968 was the implementation of the National Office. The rental was quite high and only recently have we sublet one-half of that space [one of the two rooms] to a lawyer who is active in the arts. This has reduced our annual outlay by $1,800.

With the transfer of several of the duties and responsibilities from the secretary's office and the treasurer's office, to the National Office, there can be a significant saving on honoraria and expenses in the fiscal budget of 1969–1970. [On December 30, 1968, the Board approved a budget from July 1, 1969 to June 30, 1970 of an income of $39,900 and an expenditure of $41,514—a modest deficit of $1,614.]

THE *NATS BULLETIN*

In the National Survey many of our members felt that the most significant part of our organization was the *NATS Bulletin*. It continues to increase in stature, more authors are appearing, and under the dynamic leadership of **Harvey Ringel,** we can expect further exciting developments. His able assistants are **Hadley Crawford,** *Associate Editor;* **Walter Allen Stults,** *Associate Editor;* **Helen Steen Huls,** *Circulation Manager,* and his Editorial

Board, **Bernard Taylor,** *Chairman.* **Hadley Crawford, Edward Harris, Harold C. Luckstone,** and **Walter Allen Stults.**

WORKSHOPS

George Cox has been *Director of Workshops* for a number of years. Four workshops were held in 1968, all with stimulating programs. These were at Texas Technological College. Lubbock, Texas, with Charles Post, *Director,* assisted by Charles Roe and Bruce Lunkley; at Murray State University, with Carl Rogers, *Director;* at Whitworth College, with Leonard Martin, *Director,* and Charles Walton and Margaret Davis, *co-directors;* and at the University of Southern California, with Robert Gurnee, *Director,* with Ruth Miller Chamlee, William Vennard, Jerold Shephard, and Willard Bassett, *co-directors.*

The 20-year history of NATS Summer Workshops has been an interesting one for the vocal art in our country. In an endeavor to broaden the responsibility for forming the NATS summer workshops, a committee was appointed with **Stanley Hoban,** *Chairman.* The workshops are already established for the summer of 1969 and the faculty is being assembled. Presently workshops are being formed for the summer of 1970.

CHAPTERS

The chapters vary in vitality from region to region and vary as the results of the leadership within them. They represent NATS at the grass-roots. We hope that the committee in the *Council on Vocal Education* may be of assistance to the chapters in the direction of their programs. We hope that we may have publicity forms and procedures which can be used for our members, for the students of members, and for the locale in which the chapters exist. Under the direction of **Vice President Karl Trump,** we can expect a continued growth in the vitality of the chapters.

NATS ARTISTS AWARDS

There has been discussion the past few years concerning the title of SOTY for our national auditions. After several communications with the Board, the title was changed to NATS **Artists Awards.** These auditions are one of our most important activities in terms of encouraging our students and in our public relations. They are a means of attracting attention to the vitality of NATS. They have been most successfully implemented by **Vice President Gean Greenwell.**

There has been increasing success in chapter, state and regional auditions. I must say that the Southwestern Region has had great success with a total of 300 to 400 singers participating, and approximately 600 registered in attendance. It is hoped that the national organization can assist in stimulating more auditions in areas where guidance is needed.

FELLOW IN NATS

The **Fellow in NATS** program although having five modifications and editions of its structure, did not become a successful endeavor for our organization. An *Ad Hoc Committee* of **Oren Brown,** *Chairman,* **Bruce Foote,** and **Dale Moore** were appointed to study further procedures in this area. A report has been made concerning its implementation as a graduate endeavor in colleges and universities.

THE DEPARTED

Sixteen NATS members have left this fellowship for that of the Beyond. Will you please stand and remain standing a few moments after I have finished reading their names: Donald Armand, Berthold Busch, Marie Antoinette Comeau, Loren D. Davidson, Vern DeLaney, Lucille Diano, G. Wade Ferguson, Carolyn Beeson Fry, Adam Edmund Furgiuele, Cecile Jacobson,

Lucile Lippincot, D'Alton McLaughlin, Bertyne NeCollins, John Wilbur Seale, Edgar Milton Wells, Harry Robert Wilson— Thank you. Please be seated.

SUMMARY

In summation, I think we can all look back on 1968 as a year of great change in our organization; at the new structures that have resulted in two active Councils for Research, and Vocal Education; at the involvement of approximately 150 members in various committees; at the growth of our membership and its future potential; at the stimulating auditions for our students at all levels; at the closer fellowship of our officers; and at the great future that is before us as we prepare for our 25th Anniversary Year and all that it portends. The splendid cooperation from each of you is deeply appreciated by your President, who proposes to continue to bend every effort in your behalf, to the Art of Teaching Singing, and **to music.**

**Since singing is so good a thing,
I wish all men would learne to singe.**

—William Byrd, 1588.*

In the almost four centuries since William Byrd's statement as to why men should "singe," no one has better stated the reasons. *But* in this age of historical transformation we need to be aware that the *values* of singing are *increasing* and that teachers of singing are faced with *responsibilities* and *opportunities* never faced before. *The value of the individual is at stake.*

At the time of Byrd, 400 million men were on the face of the earth; now, there are close to four billion! Historian Arnold Toynbee states the heart of the meaning of the population explo-

NATS Bulletin, May–June 1969.

sion thus, "The issue is a religious one in that it raises the questions, 'What is the true end of Man? Is it to populate the Earth with the maximum number of human beings—or is it to enable human beings to lead the best kind of a life that the spiritual limitations of human nature allow?' "

Surely our profession exists to raise the quality of human life. One of the priority skills in our culture is the use of the human voice by which most of our communications take place—we may call ourselves teachers of singing, or we may call ourselves teachers of voice. Both pertain to the use of the same wonderful instrument as a means of communication. The teaching of singing and of voice should be inextricably interwoven. Our efforts should be directed both to stardom on the musical stage, and success in daily life—as teachers, preachers, salesmen, legislators or business men through the use of the vocal instrument.

It is to the auxiliary benefits of singing to which I desire to address myself at this writing. With the population increase and the resultant depersonalizing forces of modern society, the importance of singing increases by giving an individual a greater value in today's society. Singing brings about an aesthetic, social, psychological and physiological transformation of the personality. The voice is never the same after vocal study. The laughter is more exuberant, there is greater poise of the individual, and the qualities of the voice forever changed—the personality has been augmented.

Ours is more than an intellectual society for we know that the quality of voice has a subliminal effect on people. Each of us has been moved by a speaking voice because of the unique quality of its sound. It may have said the same thing as another, but its color and delivery carried a greater depth of meaning. We are affected many times a day in this way whether we are aware of it or not, and we affect others in the same manner.

Our culture is extremely aware of the visual attributes of personality, so we have hair stylists, tailors, etc., but do we have groomers of the voice? Political, legal, artistic, religious, and business leaders in our society, take great care of their visual images. What do they do to maintain their images of vocal communication? We have heard of actors and of political figures who have been under the care of vocal therapists. Why only the corrective approach? Why can we not concern ourselves with extending the communicative techniques of the human voice which are a direct consequence of the teaching of singing?

The above results can come about when the teacher of singing is concerned with obtaining more vocal colors, a wider pitch range, a broader dynamic range and an improved diction by which the great poetry of a Goethe, and the great music of a Schubert can be communicated to an audience. Are these not similar qualities needed by all in our present society? William Byrd said it more simply, "It is the best means to procure a perfect pronunciation, and to make a good Orator."

Cannot human values be increased as participants in this art rather than as spectators? We are at a time when too much of our entertaining is done by others. What is the best idiom of artistic participation? Why not participate with an instrument which we carry with us all our lives? Why not study singing? "It doth strengthen all parts of the brest, and doth open the pipes." We can say that singing helps stay the ravages of time and that the use of the lungs, thorax, intrinsic and extrinsic muscles of the larynx has a life-giving effect for all of us. Singing is "good to preserve the health of Man."

As individual teachers of singing, one thought presents itself in relationship to our own singing. If a teacher is not currently engaged in a singing career, perhaps he should nevertheless continue his own singing, whether it is in the realm of vocal repertoire, or purely as a matter of keeping the voice healthy through daily vocalization. Are we not better teachers by reason of some form of active and personal practice? We too should gain further self-realization in this spirit-invigorating process?

It has been said that one is as old as his ligaments—those sinews which hold a body together. Probably the same thing can be said of a society. As we read the head-lines today we may feel that the "lunatics are running the asylum" and that our civilization is being dismembered. We, of the majority, must be resolute. The minority of our society shall not "break our bonds asunder.'' Or positively stated, we shall endeavor in every way to strengthen our kinship with one another. Many observers feel the generation gap is due to the younger generation having been given everything but individual attention. Where can better attention be given than in the one-to-one relationship of a singing lesson? Outside of your family and clergy, who has had more influence on your life than a teacher of singing? Where was your individual worth increased more than in your singing lessons?

And ''ligament'' is the basis of the word *religion*—that which ties, that which binds. Singing is an art which has come to us from the scholae cantorum of the past. Singing has historically been a part of the religions in our civilization; and religions have been used by governments to unite states. Thus, music has historically been a part of the cohesive force of a society. Singing must continue to do so and must become more powerful in the ''religious'' part of our mission. Eras ago, William Byrd pointed out that ''The better a voyce is, the meeter it is to honour and serve God therewith: and the voyce of man is chiefly to be imployed to that ende.''

We must think of the teaching of singing in a very broad spectrum. If we train only performers and spectators, we have not taught as much of the human values of singing and of voice as the present requires. We must keep apace with our times and our profession must be increasingly vital in the future.

NATS with its growth in personnel and financial resources is an agency which can assist all in realizing these opportunities.

The Heart Is Wiser Than the Schools

—Milton, *Comus**

The human voice is an instrument of the senses and attuned to the senses. By evolution, it is the most expressive instrument known

*NATS Bulletin, October 1969.

to man, both on the creating and receiving ends, for the voice communicates the value of our emotional utterances and the ear, acoustically and psychologically, receives the transmitted message. Civilization cannot function without the human voice, for without the oral word, man's basic communications would be no higher than the animals. Statesmen, using their voices as orators, have created great states. Religious leaders have used the human voice to give us the great religions. The voice has been used to arouse men to combat and soldiers have sung their songs marching into battle. Great social changes have occurred with such songs as "La Marseillaise," the "Battle Hymn of the Republic," and "A Mighty Fortress Is Our God." Characteristically they were sung with great fervor. *They were all sung in the vernacular!*

Singing in our time must have the greatest significance and meaning. Without a thorough understanding of the meaning of a song, there cannot be the impassioned enunciation and vocal inflections which reach the senses. To do this most effectively, we must sing in our own language! There are many folk songs— American, English, Irish, Scottish. There are many art songs originally written in English which have been overlooked. It is time that they and new ones are included in our repertoires. Many fine songs by Vaughan Williams, Quilter, Sandford, Griffes, Carpenter, Bantock, Ives, etc. will be found to be of high quality when reexamined. We have been short-changed on the value of our own language in singing. The typical four-languaged recital needs to be reevaluated. Perhaps the format was valid at one time. Is it still? Would German, French and Italian art songs be more effective if sung in English translations, at least some of the time? Are we in a position where we should consider the tastes of our audiences as did Rolf Liebermann, Intendant of the Hamburg Opera, who polled those who attended that theater as to whether Italian opera should be given in German or Italian. There were enough who wanted each, so he cast the Italian operas bilingually, alternating German and Italian performances.

We should consider doing the same in our studios for several reasons. A singer can best color his voice in a language he understands. Admittedly, singing is a modification of a spoken language. Why not approach it as a modification of the student's own language? The singer must sing that which he feels to be expressive—it will usually be in his own language. Why not sing at least some of the art songs in performance in a language understood by most of those in the audience? Even sacred services traditionally held in Latin are now being given in the vernacular. That which has been lost in mysticism has more than been gained in understanding. Can we not revitalize our art by exploring a more direct means of communication?

COLOR

Is our singing going to be monochromatic or polychromatic—of one color or of many colors? Music history, at least until the time of Haydn, is largely that of vocal music. As teachers of singing we should be more aware of our heritage. The "schools" of musicology and the recording studios have effected a standardization of styles to such an extent that singers are sounding and performing more and more alike. We all realize that until Thomas Edison first recorded singing, there had never been a duplicate performance of a song or an aria in the world. In fact it was not desired. The quality of a singer was evaluated by his ability to *change* interpretations from performance to performance. There was no standardized performance unless the word "changed" is used as being the adjective for "standardized." The singer either went into flights of song or of unique expressivity of the word. Each performance of a song was an improvisation—a newly created "role." The "heart," although well-schooled, directed the singing. History tells us that "the senses" did not "always reason well," but at least the performances were spontaneous and had meaning. Let us again have strong personalities in song.

Color can be given in many ways, by altering the brightness and darkness of tone, the stress of vowel, the stress of consonant, the inflection, etc.—all seemingly occurring "intuitively." The great singers of a century ago were so thoroughly schooled that the improvisation which occurred on the spur of the moment was already a part of the pattern of their vocal instrument. *Schools certainly have their places—they must assist in forming the vocal instrument and in highlighting the meaning of a song.* Basically, one's song is powerless without the meaning of the word. When one is singing in a foreign language, one must know exactly the meaning of each word sung. Mathilde Marchesi insisted that her students had to have the exact meaning of the word written above the foreign word sung. This principle is an eternal truth and must be stressed continually with our students.

Instrumentalists are having a day of great facility but such a conductor as Eric Leinsdorf stresses that instrumental music cannot be well played unless the artists know the song literature which is the basis for the instrumental. Musicologists have treated very lightly the folk and solo vocal literature upon which serious music is based. The accents, climaxes and melodies of serious music are derived from the linguistic expression of man. He simply is conditioned to linguistic communication, and the further music departs from its language basis, the less interested audiences become. Why are the best symphonic conductors from the pits of the opera houses—because they know language and drama as they relate to music.

As we note the subjects of the songs of the vocal masterpieces, we find songs of adventure, of love, of mystery, of other-worldliness, of communication with the Infinite, of the conflict between good and evil, of relating the individual and his environment, and of the struggle within one's self. Are not these subjects of interest today? They must be, for they appear daily in the newspapers and magazines, and on radio and television. They are also found in the Dead Sea Scrolls and, of course, are not dead today. Man's interests have changed very little in the two thousand years since the time of Christ, in the three and one-half centuries since the Camerata, in the century and a half since Schubert and Rossini, or in the century since Brahms and Wagner.

There is no doubt that today we have placed a higher stress on the intellectual, and that we have played down the importance of the "heart." In this decade, serious composers are not setting the above mentioned subjects to song. Perhaps their musical language does not fit these subjects.

The recital halls are partially full today. Does this prove that the vocal masterpieces are "irrelevant?" I would rather think that they have been *performed* irrelevantly. I have heard it said that today's performers have a higher level of mediocrity than twenty and thirty years ago. We must set ourselves to a more meaningful performance in halls which are acoustically fitting for the voice. Many modern American auditoriums are too large for the intimate art of solo singing which should be heard in halls seating less than 1500 people.

Singing is a unique art form. Just because one person prefers one art is no reason another person should have the same preference. We should promote and organize audiences for our particular art. The "Friends of Music" idea has proven to be valid. Why not form our own organizations such as "Amici di Musica"— Friends of Lyric Poetry. Why not begin small? From twelve apostles came a movement which changed the Roman world. Our numbers may be relatively small, but our influence can be ever greater in our technological society if we reclaim our heritage of performance practices and the truth of dramatic utterance through the musical instrument of the human voice.

Breathe life into your songs, let them glow with incandescence, let there be spirit, let there be light. We are all participating in a glorious and creative art!

YOUR WORLD OF SINGING*

What did you think when you stood inside the enormous geodesic dome of the United States Exhibit at Expo '67 in Montreal? Did you say, "what a place to sing!"—"would Brunhilde have liked this!" or "look at all those facets!" Interestingly enough, that form was not invented until the passage of over 5,000 years of human history. It was a spherical phenomenon. You could see

---

NATS Bulletin, December 1969.

the whole. You could see the parts. How long will it take Man to see the *whole* as well as the parts? Will it be another millenium? I doubt it, because on all sides we are beginning to see things in *both* entities. Our art of teaching is seriously limited if we cannot see the "forest because of the trees" [or the "trees because of the forest"]

Are all parts of an art or body equally valuable? No. We all well remember the thrill of the first "successful" heart transplant. A vital organ was transplanted to sustain the life of a person. We know from that history that there is an interplay between a part and the whole [in this case, the body]. The "new" vital organ enabled a life to be sustained but eventually the whole rejected the part and with that rejection, perished.

Certain organs are vital to life—the heart, the brain, spinal column, etc. Certain aspects of the vocal art are necessary for self-fulfillment in singing—drive, musicianship, rhythm, memory, etc., and certain things have been necessary in an organization of singing teachers to bring them to their Silver Anniversary with its largest and most active membership. One senses in the conventions, workshops, and chapter meetings a magnificent spirit which is released in members by our art. René Dubos in his Pulitzer Prize winning book, *So Human an Animal* says that "We know almost nothing about the process through which every man converts his innate potentialities to his individuality." We may not know too much about how it is done, but teachers of singing are all aware of the release of energy and enthusiasm when it occurs. And what excitement for both the teacher and student! No wonder so many in our profession are such avid students through all the years of their teaching careers.

Creativity is forced upon us in our work, for as Dubos states, "Each human being is unique, unprecedented and unrepeatable." "We recognize him as a unique person by his voice, his facial expression, the way he walks—and even more by his creative responses to his surroundings and events." How many professions touch *all* of the above mentioned aspects of personality: the *voice*, the *facial expression*, the *walk*, and *creative response?* Ours is one of the few. Ours is almost a "called" profession with its value far above its renown. We are miners of talent. Some teachers craft their talent in one way, others in their own manner. We are all working within the same sphere of teaching singing, but each of us has certain facets which form "his world" of teaching singing.

It is the purpose of NATS to continually assist in enlarging and clarifying each person's "vocal world." We can help in several ways. Basically the organization can generate spirit and stimulate know-how. No teacher has ever known too much about the teaching of singing. A knowledge supplementing an intuition is surely the most effective way of forming an art. The *NATS Bulletin* is the sole journal of technical and philosophical offerings related to the teaching of singing.

Certainly NATS auditions are a most important part of our organization for "hope" is a great motivator of action. Man learned from the Greeks to aspire without limit. Our auditions allow our students to reach and to sometimes succeed. As Jenkin Lloyd Jones said, "Man was not made for fulfillment, he was made for hope. He was designed to reach and usually fail. He really doesn't want to win all of the time." The competitiveness of our society is such that the winners are the ones who have a high level of frustration and keep going. Those who have a low level of frustration are not highly rewarded in spirit.

Ours is an endeavor which requires great courage, faith, and dedication. Voltaire was surely speaking of our art when he said, "Perfection is attained by slow degrees: it requires the hand of time." And during that time our work has its daily rejuvenating rewards! So, it is our destiny and joy to mine the greatest talent of all—human individualism.

Why is the individual so important? Because he is the basis of our western civilization. We cannot have leaders without individuality. We cannot have leaders unless there is a high development of personality. There are human arts, and ours, the art of singing, pertains to many of the most important personality and communicative traits of all.

We have many prophets of doom who are about willing to cash in the chips for the human species. Because of their spectacular observations, they are able to get press coverage. Their statements are oversimplified. They see a facet and not a whole. Man is a very adaptive creature and his way of living and his arts are changing. Man will endure, says René Dubos, because he is able to make decisions. There is hope for the future. Our art is based on Man's hopes, aspirations, and expressions. It is needed more now than ever before and all of us *must join the Crusade* for the betterment of Man in his fractured, technological society.

THE PRESIDENT'S REPORT, 1969*

Ladies and Gentlemen: It seems to me that the best time to state the purposes of an administration is at its close because at that time the issues have become more clearly defined! The keynote address in Chicago by Louis Nicholas was **Renewal.** This is a psychological need of men and of societies.

I stated in Chicago in 1967 that I hoped that my service would be of value to all members of NATS. To attempt this we formed a National Survey with the assistance and guidance of the Board of Directors to better know our members, their talents, their interests, and their problems. We hoped we could serve and involve people in present activities, and some which did not yet exist. Our objective was *involvement* and *renewal.*

Approximately 700 answers were received to the Survey. We did find outstanding talent of all ages, but especial care was taken that younger members should be involved in activities because from them will come our leaders of the next decades.

We had a special anniversary to commemorate so we had an objective of bringing statements and lists up to date. This was brought about by a special council and committee structure. Many reports have already been made through the *NATS Bulletin* and *InterNos.* Others will be forthcoming.

Many members felt a directory of members would be most valuable for use in referral of students in this period of high mobility of population. This was felt to be most important to the

*NATS Bulletin, February–March 1970.

private teacher. I encourage your use of this booklet which can be kept up to date by the changes listed in *InterNos*.

The private teacher has been a special concern of this administration because there is the feeling, shared by many, that singing in its highest art can exist only through the added years of training which extend beyond that of the time spent in conservatories, colleges and universities. Also, we rely very heavily on the work of the private teacher during the early years and during the time of collegiate work. We must do the best we can to keep the art of singing developing in the private studio.

I was thrilled at your response to the keynote address of Earl William Jones because he seemed to express your inmost feelings concerning the value and worth of our art. If we sense that the arts are in danger; if we realize that the clock can not be turned back and that it is our responsibility to keep things going [not only for our art but for the survival of our society], then we can more easily hold and nurture that which we cherish.

I wish to thank many, many people for overtime work and for their willingness to serve. We are dealing with the dynamics of change. And change is motion. Motion is a result of energy, the laws of which Newton stated over two centuries ago. We must concern ourselves with supplying the energy towards *guiding and speeding the motion in the direction we desire*. To do otherwise is to drift upon the tide. The currents of the tides are against us in many ways, but wise sailors know how to use the tides and the energies of a ship to best advantage. This, as I perceive it, is the purpose of this national organization of teachers of singing—to direct the ship of our vocal art.

Never have we had more "know-how" than at this time when your wishes and desires have been known and when present officers, regional governors, and past presidents have been involved in the sailing of this ship. The spirit has been exhilarating and I believe our pulses are high as we face the future. I believe we have a vibrant association and that there will be many, many teachers of singing who will desire to be where the action is. We have had a marvelous team and I want to specifically thank those who have been of great assistance to this administration.

THE NATIONAL CONVENTION

I am sure that we are finding the Silver Jubilee Convention to be one of the most exciting of all conventions. This was a result of careful planning under the direction of **Irvin Bushman,** *Convention Chairman,* **Melvin Hakola,** *Convention Co-Chairman;* and **Howard Hatton,** and **Karl Trump,** *Program Co-Chairmen.* Their many meetings, with the North Central Ohio Chapter have evolved for us a Convention which will, without doubt, stand as one of our great landmarks. We are all most grateful to them for their outstanding services.

THE BOARD

The President's Advisory Committee, made up of the four vice-presidents, secretary and treasurer, has been a source of great strength as the President has attempted to functionalize the Office of Executive Secretary and to make NATS a stronger organization for our times.

John Thut, *Secretary,* and *Chairman of the Committee on Admissions,* has been a tower of strength. He has been diligent and punctual in processing new membership applications, in keeping the mailing list up-to-date and in the reports prepared by that office. I have found his services in this critical office to be invaluable as have past administrations.

Eugene E. Pence, *Treasurer,* has efficiently formulated the financial records in such a manner that we can more easily make monthly and yearly comparisons of NATS fiscal matters. Our finances are secure in his hands.

Karl Trump, *Vice-President of Field Activities,* has done an outstanding piece of work with the stimulation of chapter and regional activities. We look forward to a strong administration under his guidance during the next two years.

Gean Greenwell, *Vice-President and Co-ordinator of the NATS Artist Awards,* on the basis of a study of three adjudication procedures at the Portland Convention has, with Board approval, instituted a new technique of evaluation which we hope will lead us to our best possible auditions. The activities of past winners indicates the NATS Artist Awards are one of our most successful endeavors.

Jean Ludman, *Vice-President for Foundations and Arts Councils,* has been our representative to the meetings of the National Music Council and is our adviser on what is occurring in the relationship of our government and the arts. Her guidance has been greatly appreciated by the officers and the Board.

Vice-President **Thomas Abbott** has been in charge of publications other than the *NATS Bulletin, InterNos,* and the Silver Anniversary publications. His efforts in this function are highly respected.

Hadley Crawford, *Archivist,* has begun a collection of NATS pictures, stories, and memorabilia in the National Office. He has also been diligent in his work as a member of the Admissions Committee.

Philip A. Duey, *Past President,* has served as an Ad Hoc member of the Advisers Committee and as such has been most helpful in his perceptive judgment related to the many issues before us. I am evermore grateful for the in-depth discussion with him in 1967 on the affairs of NATS which enabled planning procedures for the past two years. His administration brought about structural changes which challenged this administration to take several steps forward, including the establishment of the Office of the Executive Secretary.

Directors of the Board without portfolio have been William A. Eberl, Victor A. Fields, Stanley John Hoban, Vera Redgrove Neilson, George Newton, Ohm W. Pauli, Paul W. Peterson, Florence Mildred Russell, and Mary Wolfman. These directors, with the officers, have worked arduously both in correspondence and meetings in the guidance and legislation of the past two years.

EXECUTIVE SECRETARY

With **Martha Moore Smith,** the National Office has been functionalized for the first time. Through advisers' meetings in

Chicago and New York, liaison has been established and activities expedited so that we have a central office efficiently working in behalf of NATS. The specific duties of this half-time office are chronicled in the Annual Report which is in your hands. This has been one of the major activities of this administration.

There has been a feeling by many that there should be a closer relationship between the national and regional officers so that there can be a better mutual understanding of the total panorama of NATS as a national organization. The regional governors have received Board letters and have been invited to attend the Board sessions, both in Portland and Cleveland. They have proven to be of valuable assistance to the Board in its deliberations. I should like to thank the regional governors for their work. They are: Oliver A. Mogck, Gail A. Gingery, Bruce Lunkley, Margaret Souders Enrico, Annemarie Gerts, Paul R. Zeller, Lawrence Rickert, and Ruth Miller Chamlee.

LIEUTENANT GOVERNORS

The lieutenant governors also deserve our sincere thanks and appreciation for their work in assisting the regional governors and the national organization in keeping in close touch with NATS at the local level. Their effort in recruiting new members is most important.

PAST PRESIDENTS

The men who have headed administrations which have brought NATS to its Silver Anniversary have received Board letters and, as in the past, have been invited to Board deliberations. We are deeply grateful to them for their wise counsel and assistance. They are most knowledgeable of our aims and objectives and are presently involved with a study of the By-Laws to survey the needs which might propitiously be incorporated.

COUNCILS AND COMMITTEES

The councils with their committees have been task forces of exploration. There are few areas of our art which have not been studied. The committees were charged with forming statements, possible bibliographies and procedures related to their areas in vocal education and in vocal research. They were also charged with defining any fundable projects which became evident in their area. **Oren Brown,** *Coordinator of the Council on Vocal Education,* and **Arthur Schoep,** *Coordinator of the Council on Research* have done outstanding work expediting the activities of member committees. Reports of the following committees have been or will soon be published:

- Singing in Contemporary Society, Earl William Jones, *chairman;*
- Vocal Affairs in the Private Studio, Jessie May Perry, *chairman;*
- Vocal Clinics, Robert T. Gurnee, *chairman;*
- The Solo Voice and Choral Singing, Paul Peterson, *chairman;*
- Opera, Opera Workshop, Musical Theatre, Muriel Wolf, *chairman;* and
- Interdisciplinary Research, John W. Large, *chairman.*

Silver Anniversary song-lists presently available were formed by the following committees:

- Art Song—German: Oscar McCullough, *chairman;*
- Art Song—Italian: Ruth Lakeway, *chairman;*
- Art Song—Scandinavian and Finnish: Hazel Peterson, *chairman;*
- Repertoire for Young Voices: Helen Steen Huls, *chairman;*
- Sacred Song: Walter Martin, and Oratorio: Jay W. Wilkey, *chairmen;* and
- Voice and Instruments: Donald Hoiness, *chairman.*

The French Art Song list will soon be available. Charles Post is chairman of that committee.

AD HOC COMMITTEES

Our special thanks go to the members of the **Nominating Committee,** headed by Louis Nicholas, which has nominated the officers for the 1970–1971 administration, to the **Resolutions Committee,** with Barbara Kinsey and Exine Bailey, Mrs. Bailey reporting, and to the **Ad Hoc Committee** to study the **Fellowship in NATS Program,** Oren Brown, *chairman.*

MEMBERSHIP

Mailings concerning NATS as the only national organization existing for teachers of singing were made to non-NATS member voice teachers in the College Music Society Directory. Also ''Invitations to Membership'' were included in *the NATS Bulletins* of February and May 1969. Through efforts directed by the Board and many NATS agencies, the membership has increased by over 150 members during the 1969 calendar year.

FINANCES

One of the benefits of the Adviser's meetings this year pertained to the evaluation of a unit cost accounting procedure for the national conventions and workshops. This is necessary for year-to-year comparison.

We had feared that our expenditures would exceed our available cash at year's end, however, income was such that we have been able to get through the end of the year without delving into our investments.

We need monies beyond those from dues, advertising, and the sale of materials to increase the influence of our organization. We are hopeful that we will soon have a procedure for receiving tax deductible gifts and bequests. It is our belief that there are members who would like to see their influence on the Art of Singing extended into the future through this facet of NATS.

Expenses have been quite heavy this year with the two meetings of the Advisers, and other meetings of some of the officers which were called to expedite the activities of NATS. We believe the money was well spent and that we have a financially shipshape organization to meet the modest forseeable future needs of our organization.

NATS BULLETIN AND INTER NOS

One of the primary interests of present and past administrations has been to elevate *the NATS Bulletin* to the status of a learned journal. Such has been activated by the creation of *Inter Nos,* the newsletter to members concerning organizational activities. This has allowed earlier announcements of workshops and conventions and should increase attendance at these events. Also, *InterNos* has become a mouthpiece for the officers which should give members a better understanding of NATS activities. The work of more authors is appearing in the *NATS Bulletin* under the dynamic leadership of **Harvey Ringel,** *Editor.* His able assistants are Hadley Crawford, Walter Allen Stults, Bernard Taylor, Edward Harris, Harold Luckstone, and Helen Steen Huls. We are deeply appreciative of their efforts. After this Anniversary Year, *InterNos* will return to the newsletter format of September 1968.

WORKSHOPS

The workshops have come of age, literally, with the 21st series being held during the summer of 1969. **Stanley John Hoban,** *Chairman of Workshops,* and the members of that committee, George Newton, Jerold Shepherd, Walter James, and Ward Abusamra, have worked diligently to make the workshops more vital and interesting through long-term planning. I believe this was a major factor of the successes this summer. We are grateful to the directors and co-directors who staged the workshops for their vision and hard work. They are as follows: Ward Abusamra and Mary Wolfman of the *Rhode Island University Workshop;* Orcenith Smith and Margret Kommel of the *Wittenburg University Workshop;* George D. Lewis, John Lester, and Jane Havener Lea of the *University of Montana Workshop;* Thomas D. Abbott and Helen Steen Huls of the *St. Cloud State College Workshop;* and Lyneer C. Smith and Jessie May Perry of the *Weber State College Workshop.*

May I encourage each of you to attend at least one of the five workshops this coming summer which will be held in Portales, New Mexico; Eugene, Oregon; Los Angeles, California; Pittsburgh, Pennsylvania; and Carrolton, Georgia. More inspiration, discovery and fellowship for all. The dates will be announced in the January *InterNos.*

THE DEPARTED

Eleven NATS members have passed from this fellowship to that of the Beyond. Will you please stand and remain standing for a moment after their names are read: Ludwig Bergman, Lillian M. Cooper, Carl E. Duckwall, Mynard Jones, Edward L. Kemp, Katherine G. McDonald, Myrtle Louise Ornes, Eve Roine Richmond, Ellis E. Snyder, Earl Tanner, Evelyn Wienke.

SUMMARY

We hope that we have activated our organization so that it is capable of change, renewal and responsiveness. Surely an organization which develops to the fullest its human resources, that removes obstacles to individual fulfillment, life-long yearning and self-discovery is worthy of an esteemed place in society.

Statements have been made that singing is losing its relevance in our society. We believe this is an unpleasant illusion as the result of a constant tendency to over-simplify. The art of singing has existed for centuries and has varied from culture to culture and from period to period. We may be entering a cycle of greater participation as in the pre–19th Century. There are phases of all artistic endeavor. We need to be stimulating new "song" forms and new sounds for our art. We need to do our part in the stimulation of genius in the area of vocal literature. And, we will probably need to be content with the role of indirect cause of this type of phenomena. The effect may be immediate or it may be remote. This influence should come from both the individual members as well as by our National Association. History will surely record that singing continued as one of the important arts of man.

In the words of Herbert Witherspoon, who may be considered a pre-founder of NATS, "Let us take up our task as we find it, ready with a strong love of our art to try simply and honestly to clear the way for those who are to follow."

In conclusion, may I thank you for the honor of having been the captain of your ship. May it sail on and on, on and on.

Appendix H: The Singer's Diction

The teacher of singing is faced with many, many challenges—
the forming of an individual voice for each of his students, the
appropriate use of repertoire for each voice, the teaching of individualized diction of songs in several languages and the stimulation of vocal artistry. Few fields are larger in scope and more
challenging than that faced by the serious teacher of singing.

One of the most persistent problems is that of diction in the
four principal languages of singing. Molding the pronunciation of
lyrics of the basic repertoire of the *young singer* may be relatively
easy but the need for teaching the same pronunciation of the same
songs to students over a period of years can easily become an
activity of devitalization.

Another problem is involved with the song needs of the
advanced singer. Each individual voice will need its own repertoire. A teacher may not use a certain song for years, but when
the time comes, that song must be taught correctly and efficiently
as a language. Furthermore, the burden of proof is upon the
teacher. He, and he alone, must form the diction, for teachers of
languages in the classes of our colleges and universities have
little time to serve the individual language needs of students of
singing.

By means of the text, *Phonetic Readings of Songs and Arias,*
an oral assignment can now be made before actual singing is
begun. Many teachers recommend the learning of a lyric prior to

Reprinted from the *NATS Bulletin* [now *Journal*], February 1964. This
article is related to *Phonetic Readings of Songs and Arias* by Coffin,
Errolle, Singer, and Delattre. It offers a timely discussion of a valid part
of the singer's development from the beginner to the professional.
(*Mildred W. Coffin*)

the preparation of a song as being an efficient memory device. A fabled teacher was known for her desire to have her students *read aloud* the poetry of their songs early in the day as an inflective and interpretative device for preparing songs and arias for performance. It was with the above concept in mind that this book of phonetic transcriptions was formed as a reader.

Many students desire to hurry the process of learning to sing. Time may be gained in the area of language work faster than in other areas. And, if a language can be learned from the first without the necessity of correction of mistakes, learning can indeed be fast, and the attention of the teacher directed to the use of the language art as it relates to the use of vocal resources and interpretation. Instrumentalists usually observe long practice hours but the singer's work must be accomplished in a shorter length of time because of the nature of the vocal instrument. With the procedure of learning the diction of songs and arias through phonetics more work can be accomplished in a limited time and a larger and more dependable repertoire should evolve.

The *singer* today is faced with the problem that his art is more international than ever before. Hundreds of American singers are active in Europe. With the advent of fast transportation a singer is frequently called upon to sing in several countries and several languages within a very short time. Furthermore, he is expected to sing each language with standardized diction. The singer who performs only in our country is still faced with the singing of various languages, and wherever he appears can be relatively sure that several persons in his audience will know correct pronunciation of languages due to our traveling, sophisticated culture and to the enormous influence of recordings by world renowned artists. Now, as never before, the student must sing well and with correct diction.

In traveling through such countries as Italy, Germany, France, England, and the United States, one is constantly aware of the changing of language within each nation. Almost any area of a country may be represented by our language teachers. But as far as singing is concerned, there are standards to be used and the standards are subtly changing—witness the continued revisions of Webster dictionaries in this country. Suffice it to say that the transcriptions found in this text have been made according to the most recent techniques of phonetic transcriptions and accepted standards of language. The phonetics used are those of the International Phonetic Association of which at least half of the symbols are already known to the singer. With the memorization of the remaining symbols the pronunciation of the basic lyric repertoire will be easily available to every singer. A clear statement concerning the symbols of each of the languages is found in the foreword of each of the divisions.

The Italian standard, used by Italian radio announcers and actors, is Zingarelli—*Vocabulario della Lingua Italiana.* Although this reference does not use the International Phonetic Alphabet, pronunciation is clearly marked and is in this text transferred to I.P.A. symbols with few changes. A few exceptions of the unaccented e and o vowels have been transcribed open [Ɛ-*eh* and ɔ] for singing, however, *the authors hope that these exceptions do not serve as license to open all other unaccented e and o vowels.*

The German standard used has been Siebs—*Deutsche Hochsprache,* the use of which has been further strengthened by the reference, *Deutsche Phonetik,* by Martens. These sources differ from earlier use of I.P.A. transcriptions primarily in the treatment of diphthongs.

Haus	is now	ao	rather than au
Eis	is now	ae	rather than aɪ
Leute	is now	ɔø	rather than ɔɪ

French, the most standardized of the languages, is written in open syllabification for better flow of the language in this text, designed as a phonetic reader. French is essentially a language of open syllables. In this reference the closing consonant has been transposed to the right, becoming a part of the consonant cluster at the beginning of the next syllable. Americans have the tendency of closing the syllables, thus anglicizing the French. The standard for the French transcription has been Fouché's *Traité de Prononciation Française.*

For the experienced singer who kinesthetically knows the following modifications or for the teacher of singing or coach with a sensitive ear, the phenomenon herein described is probably already observed but not categorized. For the untrained singer, the teacher of singing, and coach with limited experience, a *definition of vowel modification* is probably necessary in a book of phonetic transcription to avoid a forced, uniform phonetic forming of vowels on all pitches of all voices. Such inflexible treatment might impair the musicality, expressiveness and survival of many voices.

Italian teachers have long preferred the vowel *a* for the vocalization and training of the singing voice. There is a fundamental reason why this is true which is also related to the modification of other vowels. In short, the phenomenon is as follows:

1. Vowels are caused by two cavities, the cavity of the mouth, and the cavity of the pharynx.
2. *The frequencies of these cavities for the various vowels are the same for men and women.*
3. The frequency of the buccal cavity may be heard by *whispering* the vowel.
4. The frequency of the pharyngeal cavity may be heard by forming the vowel then *thumping* on the base of the tongue, below the jaw bone. The frequencies are better heard when the glottis is closed as before the explosion of a cough. The vowels i-e-a-o-u in order will give a rising and falling pattern of frequencies. (A vowel sung above that frequency will need to be modified.)
5. Frequencies of the pharyngeal cavity for the various vowels in *male and female* throats are:

æ	a	ɑ (750 cps)	roughly g^2
ɛ	œ	ɔ (600 cps)	roughly d^2
e	ø	o (456 cps)	roughly a^1
i	y	u (350 cps)	roughly f^1
I	II	III Series	[Modified from Howie and De-lattre.]

6. There are three series of vowel modifications, I—front vowels, II—middle vowels, and III—back vowels.

7. There is loss of understandability of a given vowel when it is sung on a pitch above the frequency of the larynx cavity of that vowel, and it will tend to sound like the vowel in its series on that particular note, i.e. the vowel i [see Series I in No. 5] will tend to sound like ae [*at*] on g^2, ε [*eh*] on d^2, and e on a^1. The same is true of any vowel in its particular series.

8. Vowels sung on pitches higher than their indicated frequencies tend to be harsh when an unmodified form is forced upon the voice.

9. The law of cavity frequency and vowel modification is primarily concerned with *female voices* because this phenomenon occurs between f^1 and g^2.

10. The observation can be made in the above chart that in the female voice 12 vowels are possible on f^1, 9 vowels possible on a^1, 6 vowels possible on d^2 and three vowels possible on g^2. An adroit use of modified vowels in context with consonants should create the illusion of good diction. At the same time the fundamental of the pitch being sung will be heard. If it is not, the tone will be a fraction of what it should be.

11. If the law is disregarded [without intuitive change] there may be difficulty with timbre, pitch, agility and flexibility of dynamics.

12. The above definition is a substantiation of the preferable *a* vowel of the Italians—it is the only vowel that can be sung freely on all pitches! Albert Bach in ''Musical Education and Vocal Culture'' quotes Anna Maria Celoni as saying, ''Le vocali l'i ed l'u si devono evitare a lasciarle a coloro che avessero la mania d'imitare i cavalli ed i lupi.'' [The vowels *i* and *u* should be left for those who desire to imitate horses and wolves.] Apparently *i* and *u* were considered to be unfavorable vowels for training most voices. BUT we must sing on these vowels in all languages. The above law indicates how these and related vowels can be sung.

13. The stated law should indicate approximately how the vowels will be used by the various voice classifications. In

female voices there must be a great deal of modification. Male voices are hardly touched by this law.

14. The law of modification of *male voices* is that in ascending, open vowels close and close vowels open [Witherspoon].

Thus, there is a high art with which the wedding of language and musical line [vocal line] must be accomplished. Traditionally this has occurred quite late in study and is the mark of an artist. Why can it not occur earlier if the above phenomena are understood and observed with the study of standardized languages through phonetics?

Appendix I: Remembering Berton Coffin

Berton Coffin, internationally recognized vocal instructor and professor emeritus at the University of Colorado, died Wednesday, January 28, at his Boulder, Colorado home. He was 76.

The teaching of singing, as every teacher (and student) knows, is an enormously complex activity, for not only is the teacher concerned with the pupil's relationship to his or her instrument as a means of musical expression, as are all music teachers, but in our case one is dealing with an instrument which lies hidden from view, buried, as it were, in the throat of the pupil. It concerns, among many other things, the training and physical development of an organ of the human body, an organ with several functions in addition to that of speech.

Berton Coffin was an outstanding teacher because he understood the complexity of his art. He understood the physical and emotional nature of the human larynx as a musical instrument, and eagerly passed this knowledge on to those of his pupils who were open to receive it. His many books and articles on the various aspects of singing, and the teaching of singing, stand as testimony to his expertise on these subjects.

But he was more than this. More than the dedicated researcher who found such joy in the discovery and study of the relationships of vowel resonance to sung pitch; more than the pedagogue who conceived a system whereby such knowledge could be understood and taught by others; more than the author, lecturer, past president of the National Association of Teachers of

Reprinted from *NATS InterNos,* May 1987.

Singing, and member of the American Academy of Singing Teachers; more than all of these, he was a wonderfully warm and simple man. A man who loved studio teaching more than all other of his endeavors; a teacher who took a deep personal interest in each of his students; a man whose love of being around young people kept him perpetually young at heart; a man who had a wonderful sense of humor, and who loved the occasional bawdy joke, and for me, just the healthy deep sound of his laughter was enough to keep me always scratching around for new material.

He was an intensely moral and ethical man, perhaps due to his strict Quaker upbringing. This was a trait which one could sense just being in his presence, and which meant for his students that he wouldn't just be there to take credit when things were going well, but was more apt to be there providing support when things weren't going so well. He once remarked that "if you are going to take credit for the good students, you must take credit for the other ones as well", and he did.

It was this love of teaching, this simple joy he found in the mysteries of the singing voice that kept him and Mildred Eurailing around Europe year after year, for months on end, after his retirement from the University of Colorado, attending an astonishing number and variety of opera and concert performances in the evenings, and teaching during the day, all with the exuberance of teenagers, (a schedule which tired me just hearing them tell of it). But a passion for the human voice such as he had, only fostered a seemingly unquenchable thirst for more.

It was in his graduate vocal pedagogy course at the University of Colorado, that I first remember studying "Gestalt Psychology," which, stated quite simply and in his words, teaches that "the whole is equal to more than the sum of the parts," an idea which he seemed to embody. He was at once researcher, author, lecturer, administrator, vocal pedagogue, and above all teacher of singing, and was highly respected as each. But he was certainly more than these things to me, and he was more than these things to thousands of other wide eyed and hopeful young singers

who were fortunate enough to pass through his studio and class-
room during his long and distinguished teaching career.

He will be sorely missed, but he certainly won't be forgotten.

Jérôme Pruett
Paris
February 4, 1987

Appendix J: Biography of Berton Coffin

Dr. Berton Coffin (April 11, 1910–January 28, 1987), internationally known vocal pedagogue, was a Professor Emeritus and formerly Chairman, Division of Voice, College of Music, University of Colorado, Boulder. Posthumously the faculty of the College of Music selected him for their first "Distinguished Faculty" Award, March 30, 1987. He is also remembered for his legacy as a voice teacher and vocal pedagogue among his colleagues at the university.

On April 17, 1977, the Berton Coffin Scholarship for graduate students in the College of Music was established. At the May CU Commencement, 1977, Professor Coffin and his wife Mildred were the first dual recipients of the Robert L. Stearns Award for distinguished service to the university. Their tenure represented a combined total of 59 years in teaching and arts administration.

On May 30 the Coffins moved to Europe, where he established a private vocal studio for professional singers in Vienna, Austria, as well as for those from German opera houses, September 1977 to mid-April 1979. In addition, Professor Coffin was a member of the voice faculty of the American Institute of Musical Studies, Graz, Austria, for seven summers, 1976–82.

Before moving to Vienna in 1977, Professor and Mrs. Coffin made annual and semiannual trips to Europe for a number of years. Between 1963 and 1983 they heard over 400 operatic performances in some 70 opera houses in many countries of Western and Eastern Europe. He maintained a broad overview of today's singing world while living in Europe. Even at that time he was also consulting with leading vocal and acoustical authorities in Europe.

Coffin's career included an appointment at the University of Cincinnati, Ohio, College-Conservatory of Music, 1981–82, as a

Visiting Professor of Voice and Vocal Pedagogy. In 1982–85 he went to Southern Methodist University, Dallas, Texas, as a Visiting Professor in the same areas of teaching. During that time (October 1983) he was an invited guest at the centennial celebrations of music on the CU campus, and the 60th anniversary of the founding of the College of Music in which he later played an important role. Due to ill health, Berton Coffin returned to Boulder, Colorado, in May 1985, but continued to use his vocal technical skills as a private consultant and pursued his pedagogical writings.

Although Dr. Coffin began his academic life at Earlham College as a physics major, he graduated with an English major from Earlham College, Richmond, Indiana, in 1932, but had already begun vocal study. Subsequently he added a B.M. in performance, Chicago Musical College, 1935, an M.M. from the Eastman School of Music, University of Rochester, New York, 1938, and an M.A. in 1946 and a doctorate in 1950 from Columbia University, New York City. He was singing professionally during that study period. Additional work was done at the Juilliard School of Music, New York City, and at Northwestern University, Evanston, Illinois. His private study with several teachers of singing and vocal coaches included such notables as Graham Reed (assistant to Herbert Witherspoon), Paola Novikova, Mack Harrell, and Werner Singer.

He married Mildred Wantland on August 26, 1936, in Mc-Alester, Oklahoma, and they celebrated their 50th wedding anniversary in 1986. Their daughter, Dr. Martha Coffin Smith (Mrs. James E.), lives in San Dimas, California, and is Assistant Superintendent, Educational Services, Whittier, Union H.S. District.

Between 1979 and 1983, Berton and Mildred Coffin made biannual trips to Europe where he taught singers in 21 opera houses in Austria, Denmark, Germany, Italy, and Switzerland. Among his most illustrious singers in Europe is Jérôme Pruett, lyric tenor, Paris (see his February 4, 1987, tribute to Dr. Coffin in Appendix I), who studied with Coffin at the University of Colorado as a graduate student, later in Vienna while under contract with the Vienna Volksoper, and in Paris as his career took an international direction. Kenneth Garrison, heldentenor of the Bayerische National Theater, Munich, also studied with him in Vienna, and later in Regensburg, Oldenburg, and Karlsruhe, Germany. After Drew Minter's success in Early Music in Vienna, he returned to the United States where he is currently in the limelight with his countertenor opera roles and recordings (*Opera News*, January 16, 1988).

Numerous singers worked with Professor Coffin in these 21 opera houses of whom leading sopranos Fran Luban of the Vereinigte Bühnen, Graz, Austria, and Gail Steiner-Neubert, Städtische Bühnen, Nürnberg, Germany are representative. Lars Waage, bass, of Den jydske Opera, Aarhus, Denmark, and others there were also among those singers he taught as he went to and from across the Atlantic for their 5,000 mile checkups.

Among Coffin's University of Colorado graduate students, heldenbaritone Herbert Eckhoff enjoys a very busy career in the United States and made his debut at the Metropolitan Opera, December 1987 in *La Traviata* (*Opera News*, December 19, 1987). Others have been singing with the San Francisco Opera, New York City Opera, Chicago Lyric Opera, and Houston Grand Opera. In addition to the opera singers, many performers maintain active careers in such areas as recitals, orchestral appearances, in oratorio, and as private or college/university teachers of singing.

Master classes in the teaching of singing and of vocal pedagogy principles dealing with his speciality of the acoustics of the voice and the pitch of vowels, with his own Vowel Chart, were held in Europe and the United States in conservatories, colleges, and universities. He also presented his teaching ideas via lecture-demonstrations at several conventions of the National Association of Teachers of Singing in various cities and in summer workshops of NATS.

A baritone, Berton Coffin sang professionally in New York City before joining the voice faculty as an Associate Professor in the College of Music, University of Colorado, Boulder, in 1946. He became a full professor in 1959, and later served as Chairman, Division of Voice until May 1977 when he and Mrs. Coffin moved to Europe. He remained active in oratorio and opera and as a recitalist, making what was to be his final public performance on a faculty recital at Southern Methodist University in the fall of 1982. His academic career began at Tarleton State University, Stephenville, Texas, where he was a Professor of Voice, and Head, Division of Music and Fine Arts.

During World War II, Coffin taught physics in the Army Specialized Training program at Tarleton, and later became a Weights Analyist and Mathematician at Consolidated Vultee Aircraft Corporation, Fort Worth, Texas, working on the XB 36. In addition he was a Guest Artist-in-Residence at the Fort Worth Conservatory of Music.

Berton Coffin was an innovative and creative person in various aspects of his professional life. He implemented one of the first doctoral (Doctor of Musical Arts) programs in the United States devoted to the study of both pedagogical research and vocal performance in the same degree, at the University of Colorado. He created a "town and gown" Festival Chorus of 200 voices that was devoted to performing the major oratorios. He was vitally concerned with building and recruiting an excellent vocal program and faculty. He was recognized as one of the leading internationally known acoustical researchers in the field of vocal pedagogy. This led him to authorities on acoustics as related to singing in Vienna, West Berlin, Stockholm, Zurich, Switzerland, Bell Telephone Laboratories in New Jersey, and other sources including the British Museum and the Bibliothèque Nationale in Paris. His vocal curiosity was intensified in wanting to know "why." Although he used technical/scientific methods to prove his theories, Coffin was not a vocal scientist per se. He wanted practical tools for teaching singing that were valid. He felt that no teacher has ever known too much about the teaching of singing: "A knowledge supplementing an intuition is surely the most effective way of forming an art" (*NATS Bulletin,* December 1969).

His presidency of the National Association of Teachers of Singing, 1968 and 1969, was known for the National Survey he

initiated for involvement and renewal of the wide membership of
this organization (the only one devoted to the teaching of singing
on a national basis) in areas of repertoire, vocal research, and
related areas. Coffin engaged the first Executive Secretary for
NATS and opened a national office in New York City. His articles "From the President" are found in Appendix G of this
volume. They are pertinent now for the values stressed to today's
singers and teachers and to members of NATS both past and
present.

In addition to Coffin's NATS presidency, he was a Charter
Member, served on the Board of Directors, was Chairman of the
Editorial Board of the *NATS Journal* (ex *Bulletin*), served as
program chairman for one of the Dallas national conventions, and
was director and codirector of several NATS summer workshops
at the University of Colorado, Boulder. He also formulated the
plans for the NATS Foundation.

The books Dr. Coffin authored or coauthored provide a living
memorial to his dedication to seeking the truth in the vocal field,
as he saw it, as well as linking the art of the old singing masters
of the past 250 years.

The Singer's Repertoire which appeared first in a single volume of 7,500 titles of songs and arias in American, British,
French, German, Italian, Russian, Scandinavian, and Spanish, in
752 lists for the nine voice classifications (coloratura soprano,
lyric soprano, dramatic soprano, mezzo-soprano, contralto, lyric
tenor, dramatic tenor, baritone, and bass). In 1955 it represented
the living song repertoire of today drawn from recital programs,
recordings, broadcasts, telecasts, and other sources. Coffin was a
pioneer in IBM electronic processes and techniques comprising
these indices and sorting over one million cards. A grant from the
Council on Research and Creative Work of the University of
Colorado was of vital importance in this project. The book was
separated into four parts in 1960 and is still in use as an aid in
program building by professional singers, students, and teachers,
as well as a valuable reference book in libraries. The four parts
constitute 8,200 songs and arias in 818 lists for soprano, contralto, tenor, and bass voices.

Program Notes for the Singer's Repertoire was compiled by Coffin and Werner Singer in 1962 and designed for the singing profession, as well as coaches. The *NATS Journal* (ex *Bulletin*) reviewer said it "brings to notable conclusion the most comprehensive source of authentic information concerning vocal literature presently extant!"

The year 1964 saw the publication of *Phonetic Readings of Songs and Arias* by Berton Coffin, Ralph Errolle (former Metropolitan Opera tenor), Werner Singer (eminent coach-accompanist for many leading singers), and Pierre Delattre (noted French phoneticist and former French Editor for Webster Dictionaries). A total of 413 songs and arias were selected from Coffin's *The Singer's Repertoire,* representing the most frequently performed vocal repertoire for all voice classifications. This invaluable aid to singers greatly reduces the time spent in learning the correct pronunciation of songs in foreign languages, and a second edition was released by Scarecrow Press in 1982.

Coffin, Singer, and Delattre coauthored *Word-by-Word Translations of Songs and Arias: Part I—German and French* in 1966, which allowed artists to interpret and express the feelings and emotions the songs required. An extended index of titles and first lines provides easy access to the contents. Dr. Coffin wrote the "Preface" to *Part II—Italian,* which Arthur Schoep and Daniel Harris compiled in 1972 as a part of this series of repertoire, phonetics, translations, and vocal techniques. The Italian added a broader dimension to the already established German and French translations.

The Sounds of Singing: Vocal Techniques with Vowel-Pitch Charts appeared in 1976 and was the first of Coffin's books *about* singing. It tells *how* singing principles can be used and checked by the ear, the eye, and the sense of touch. It is a sequel to *Phonetic Readings* and tells how much to "round" or "brighten" vowels in the singing voice, using the International Phonetic Alphabet. *The Sounds of Singing* is a synthesis of classic technical methods spanning the past 250 years, including the principles of the teacher of singing Paola Novikova, the acoustical phonetical principles of Pierre Delattre, and Coffin's original modern chromatic Vowel Chart with exercises. The Vowel Chart put vocalises of the past and present in notation form. Pruett Publishing Company, Boulder, Colorado, initially published it, then Scarecrow Press purchased the inventory, and the book is now out-of-print.

The revised and expanded second edition of *Coffin's Sounds of Singing: Principles and Applications of Vocal Techniques with Chromatic Vowel Chart* was posthumously published by Scarecrow Press in September 1987. Both editions of this work were dedicated to the famous and much recorded Swedish tenor Nicolai Gedda. The 1987 volume contains a Foreword by Gedda that gives insight into the teaching of Novikova (a student of Mattia Battistini), with whom Coffin studied for ten years. In a letter to Mrs. Coffin on November 9, 1987, Gedda said, "The book is fantastic! Bert left a wonderful heritage—a work of enormous value of instruction for singers, teachers, researchers, etc. I am so proud that Bert asked me to write the foreword."

Coffin's Overtones of Bel Canto: Phonetic Basis of Artistic Singing with 100 Chromatic Vowel-Chart Exercises realistically should have preceeded the 1976 *Sounds of Singing,* but the research for *Overtones* was done in Vienna in his private studio and in the Academy of Sciences; in Stockholm with Dr. Johan Sundberg at the Royal Institute of Technology; in the opera houses in Vienna; and in the European opera houses where he had begun to teach quite a number of singers. After publication of *Overtones,* Professor Coffin added (for his personal reference) specific vocalises for various singers. He had hoped to form an appendix of these vocal exercises in a later edition of *Overtones of Bel Canto* since it was of such practical use.

When Scarecrow Press published *Overtones,* the press prepared a special brochure on "Classics for Singers and Teachers of Singing" which featured all of Coffin's publications to date, plus a selected group of six other publications pertaining to the singing voice. The book stressed the phonetic basis of artistic singing as reflected in *bel canto* (beautiful singing), which is basically a linguistic musical art. Vowels have pitch, the melodic line has pitch, and there is sympathetic resonance. Coffin prepared a new Vowel Chart for this volume which was for male and female voices. The purpose of the book and the Chromatic Vowel Chart was to set forth in acoustic phonetics, register, and musical notation, many exercises that would collect and make the voice stronger and more musical according to the precepts of *bel canto*. The chart is part of *Overtones* and may also be purchased separately. It is included in the 1987 *Sounds of Singing*, with a few minor changes; again available separately.

During the past 25 years, Berton Coffin became well known in this country, Europe, Australia, New Zealand, England, and other countries as an author and/or coauthor of this diversified series of books. His biography appears in the *International Who's Who in Music and Musicians' Directory;* the *International Authors and Writers Who's Who; Dictionary of International Biography; Contemporary Authors; World Who's Who of Musicians; Men of Achievement; Who's Who in Music; Who's Who in Colorado;* and other publications.

As previously mentioned, the Berton Coffin Scholarship, College of Music, University of Colorado, was established in 1977. Another Berton Coffin Scholarship was set up in 1986 through the NATS Foundation with an award being presented to one of the finalists of the NATSSA Competition at the national conventions held every 18 months.

In a biography of Berton Coffin it seems appropriate that in summation it should be said that he was a very unusual and many-faceted person in his teaching attitudes and approaches to singing. He taught many professional singers as well as countless undergraduate and graduate students. Above all, he was concerned with the level (quality) of the teaching of singing. He wanted this high quality of teaching to be evident and tried to foster this throughout his service in the National Association of Teachers of Singing (NATS).

Dr. Coffin gave a legacy to his students who are now teaching because they will also impart much of his vocal knowledge. In turn, these principles will be handed down from teacher to student whether they themselves pursue a career as teachers or as performers. He will be remembered for a long time by those who worked with him and by their students whether in the academic world or in the private sector.

Professor Coffin was unique in that he appreciated the success of other teachers and was willing to share his knowledge. When colleagues asked him for help with specific vocal problems in their students, he would take the time to work with the students and their teachers in suggesting practical ways in which to deal with a given situation—usually tuning a vowel or vowels, or an easy approach to the passaggio or some other critical vocal area. He found this professional camaraderie very rewarding and there was no jealousy or one-upmanship.

As a member of the two most prestigious groups of singing teachers, the large National Association of Teachers of Singing and the smaller American Academy of Teachers of Singing, Coffin was interested in the functions of these two organizations. They had wide geographic representation among the members, and in recent years NATS has had affiliate members in several foreign countries. The reader is no doubt aware of this evidence in the preceding pages. In consultation with other academy members a special pronouncement was drawn up for the American Academy and is found in Appendix B.

It is hoped that this biography reveals the man as well as his accomplishments.

Mildred W. Coffin
Editorial Assistant

Appendix K: Delle Sedie's Modifications of the French A in the Modulated Voice of Singing

TAVOLA COMPARATIVA	TABLE COMPARATIVE	COMPARATIVE TABLE
DELLE GRADAZIONI FONICHE INE- RENTI ALLA SCALLA VOCALE	*DES NUANCES PHONIQUES INHE- RENTES A LA GAMME VOCALE*	*OF THE PHONICAL SHADES IN- HERENT TO THE VOCAL SCALE*
La parola posta contro la nota musicale serve per indicare l'accen. tofonico delle vocale corrispondente al suono di quella nota. Questa vo. cale è messa in evidenza per mezzo di segni speziali apposti alla vira le citata.	*Les mots mis en regard des notes servent à indiquer l'accent phoni- que de la voyelle correspondant au son vocal, et celle-ci est signalée par des lignes speciales posées auprès de la voyelle même.*	*The words placed at the sides of the notes serve to show as that the phonic accent of the vowel corre. sponding to the vocal sound, is marked by special lines and plac. ed after the same vowel.*
ā apertа come nel Bărdo la parola	ā ouvert comme dans l ă de Climāt	ā open as in the word . . . Bār
ɑ semioscura come nella parola Baulta	ɑ un peu sombré com. me dans l ɑ de Courage	ɑ a little closed as in the word . . Father
ᾱ oscura come nel la parola Farmaco	ᾱ sombré comme dans l ᾱ de Caprice	ᾱ closed as in the word . . . . . Căto

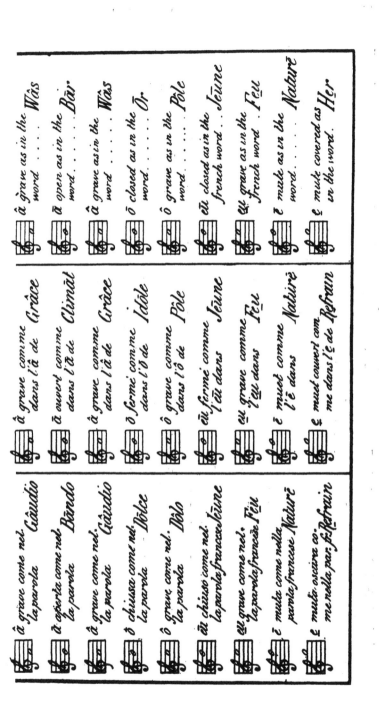

Italiano	Français	English
à grave come nel. la parola Gàudio	à grave comme dans l'à de Grâce	à grave as in the word... Wâs
ā aperta come nel. la parola Bàndo	ā ouvert comme dans l'ā de Climât	ā open as in the word... Bār
â grave come nel. la parola Gàudio	â grave comme dans l'â de Grâce	â grave as in the word... Wâs
ō chiusa come nel. la parola Dolce	ō fermé comme dans l'ō de Idôle	ō closed as in the word... Ōr
ô grave come nel. la parola Idolo	ô grave comme dans l'ô de Pole	ô grave as in the word... Pole
aū chiuso come nel. la parola francese Jeūne	eū fermé comme dans l'eū dans Jeūne	eū closed as in the french word.. Jeūne
eu grave come nel. la parola francese Feu	eu grave comme l'eu dans Feu	eu grave as in the French word. Feu
ē muta come nella. parola francese Naturē	ē muet comme l'ē dans Naturē	ē mute as in the word... Naturē
e̶ muta oscura co. me nella parola fr. Refrain	e̶ muet couvert com. me dans l'e̶ de Refrain	e̶ mute covered as in the word. Her

Bibliography: Published Books and Articles by Berton Coffin

The Singer's Repertoire. Metuchen, N.J.: Scarecrow Press, 1956. [Out of print.]

The Singer' Repertoire: Part I—Coloratura, Lyric and Dramatic Soprano; Part II—Mezzo Soprano and Contralto; Part III—Lyric and Dramatic Tenor; Part IV—Baritone and Bass. Metuchen, N.J.: Scarecrow Press, 1960.

With W. Singer. *Program Notes for the Singer's Repertoire.* Metuchen, N.J.: Scarecrow Press, 1962.

"The Singer's Diction." *NATS Bulletin,* February 1964. [Appendix H in this volume.]

With R. Errolle, W. Singer, and P. Delattre. *Phonetic Readings of Songs and Arias.* Boulder, Colo.: Pruett Publishing, 1964. [Inventory purchased by Scarecrow Press. Out of print.]

With W. Singer and P. Delattre. *Word-By-Word Translations of Songs and Arias: Part I—German and French.* Metuchen, N.J.: Scarecrow Press, 1966.

"From the President." *NATS Bulletin,* February 1968 to February-March 1970. [Nine articles.]

Schoep, A., and D. Harris, with Preface by B. Coffin. *Word-By-Word Translations of Songs and Arias: Part II—Italian.* Metuchen, N.J.: Scarecrow Press, 1972.

"The Instrumental Resonance of the Singing Voice." *NATS Bulletin*, December 1974. [Appendix D in this volume.]

"The Relationship of Phonation and Resonation." *NATS Bulletin*, February 1975. [Appendix E in this volume.]

"The Relationship of the Breath, Phonation, and Resonance in Singing." *NATS Bulletin*, December 1975. [Appendix A in this volume.]

The Sounds of Singing: Vocal Techniques with Vowel-Pitch Charts. Boulder, Colo.: Pruett Publishing, 1976. [Inventory purchased by Scarecrow Press. Out of print.]

"Articulation for Opera, Oratorio, and Recital." *NATS Bulletin*, February 1976. [Appendix F in this volume.]

Coffin's Overtones of Bel Canto: Phonetic Basis of Artistic Singing with 100 Chromatic Vowel-Chart Exercises. Metuchen, N.J.: Scarecrow Press, 1980.

With R. Errolle, W. Singer, and P. Delattre. *Phonetic Readings of Songs and Arias.* Second Edition. Metuchen, N.J.: Scarecrow Press, 1982.

Coffin's Sounds of Singing: Principles and Applications of Vocal Techniques with Chromatic Vowel Chart. Revised and enlarged second edition. Metuchen, N.J.: Scarecrow Press, 1987.

Historical Vocal Pedagogy Classics. Metuchen, N.J.: Scarecrow Press, 1989. [A series of 18 book reviews, as presented in this volume.]

Lightning Source UK Ltd.
Milton Keynes UK
UKHW01f0958150918

328882UK00001B/1/P